I0810437

IMAGES of America

SAUCON VALLEY

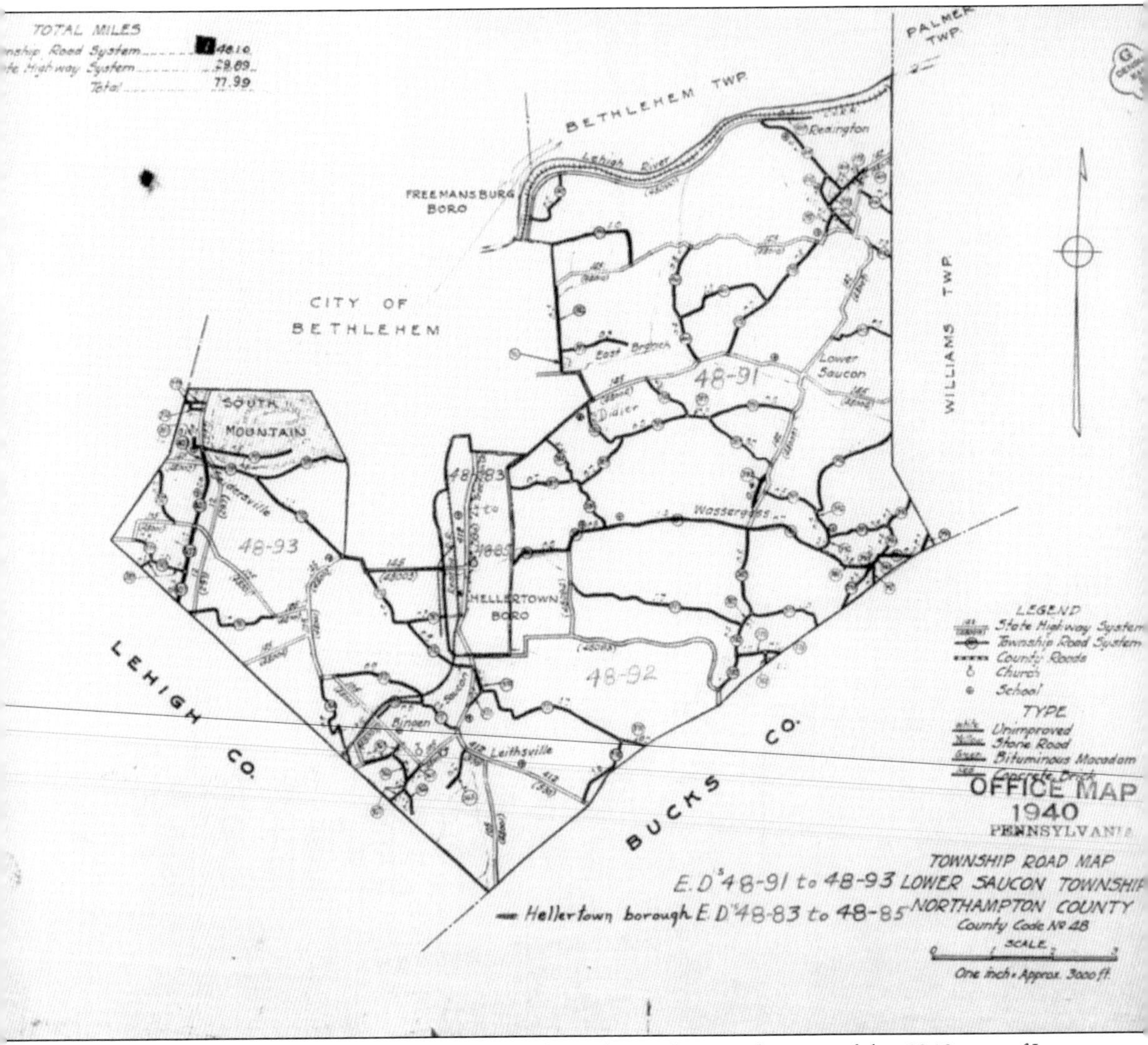

Many changes and additions have been made to the roads since the time of this 1940 map of Lower Saucon Township. Note that Pennsylvania Route 12, shown on the map, is aligned where Route 378 runs today. Route 378 was completed in 1968. Interstate Route 78 is not shown, having been completed through the Lehigh Valley section in 1989. (Courtesy of the Lower Saucon Township Historical Society Archive.)

On the Cover: This is a rare 1950s view of the inside of Guro's Luncheonette, 1105 Main Street. The "cool kids" are lined up at the soda fountain in a race to finish their drinks. Brothers Andrew and Walter Guro started the luncheonette around the corner on Thomas Avenue in 1944. Within a year, they had moved to the Main Street location. Andrew and his wife, Anna (Kozlowski), ran the business for over 30 years, closing it in the late 1970s. Andrew Guro serving the drinks on the right. (Courtesy of Edward Guro and Patricia Guro Bendrick.)

IMAGES
of America

SAUCON VALLEY

Daniel T. Ruth, Karen M. Samuels,
and Lee A. Weidner

ARCADIA
PUBLISHING

ISBN 978-1-4671-2353-2

Published by Arcadia Publishing
Charleston, South Carolina

Printed in the United States of America

Library of Congress Control Number: 2014957237

For all general information, please contact Arcadia Publishing:
Telephone 843-853-2070
Fax 843-853-0044
E-mail sales@arcadiapublishing.com
For customer service and orders:
Toll-Free 1-888-313-2665

Visit us on the Internet at www.arcadiapublishing.com

This book is dedicated to Margaret E. Fluck (1924–2013) and Dorothy L. Eyer (1948–2014). The Lower Saucon Township Historical Society was fortunate to receive the support of these two dedicated women. They were vital to the historical society's success and are missed every day.

Contents

Acknowledgments

We could not have completed this book without the help of the following persons:

Daniel thanks his wife, Joan; daughter Ann; son Jeff; and sister Cheryl Kazan. Karen is grateful to her husband, John; her sons Teddy and Tommy; and her sister Deborah and brother Richard. Lee is appreciative of the support from his children Lynn, Bobby, Laura, Chris, Lori, and Andrew.

We thank our Saucon Valley historians: Richard Kantor, Frank Fabian, Dave Jacoby, John Fischel, Diane Webber Wampole, the Ruth Collection, Bob Limons, John and Marianne Hayes, Chris Scherer, Lost River Caverns, Isabel Bauder, Fred Lucrezi, Pattie (Guro) Bendrick and Edward Guro, Mike Hansen, William Berger, Pearl Pondelek Boder, Ken Raniere, Randy Stull, Dean Shaffer, Dewey Fire Company, Sue Corvaia Hunter, St. Theresa's Church, Hellertown Borough Water Authority, Lawrence Kish, Fran Robb, Ray Shook, Dave Leidig, Pete Connor, Herman Hackman, Joanne Jones, Andrea Thrush and the Hellertown Historical Society. Once again, we thank our editors at Arcadia Publishing, Abby Henry and Lily Watkins, who were patient, supportive, and always helpful.

Unless otherwise noted, all images in this book are from the Lower Saucon Township Historical Society Archive.

INTRODUCTION

The local Native American tribes, the Lenni Lenape, named the eastern Pennsylvania creek Saucon, meaning "at the mouth of the creek." Saucon Valley refers to the area drained by the Saucon Creek, a 17-mile tributary of the Lehigh River. The creek drains into 58.2 square miles of the Lehigh basin. This area includes Hellertown and Lower Saucon Township of Northampton County. The Lenni Lenape lived in the Saucon Valley for 2,000 years before European settlers arrived in the 1600s. The Lenape established the Minsi Trail, between Philadelphia and Northampton County, which cut through Saucon Valley. This historic 41-mile road evolved into a Colonial highway called the King's Road in the 1760s. Although there were countless Lenni Lenape burial grounds in Saucon Valley, regrettably, most of them have been destroyed by development.

European traders appeared in the area prior to 1700 and carried on a peaceful relationship with the Lenni Lenape. William Penn was granted land on March 4, 1681, by King Charles II to repay a debt owed to Penn's father. The land grant included what is now Pennsylvania and Delaware. Penn decided that fairness required he make treaties with the Lenni Lenape for large parcels of this land grant as well. In 1737, Penn's sons expanded their land holdings to include most of the Lehigh Valley, including Saucon Valley, through the fraudulent Walking Purchase Treaty. Although the Lenni Lenape objected to this claim, they eventually moved out of the area, allowing Europeans to settle it. In the early 1700s, Nathaniel Irish established a farm, gristmill, and sawmill, as well as a land office for William Allen, who was the chief justice for Pennsylvania. Irish is considered the first European settler in Lower Saucon Township. His property later became known as the village of Shimersville. Irish was the first justice of the peace in the area. This book includes never-before-published photographs of Shimersville. The village was bought by Bethlehem Steel in 1915 and then demolished.

German immigrants, convinced by Penn's favorable advertisements of Pennsylvania, settled in the Saucon Valley in large numbers beginning in the 1730s. These early settlers were successful at farming and built numerous mills to provide wood, flour, textiles, paper, and gunpowder. Other early industry included limekilns and the mining of zinc and iron ore.

Early settlers included Christoph (Christopher) Heller, his wife, Veronica, and their six children, who arrived in 1738 and made a homestead at the foot of the south slope of the Lehigh Mountain. Heller built his log house and large log barn in the area now occupied by today's Saucon Valley Square on Route 378. Simon and Michael Heller, two of Christoph's sons, purchased land along the Saucon Creek. This early Heller settlement developed into the current Borough of Hellertown. Another early pioneer was Anthony Boehm, the son of Rev. John Philip Boehm. Boehm built what is now the oldest house still standing in Hellertown. Local historic buildings also include the Ehrhart's Mill Historic District, Michael and Margaret Heller House, and the Lutz-Franklin School, all listed in the National Register of Historic Places. Christopher Heller and other early European settlers of Saucon Valley lie buried in the cemetery at the Lime Kiln Schoolhouse on Creek Road.

Lower Saucon Township was chartered in 1743, when it was still a part of Bucks County. The township also included South Bethlehem until 1865 and Hellertown until 1872. Before becoming a borough in 1872, Hellertown was the largest village in Lower Saucon Township for many years.

When the North Penn Railroad, connecting Philadelphia and Bethlehem, was completed in 1856, the 55-mile line provided a catalyst to establishing iron foundries. In 1868, the railroad company erected a large brick station house near Hellertown. Stations were also built at Bingen, Saucon, and Center Valley. Today, this railroad line has been converted into a popular bicycle and pedestrian pathway.

In 1866, with the formation of the Saucon Iron Works and, later, the Thomas Iron Works in 1884, Hellertown experienced a great surge in development to accommodate the workers. In the first half of the 1900s, Bethlehem Steel Corporation was the largest employer in the area. Men took trolleys, buses, and then automobiles to the great Bethlehem Steel mills in South Bethlehem. Not only did Bethlehem Steel buy hundreds of acres in Saucon Valley for the purpose of building homes for its workers; it located coke-processing ovens just north of Hellertown.

In 1908, Charles M. Schwab, president of the Bethlehem Steel Corporation, visited the Didier-March Company in Germany to observe its process of making coke. Schwab signed a contract with Didier-March in 1912 to build a plant near Bethlehem to supply coke. However, when World War I broke out, Didier-March was forced to sell the plant to Bethlehem Steel for $8 million in 1917. The plant was located on 160 acres between Hellertown and Bethlehem and employed 30,000 at the height of production.

The Coke Works processed coal by baking it in ovens for 24 to 34 hours at temperatures as high as 2,000 degrees. The resulting coke was then used to make steel. The plant was known for its difficult working conditions. The Coke Works was the last of the Bethlehem Steel Corporation plants to close. In March 1998, 800 Coke Works employees were informed of the closure. Many of them lived in the Saucon Valley area. A warehouse complex operates on the site today.

Today, Saucon Valley residents are no longer employed in farming or mills. Most men and women work in the service industries, such as health care, education, or entertainment. Locals seek out fresh fruits and vegetables at the Saucon Valley Farmers Market in Hellertown. New businesses, such as restaurants, banks, a bike shop, and a health-food store, have found that they are a good fit for Main Street in Hellertown.

One

Our Community

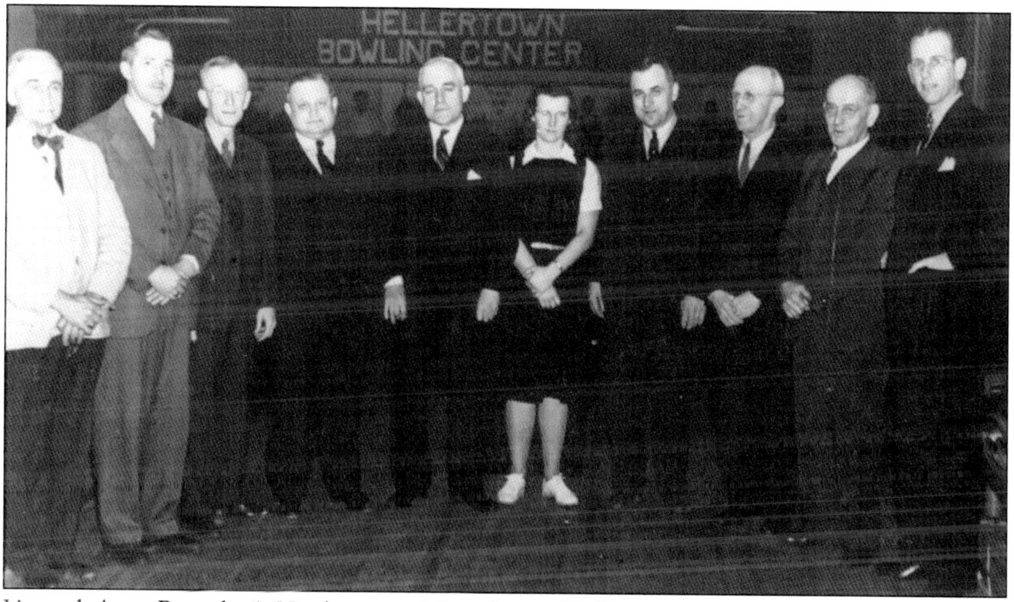

Housed above Rauscher's Hardware on Main Street, Hellertown, bowling lanes accommodated many adult and children bowling leagues. Pin boys were used to reset the pins, as automatic pinsetters were yet unavailable. Shown here on February 1, 1941, in the bowling alley, are, from left to right, unidentified, Harold Ward, Don Peffer, Stanley Yeager, Chief Burgess Morris Dimmick, Jeanette Scholl, Bill Buhecker, Herb Hoffert, John Bergstresser, and Charlie Bauder. This group is composed of the local community leaders and active bowlers. (Courtesy of the Hellertown Historical Society.)

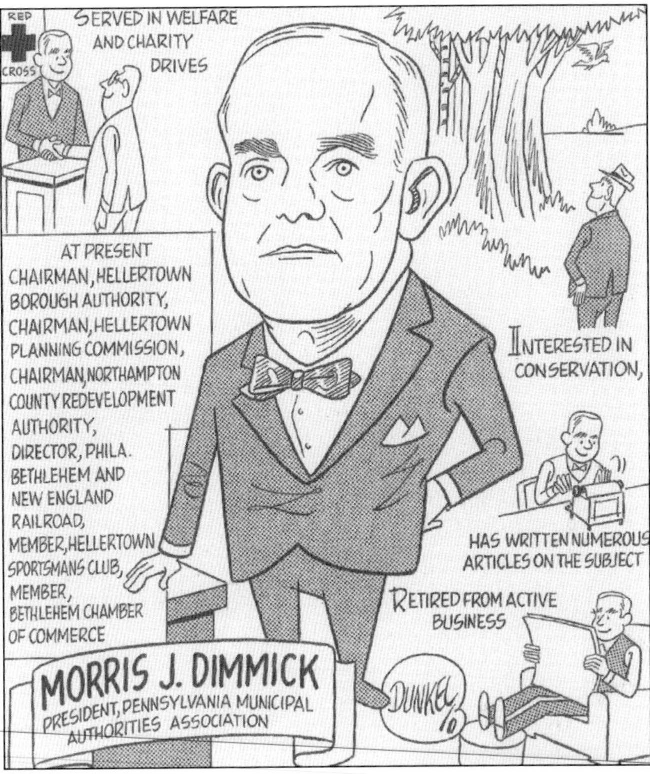

Morris Dimmick served as chief burgess (today, mayor) and was the most influential borough leader in history. He led Hellertown through the Great Depression, when funds were received from the federal government's Works Progress Administration. (Portrait below courtesy of Hellertown Borough Water Authority.)

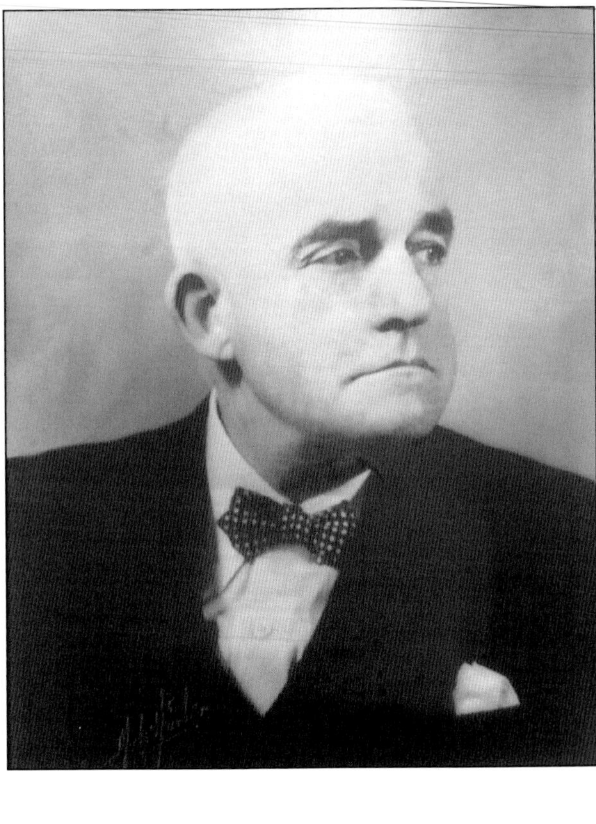

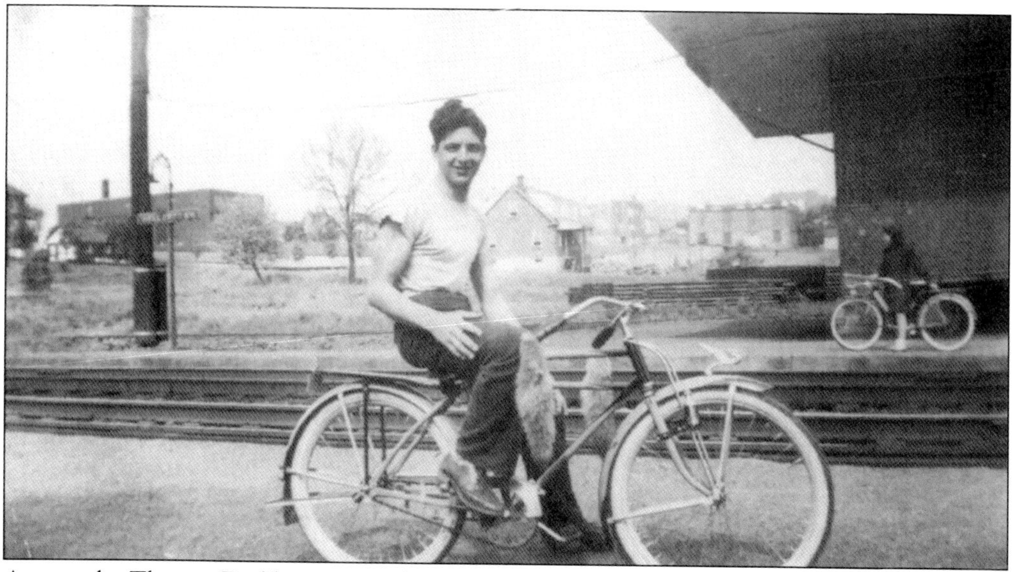

A muscular Thomas Doddy pauses at the Hellertown train station. A close look reveals what may be a bicycle license plate hanging from the rear wheel rack. A generator is attached to the fork of the front wheel, which was useful to power the bike's headlight—if there was one! (Courtesy of the Hellertown Historical Society.)

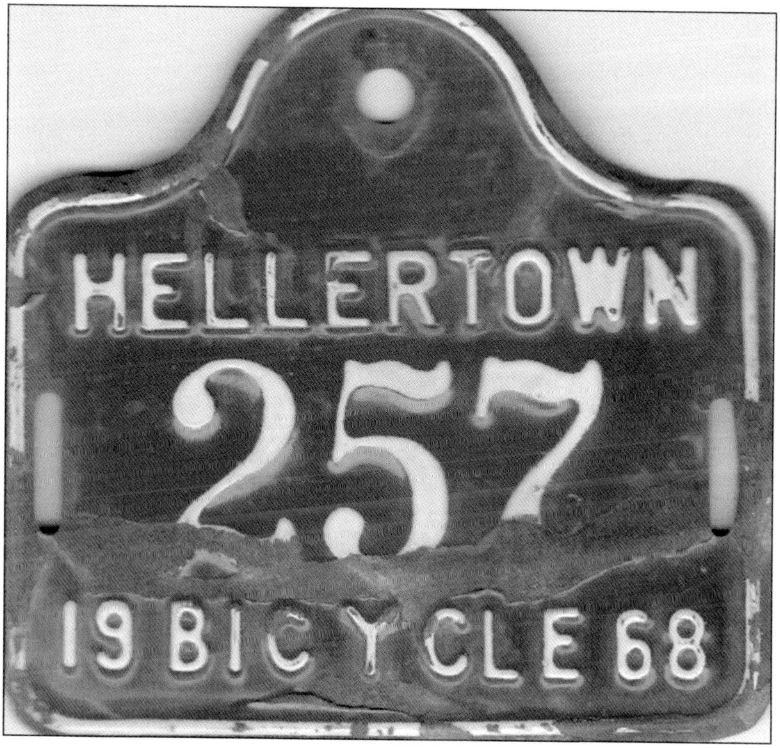

Many communities encouraged residents to register their children's bicycles to deter theft and aid in returning recovered property. Locally, these programs have all been eliminated. Such license plates provide memories for many of their favorite bicycle. (Courtesy of Randy Stull.)

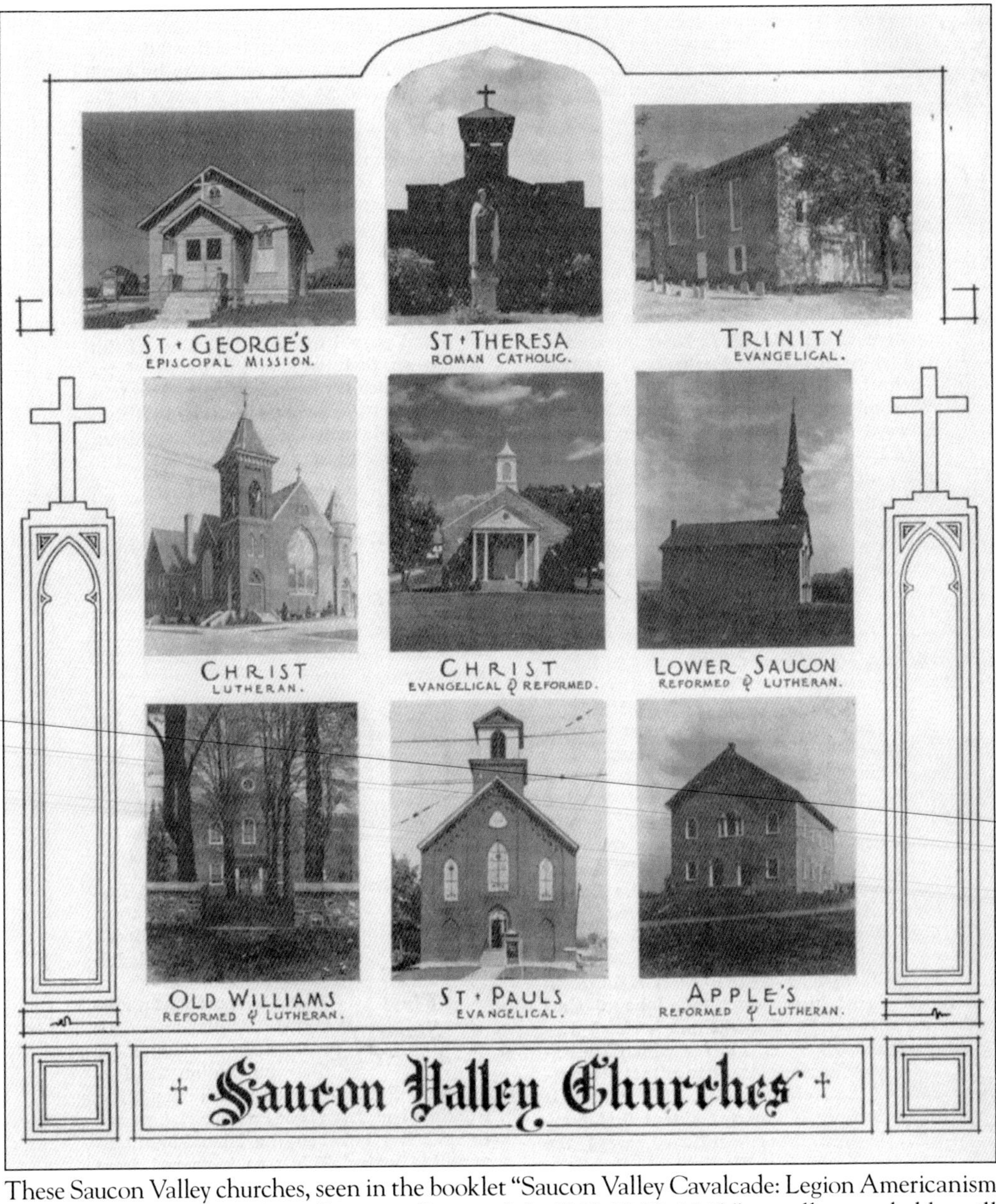

These Saucon Valley churches, seen in the booklet "Saucon Valley Cavalcade: Legion Americanism Pageant, Hellertown Park, Hellertown, Penna., July 17-18-19-20, 1940," are all, remarkably, still active today. The oldest church in the group, Lower Saucon Church, was established in 1734, soon after early settlers arrived. A German Reformed congregation built the church on what is now Easton Road.

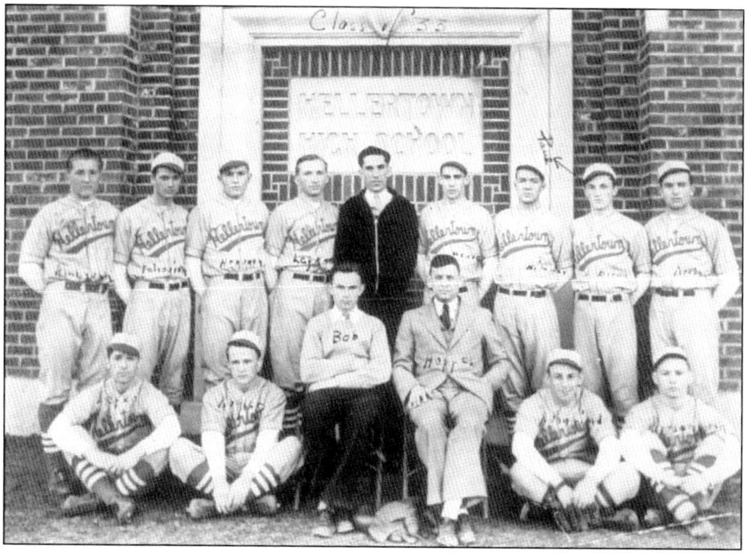

This is the 1933 Hellertown High School baseball team and its coach, Robert Hoppes. The early 1930s marked a high point for Hellertown baseball, both for the high school team and the summer teams sponsored by Ackerman Post 397 of the American Legion. Hoppes also coached soccer and basketball before the days of football.

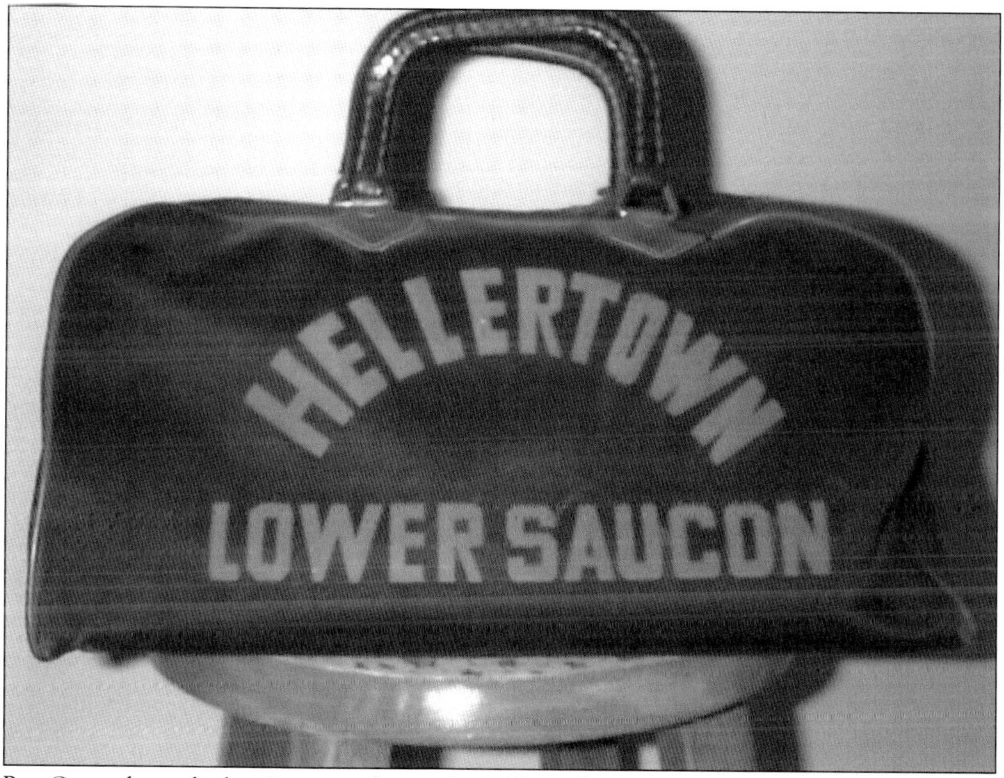

Ray Gozzard was the boys' gym teacher in the 1950s and 1960s. A gym bag was essential twice a week for a student's all-white outfit and sneakers. The bag also doubled as a book carrier in the days before backpacks became widely used.

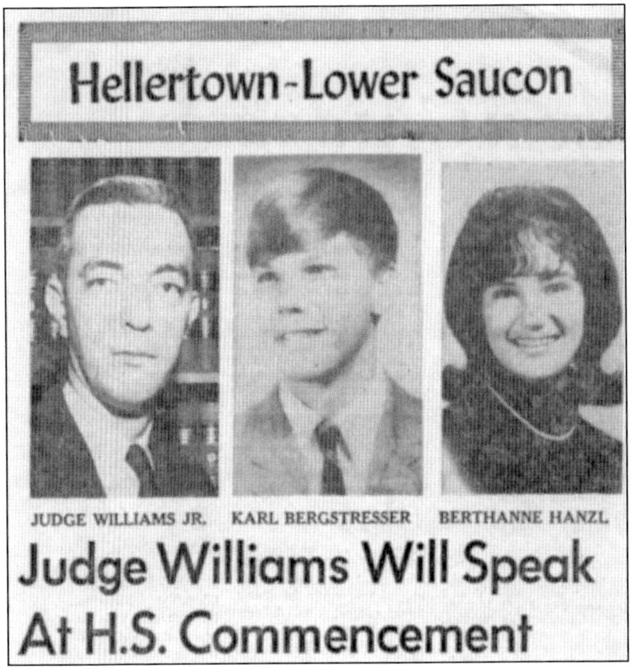
Hellertown-Lower Saucon

JUDGE WILLIAMS JR. KARL BERGSTRESSER BERTHANNE HANZL

Judge Williams Will Speak At H.S. Commencement

The *Globe Times* newspaper (1925–1991) covered Hellertown and Lower Saucon Township news. In October 1925, the *Daily Times* and the *South Bethlehem Daily Globe* merged to form the *Bethlehem Globe Times*. In 1991, when the *Express* bought out the *Globe Times*, many Bethlehem residents mourned the loss of their Pulitzer Prize–winning local paper.

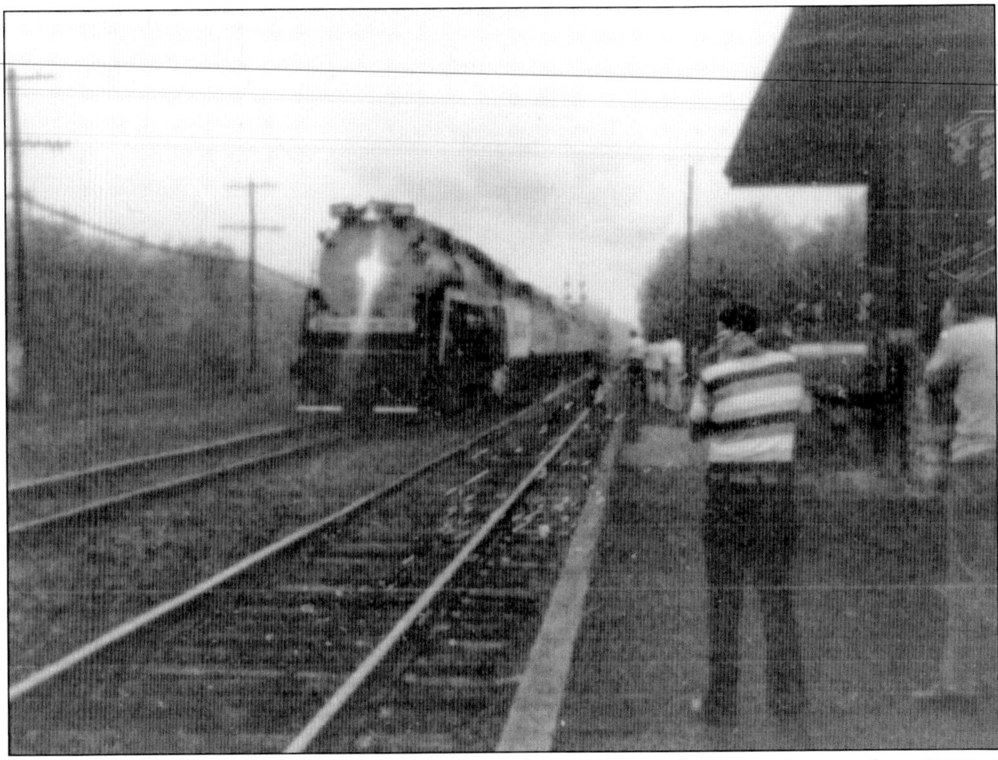

Starting in April 1977, the newly refurbished 2101 locomotive and six cars ran tours from Saucon Creek Roundhouse in Hellertown to Philadelphia and Baltimore. The train carried members of the press and devoted fans. This Chessie Steam Special train run celebrated the 150th birthday of American railroading. (Courtesy of Dean Shaffer.)

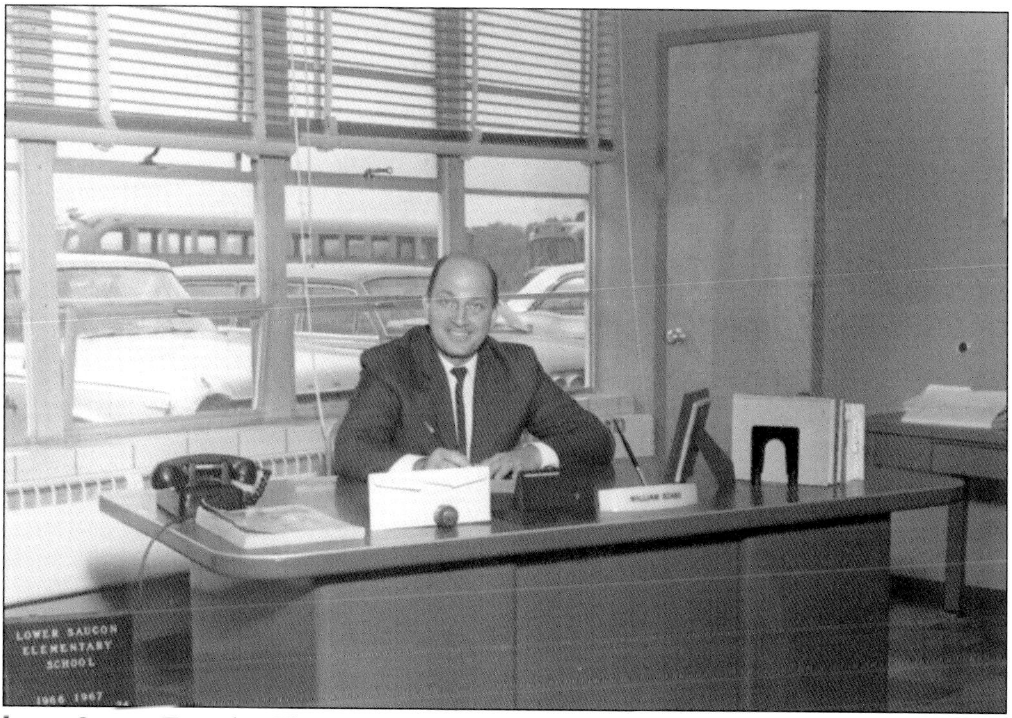

Lower Saucon Township Elementary School's first principal, William Szabo, poses at his desk in the new school in 1958. Szabo began his career in the 1950s in the school district, teaching sixth grade at the Lehigh Mountain one-room school and then at Seidersville School. He served as a principal from 1958 to 1986, when he retired. Before becoming a teacher, he was a catcher for the Washington Senators in a Class B Colonial League in Waterbury, Connecticut, from 1949 to 1952.

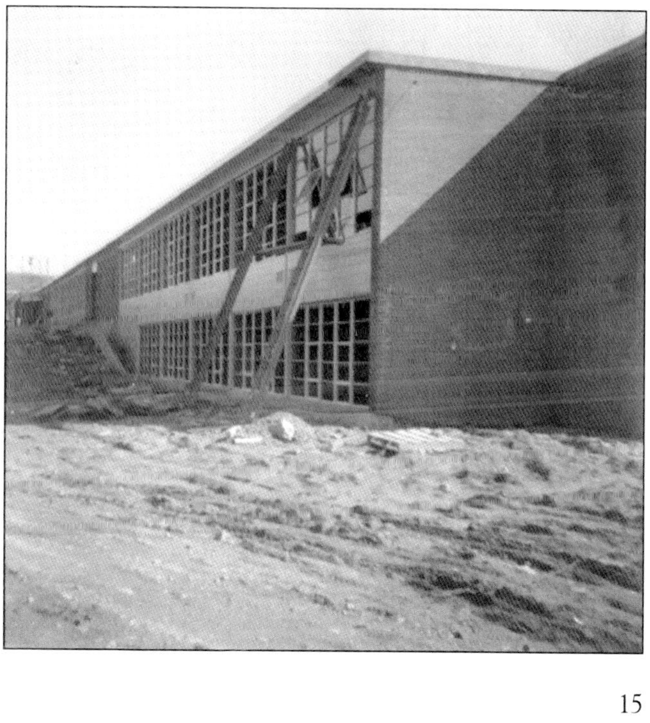

The Lower Saucon Township Elementary School is under construction in 1958 on Wassergass Road. The building would hold 22 classrooms, a library, cafeteria, and auditorium. Upon completion, it phased out the use of 14 one-room schoolhouses. The school was replaced in 1999 when new elementary and middle schools were built on the Polk Valley campus. Today, the building is owned by the Bug Company.

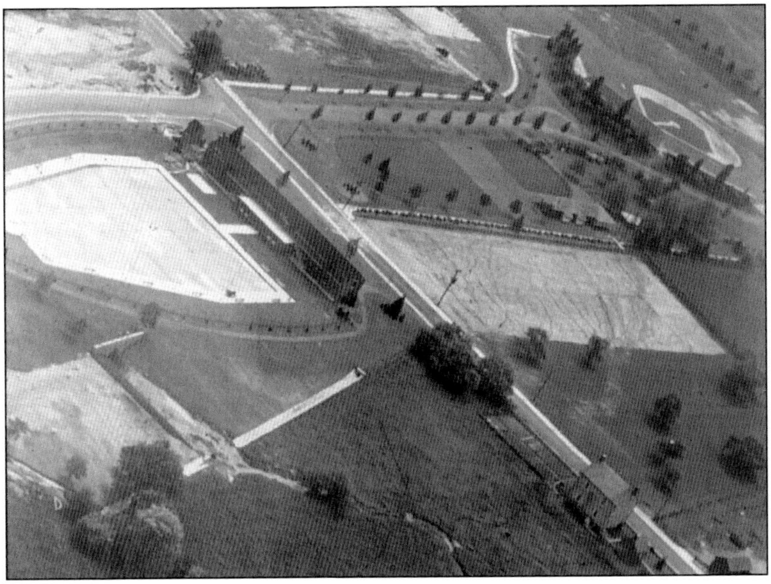

This 1939 aerial photograph shows the Hellertown Municipal Swimming Pool and Dimmick Park soon after the completion of this Works Progress Administration project. The 800,000-gallon pool was dug by hand. A.J. Oplinger was the first manager of the pool. The pool and the park are still enjoyed today by the community.

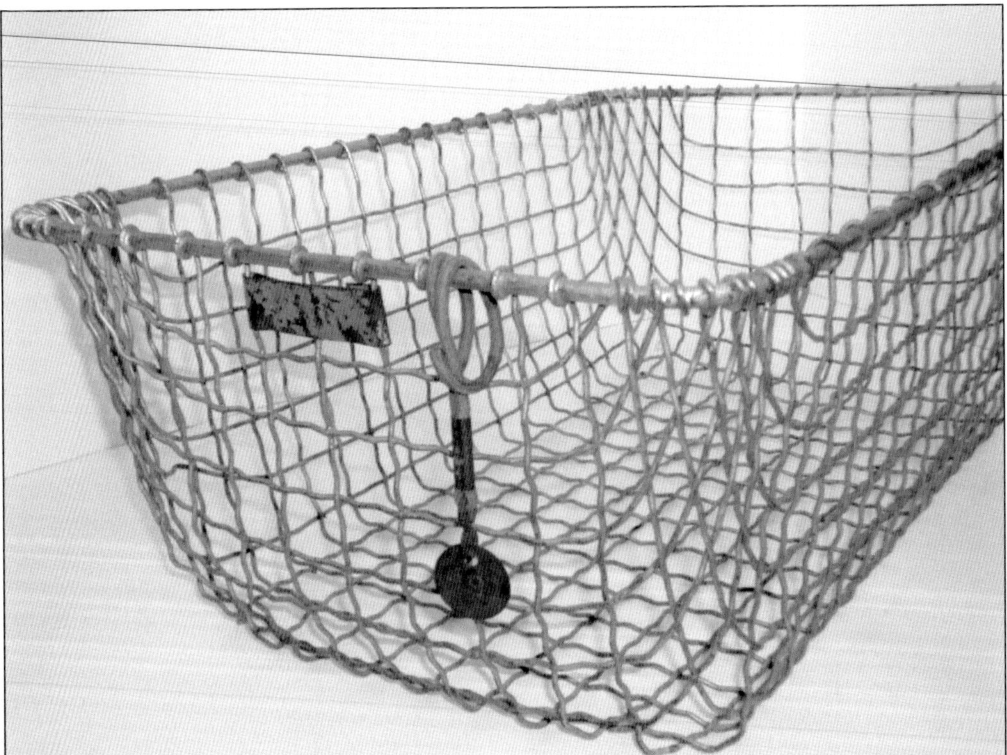

This is a Hellertown pool metal basket with a brass numbered tag. In the 1950s, swimmers stored belongings in the basket and wore the tag while they swam. They had to show the tag to the attendant to retrieve their clothes after a swim.

Vince Coughlan (1904–1992) was the Hellertown police chief for 14 years before retiring in 1968. He started on the force in 1938. After retiring, he was an officer of the court for the county of Northampton until 1983.

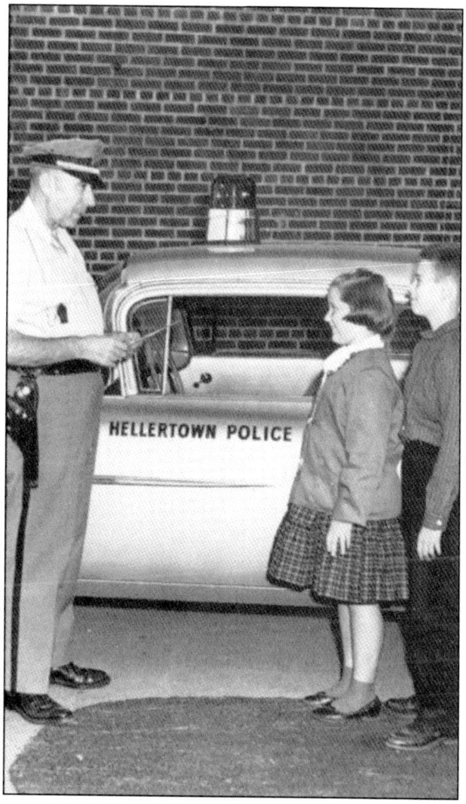

Stevie "Dabo" Szabo was a beloved fixture of the Hellertown community. Despite his handicaps, he was accepted for who he was and welcomed by all. Stevie would frequent the community businesses and offer to do chores. He would be rewarded with a meal or other treats.

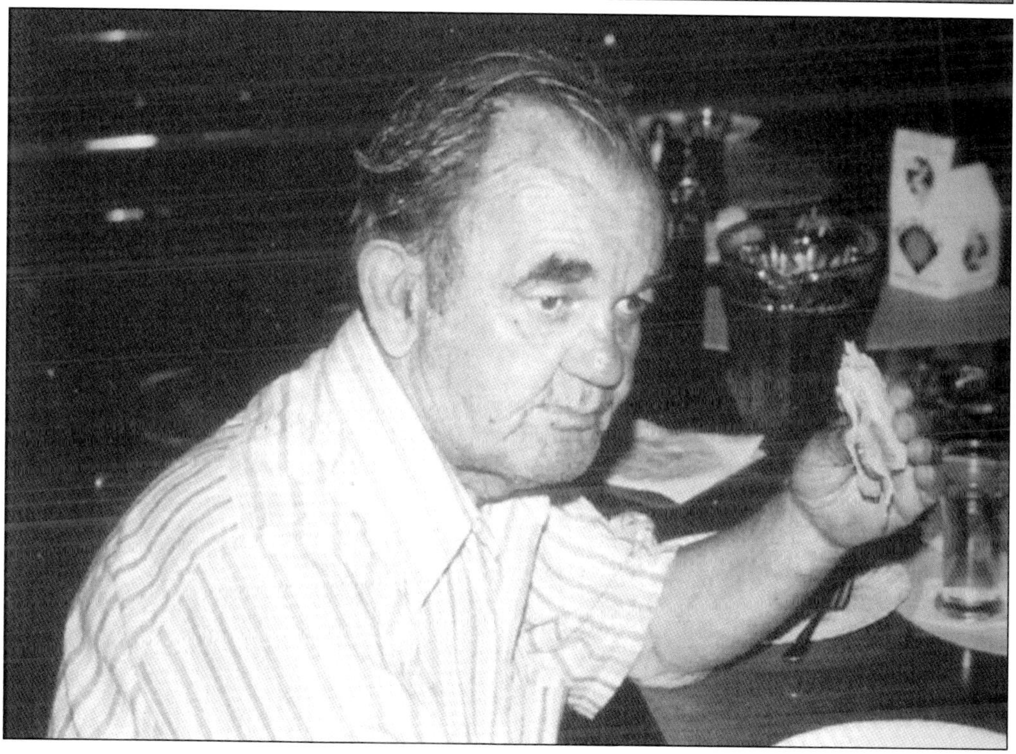

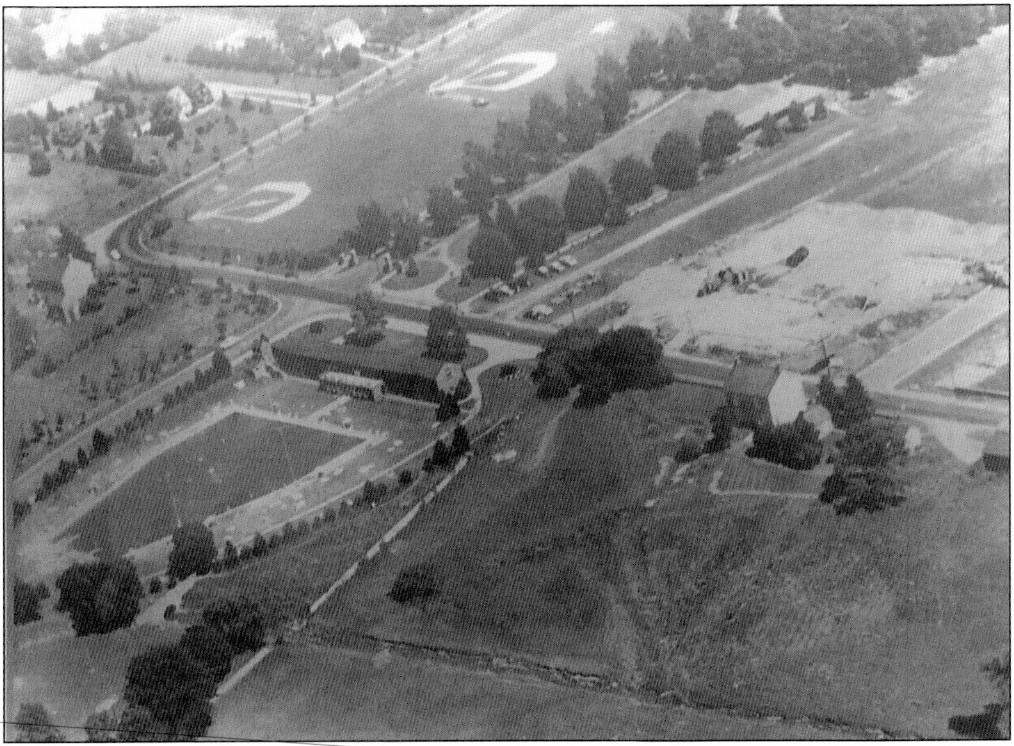

A farm previously occupied the grounds on which the second Dewey Fire Company was built. Ground breaking for the second, larger Dewey Fire Company was held in March 1954, and the dedication ceremony was held in July 1955. (Courtesy of Dewey Fire Company Archives.)

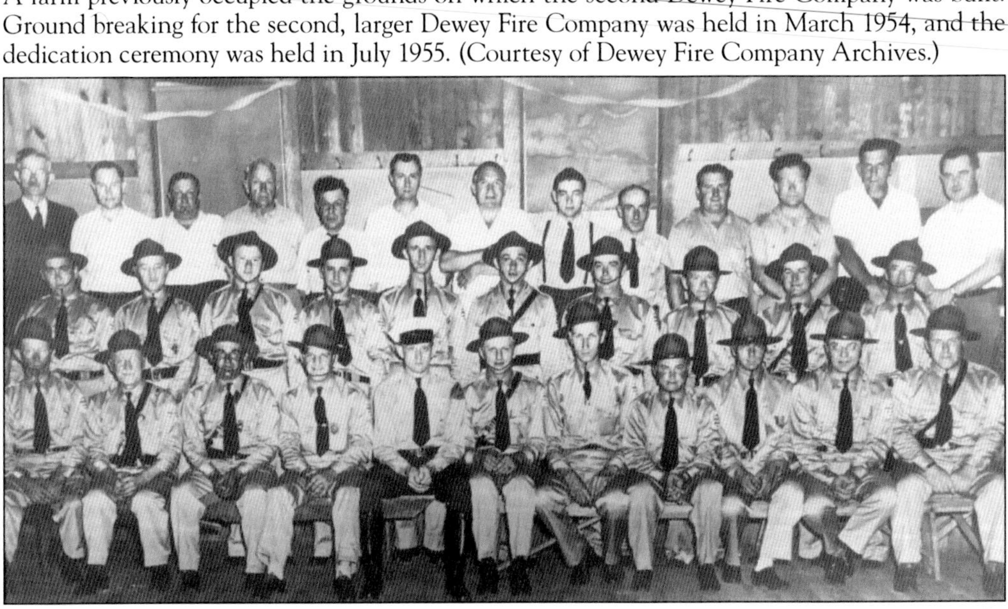

Before the evening blackout, members of Lower Saucon's Auxiliary Police meet at the Leithsville Community Hall. They are, from left to right, as follows: (first row) Officers Long, Ganser, Keshl, Raab, Dimmig, Focht, J. Kerner, Scheetz, Benner, Landis, and Fritchman; (second row) Zelko, Weiss, V. Hayes, Kichline, A. Kerner, J. Hayes, Banks, Hafler, Kelemen, and Fluck; (third row) Wilhelm, Neibauer, Mozaeki, Urich, Brader, Freed, Kravatz, DiJirolanio, Weikheiser, Vasso, Weidner, Sutton, and Calahan.

Accordion player Joseph V. Corvaia Jr. led the Joe Corvaia Quartet, a favorite band in the Lehigh Valley for over 20 years. He also operated Joe's Lawn Care of Bath and participated as a "mummer" in the Mummers Parade in Philadelphia. The Corvaia Quartet frequently played at the Beethoven Waldheim and Saucon Valley Country Club for weddings. (Courtesy of Sue Corvaia Hunter.)

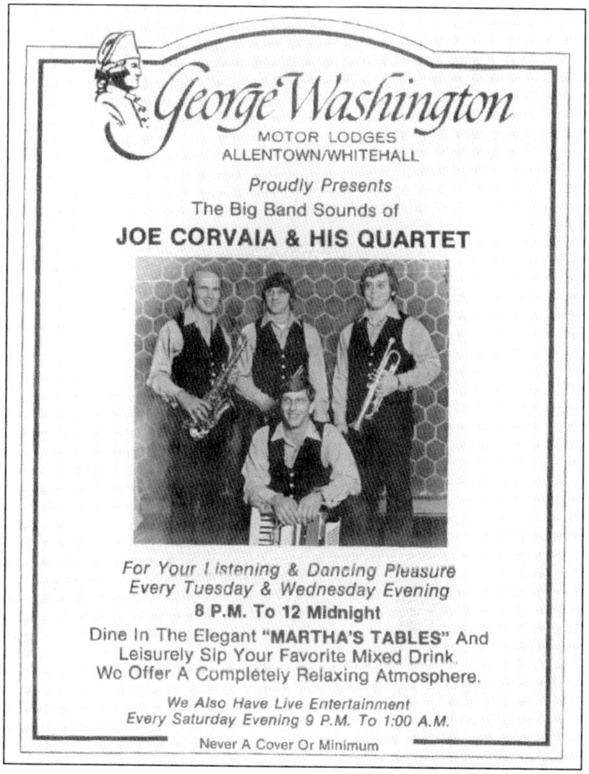

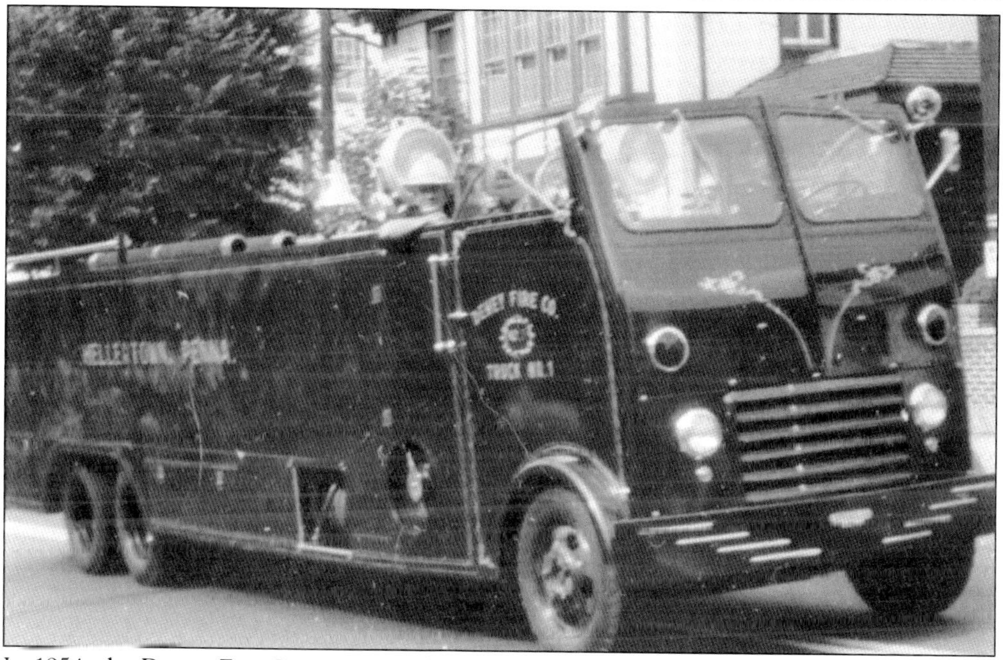

In 1954, the Dewey Fire Company purchased a Hahn pumper (pictured), equipped with two engines, two transmissions, and two differentials. The huge truck had difficulty making it around tight corners and earned the nickname "Big Bertha." This infamous Hahn pumper was replaced in 1956 by a more manageable American LaFrance pumper. (Courtesy of Dean Shaffer.)

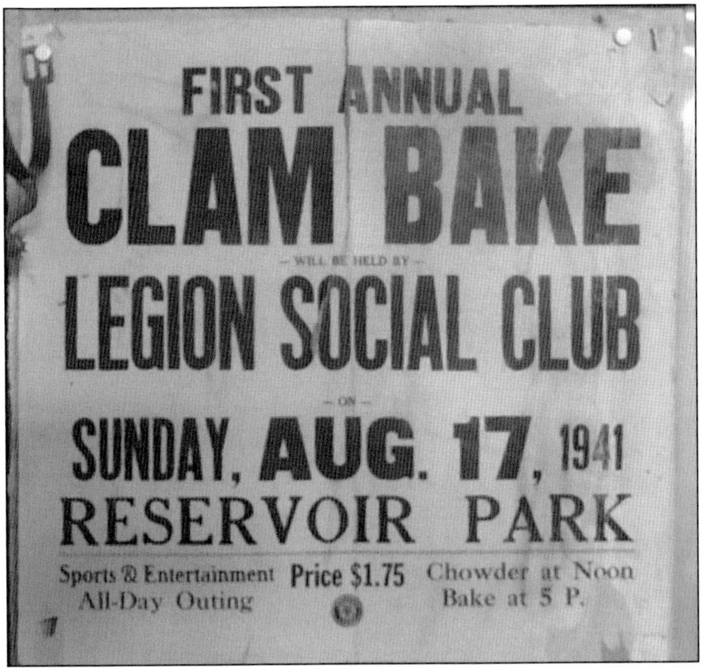

This poster announces the First Annual Clambake for the American Legion Social Club in 1941. A Sunday picnic was held on August 17, 1941, at Reservoir Park, located at 3400 Reservoir Road. The event was a great success—the American Legion carries on the tradition each year at the Meadows in Hellertown. (Courtesy of the Hellertown Historical Society.)

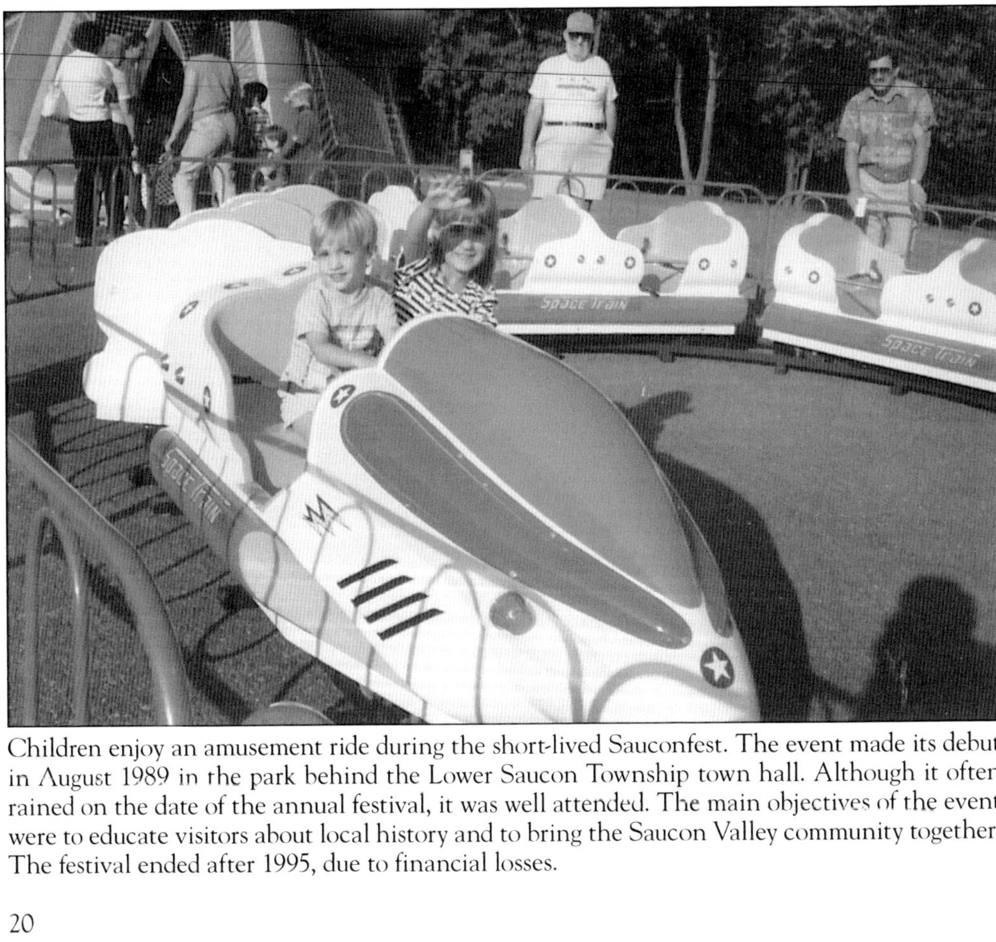

Children enjoy an amusement ride during the short-lived Sauconfest. The event made its debut in August 1989 in the park behind the Lower Saucon Township town hall. Although it often rained on the date of the annual festival, it was well attended. The main objectives of the event were to educate visitors about local history and to bring the Saucon Valley community together. The festival ended after 1995, due to financial losses.

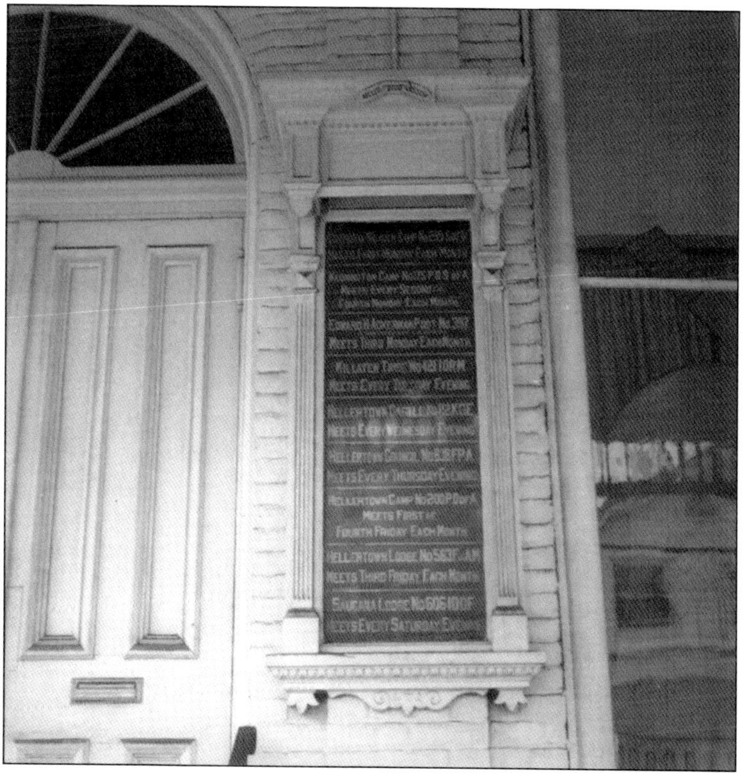

In the 1800s and early 1900s, many men's private organizations, called lodges, were established. Among these organizations were the Order of the Redmen, the Masonic Lodge, and the Corporal Weaver Camp, the latter for the Sons of Civil War Veterans. (Courtesy of the Hellertown Historical Society.)

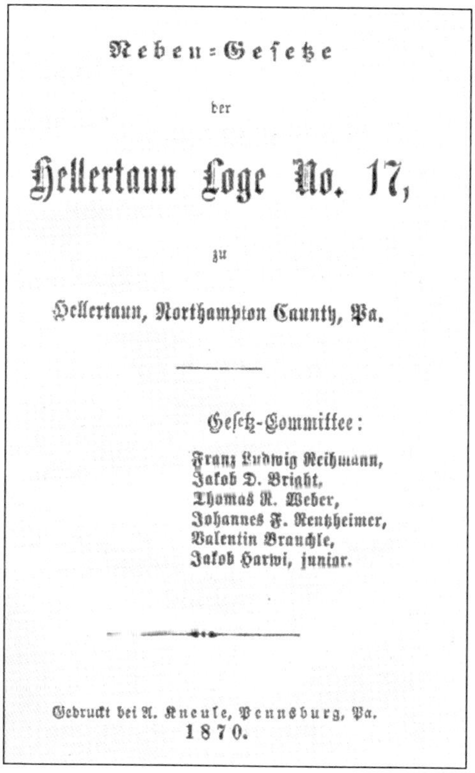

Neben-Gesetze

der

Hellertaun Loge No. 17,

zu

Hellertaun, Northampton Caunty, Pa.

Gesetz-Committee:

Franz Ludwig Reichmann,
Jakob D. Bright,
Thomas R. Weber,
Johannes F. Rentzheimer,
Valentin Brauchle,
Jakob Harwi, junior.

Gedruckt bei A. Kneule, Pennsburg, Pa.
1870.

The Order of the Sons of Hermann, also known by its German name, Der Orden der Hermann's Soehne or Hermannsshne, was formed as a social club for German immigrants in New York City on July 20, 1840. The order declined in popularity with the outbreak of World War I. A valuable benefit of joining the brotherhood was the eligibility for aid during illness. This is the charter for the Northampton County group in 1870.

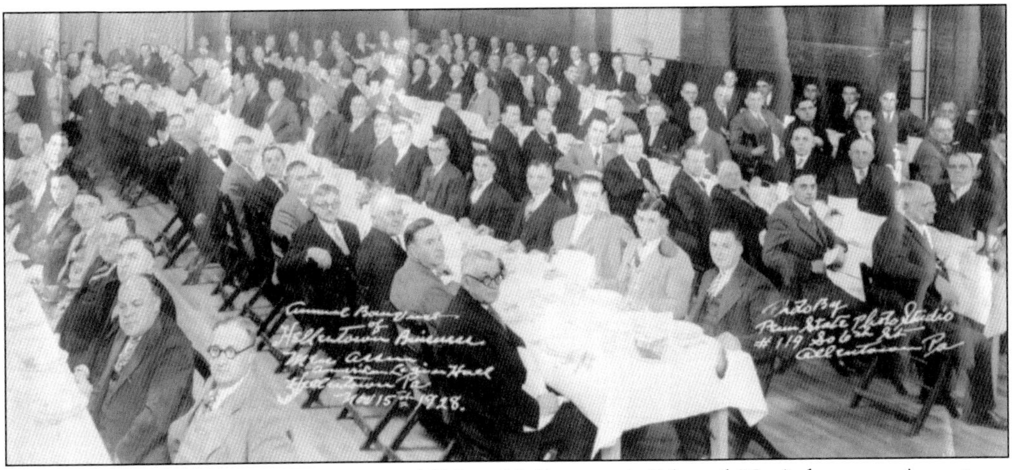

Shown here is a business meeting in 1928 at Hellertown's Edward H. Ackerman American Legion Post 397. This was one year after the building was opened in 1927. The 17,000-square-foot building is located at 935 Main Street and was named in honor of Hellertown's first casualty of World War I.

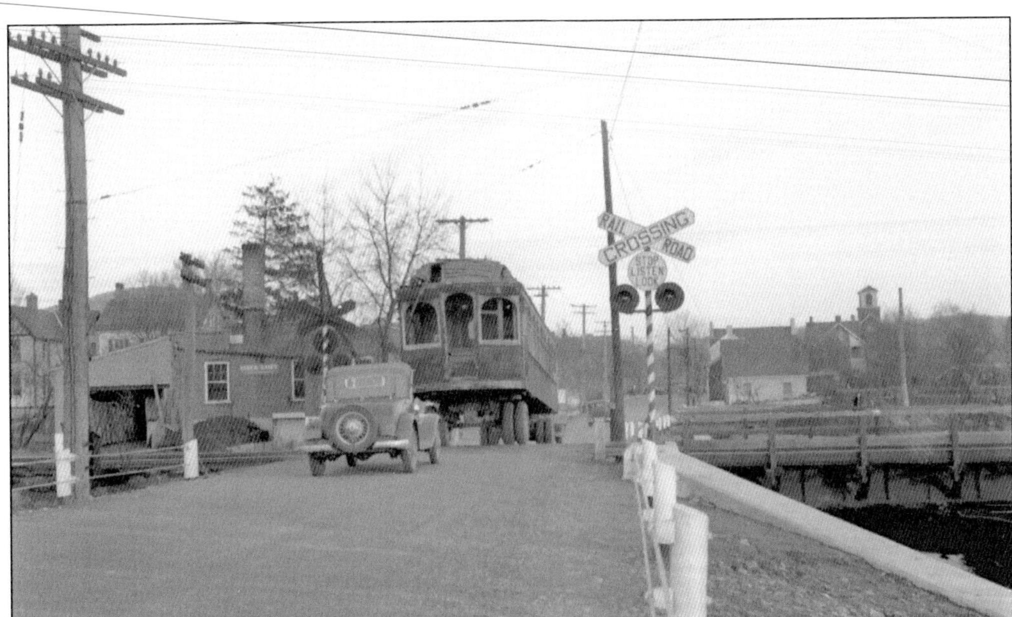

Lerch Dairy was located at Main and Clark Streets, by the North Penn Railroad tracks—now a rail trail—on Water Street. This dairy eventually became Brookfield Dairy. The trolley car being hauled on the flatbed would soon end its journey and be used as Andy Komer's Diner on the northern end of Main Street. See the trolley's final destination on page 53. (Courtesy of the Hellertown Historical Society.)

While a newspaper called the *Hellertown Herald* existed between 1946 and 1949, the publication shown here began publishing in 1962. Billed as a picture newspaper, its audience was the citizens of central eastern Lehigh Valley.

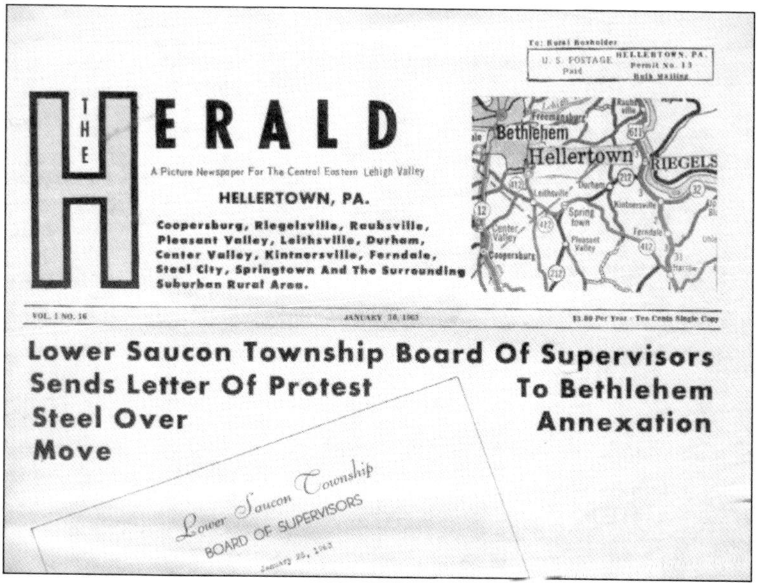

THE HERALD

A Picture Newspaper For The Central Eastern Lehigh Valley

HELLERTOWN, PA.

Coopersburg, Riegelsville, Raubsville, Pleasant Valley, Leithsville, Durham, Center Valley, Kintnersville, Ferndale, Steel City, Springtown And The Surrounding Suburban Rural Area.

U. S. POSTAGE Paid

HELLERTOWN, PA.

Lower Saucon Township Board Of Supervisors Sends Letter Of Protest To Bethlehem Steel Over Annexation Move

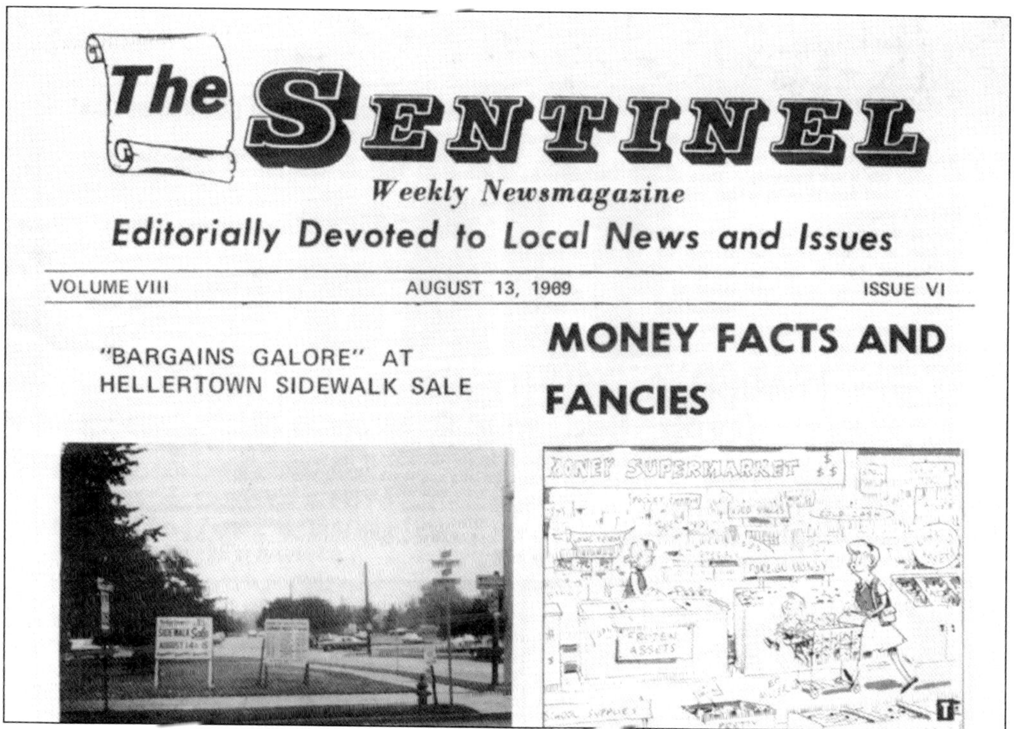

The SENTINEL

Weekly Newsmagazine

Editorially Devoted to Local News and Issues

VOLUME VIII | AUGUST 13, 1969 | ISSUE VI

"BARGAINS GALORE" AT HELLERTOWN SIDEWALK SALE

MONEY FACTS AND FANCIES

The *Sentinel* newspaper, published in Lower Saucon Township, was "Devoted to the interests of the Saucon Valley." The publisher was Beck Printing & Publishing Company on Old Philadelphia Pike in the old Hires bottling plant. The paper was distributed weekly in the late 1960s. The 24-page publication had a circulation of 6,000, and each issue cost a nickel.

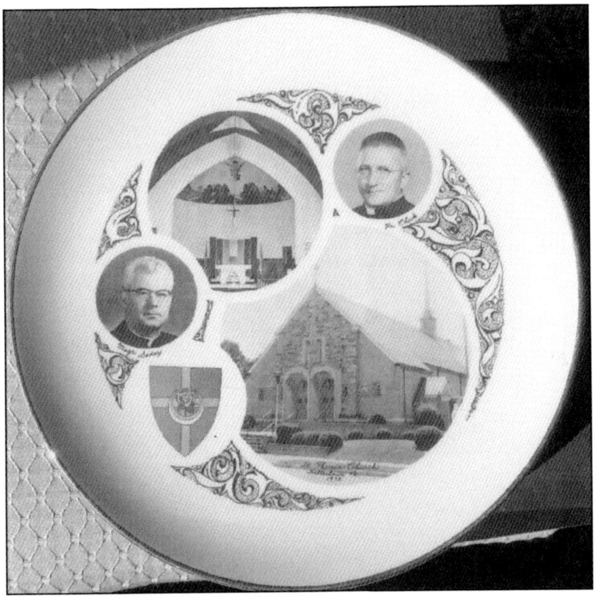

St. Theresa Parish began as a mission church attached to SS. Cyril and Methodius Church of Bethlehem in 1921. In 1923, property was purchased on Easton Road and Leonard Street, and a basement church was built. On November 12, 1925, full canonical parish status was granted, and Father George Check was named its first pastor. He served in this capacity for 40 years until his death and was succeeded by Rev. Stephen Daday, who served for 19 years. (Courtesy of St. Theresa's Church.)

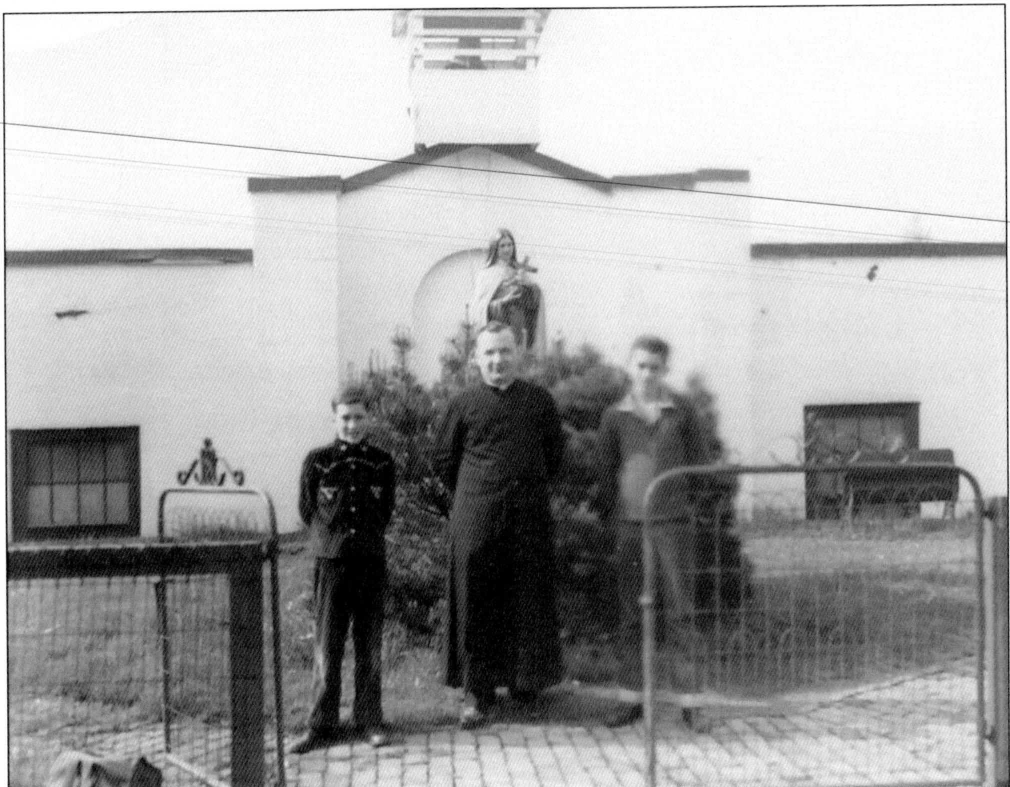

Donald Ruth (left), Rev. Joseph P. Birsh (center), and Allen Sell stand in front of St. Theresa of the Child Jesus Catholic Church at 308 Leonard Street in Hellertown. The church began in 1921 as a mission church, an offshoot of the SS. Cyril and Methodius Church in Bethlehem, Pennsylvania. It was the first Catholic church in Hellertown and held its first services in a movie studio at High and Whitaker Streets.

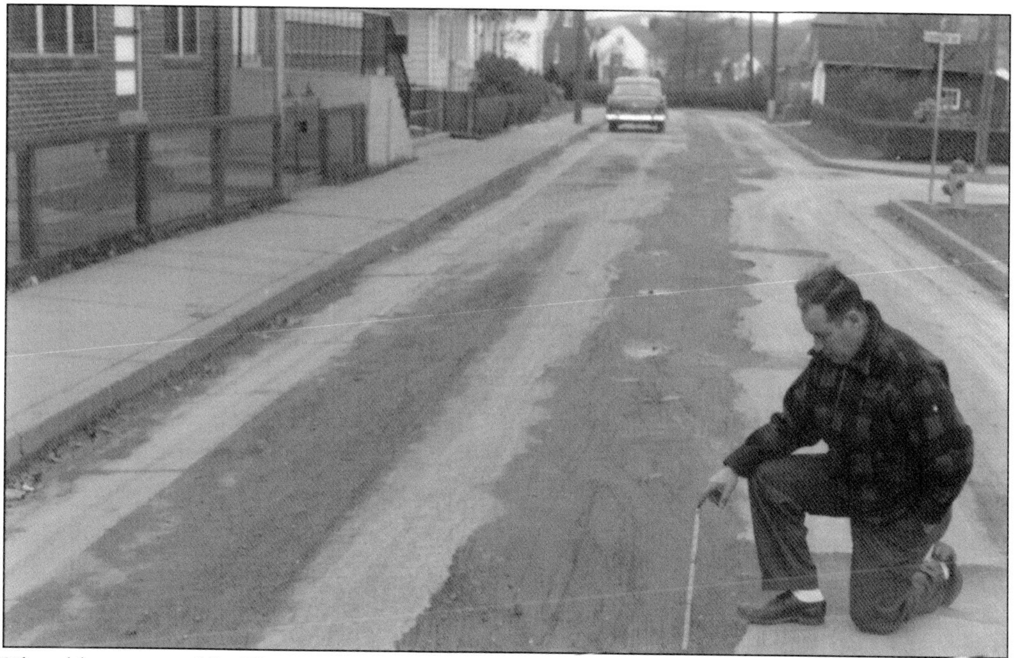

The old convent of St. Theresa's Convent is the building at far left. Next to it is the rear door and stairway to the school. Here, a member of the Hellertown Water Authority surveys Leonard Street for maintenance of the borough water mains. The convent building has since been demolished, and the convent was moved to Wilson Avenue in Hellertown. (Courtesy of Hellertown Borough Water Authority.)

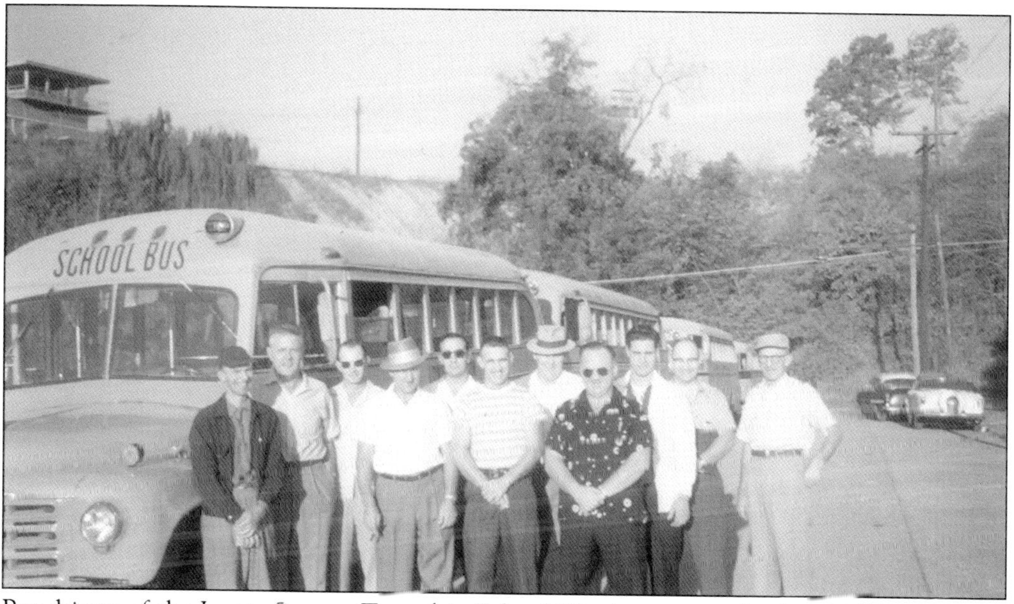

Bus drivers of the Lower Saucon Township School District pose at the Iron Hill bus stop. G. Raymond Todd is second from right, holding a clipboard. Earl Werkheiser is on the far left, and Merritt Beitler is next to him. Peter Kiss is in the black aloha shirt. These drivers traveled on 100 miles of roads to transport students to the 12 schoolhouses spread throughout the township. (Courtesy of John Fischel.)

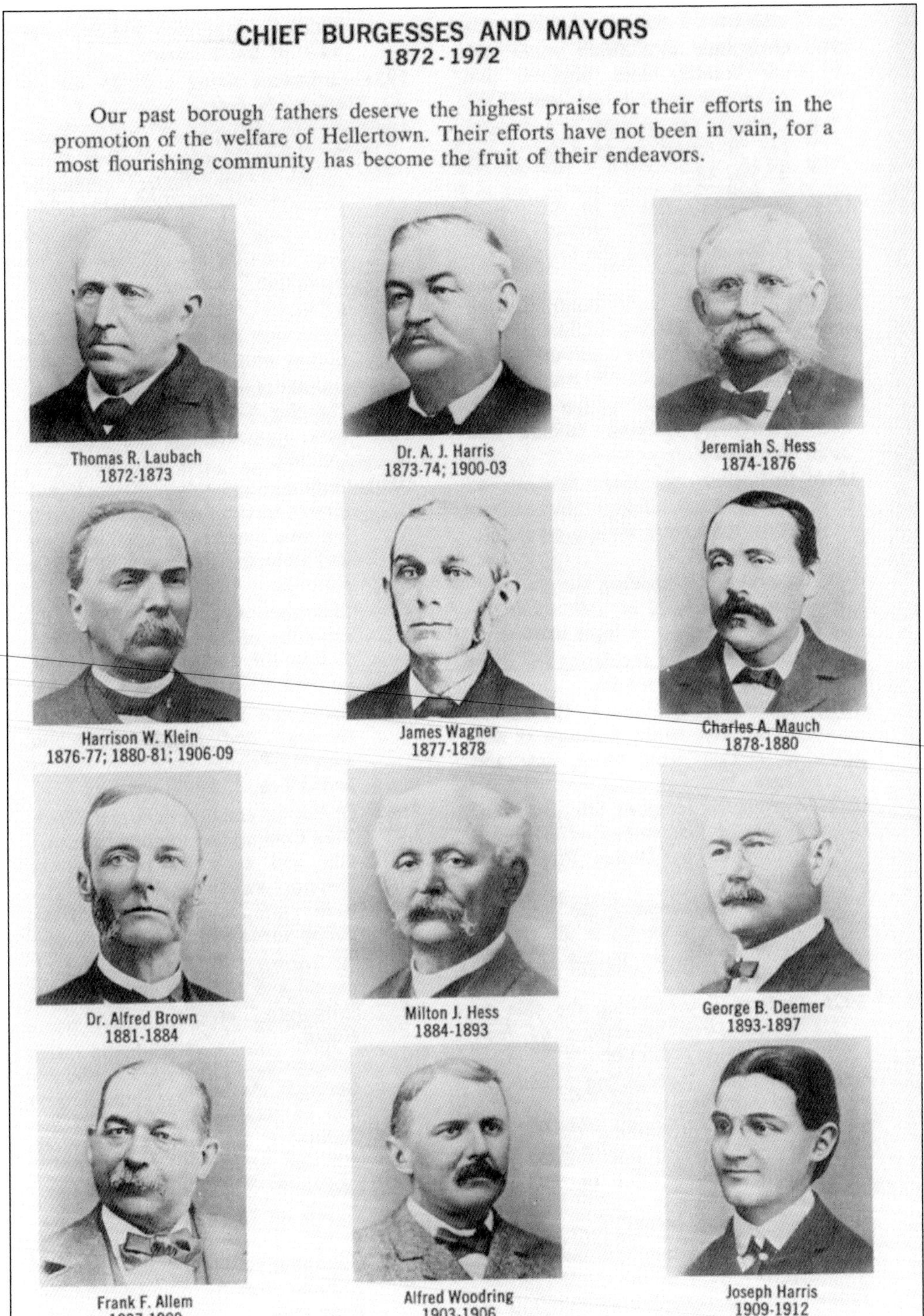

CHIEF BURGESSES AND MAYORS
1872 - 1972

Our past borough fathers deserve the highest praise for their efforts in the promotion of the welfare of Hellertown. Their efforts have not been in vain, for a most flourishing community has become the fruit of their endeavors.

Thomas R. Laubach
1872-1873

Dr. A. J. Harris
1873-74; 1900-03

Jeremiah S. Hess
1874-1876

Harrison W. Klein
1876-77; 1880-81; 1906-09

James Wagner
1877-1878

Charles A. Mauch
1878-1880

Dr. Alfred Brown
1881-1884

Milton J. Hess
1884-1893

George B. Deemer
1893-1897

Frank F. Allem
1897-1900

Alfred Woodring
1903-1906

Joseph Harris
1909-1912

On these two pages are the images and names of the chief burgesses and mayors of the borough of Hellertown, between 1872 and 1940. These pages appeared in the booklet "Saucon Valley Cavalcade: Legion Americanism Pageant, Hellertown Park, Hellertown, Penna., July 17-18-19-20, 1940." The

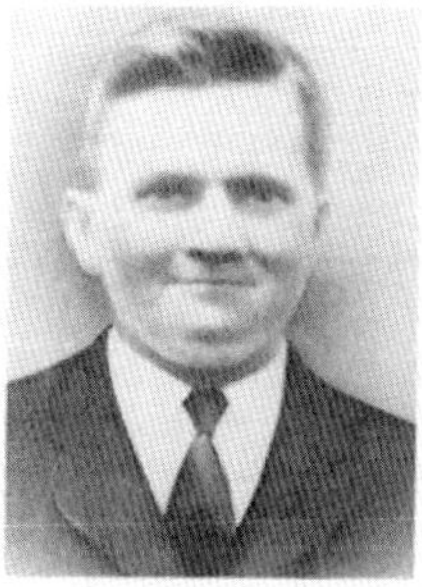

Edward Bergstresser
1912-1916

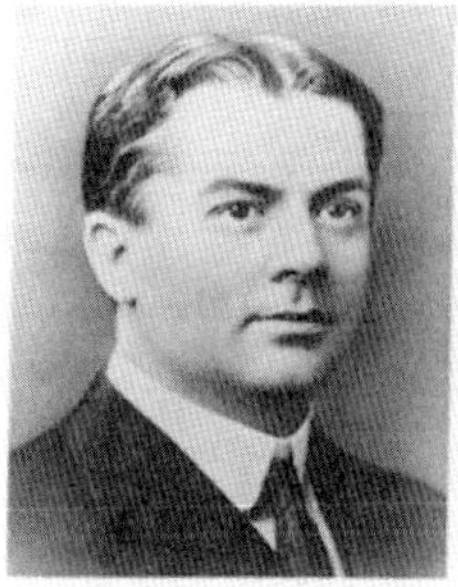

Harry L. Ache
1916-1918

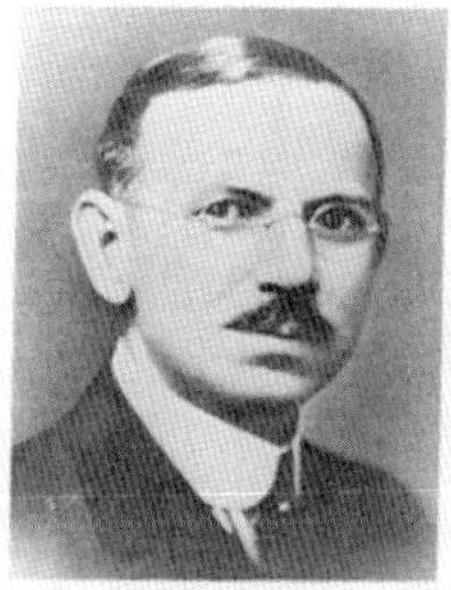

Franklin Sutton
1918-1922

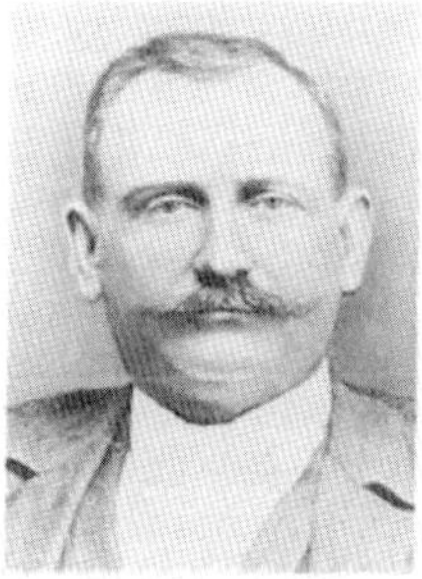

Dr. Chas. J. Waidner
1922-1923

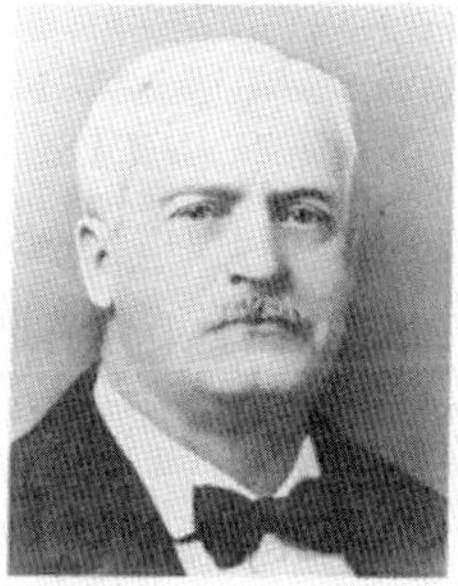

Ambrose J. Welker
1923-1926

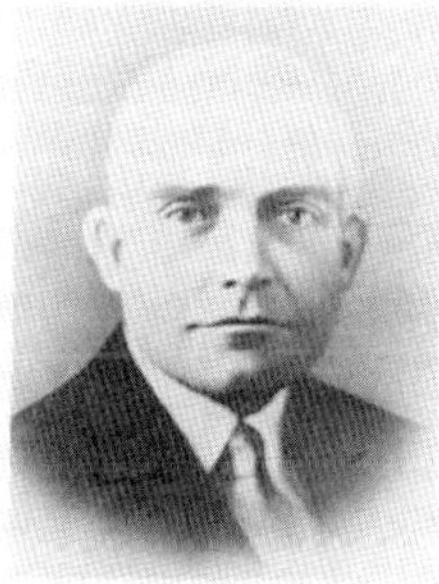

Morris J. Dimmick
1926-1946

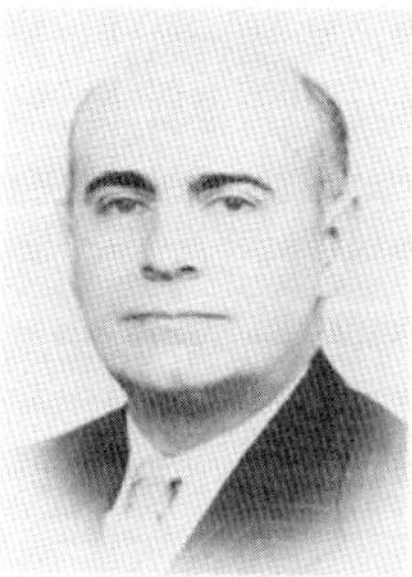

Howard S. Hess
1946-1949

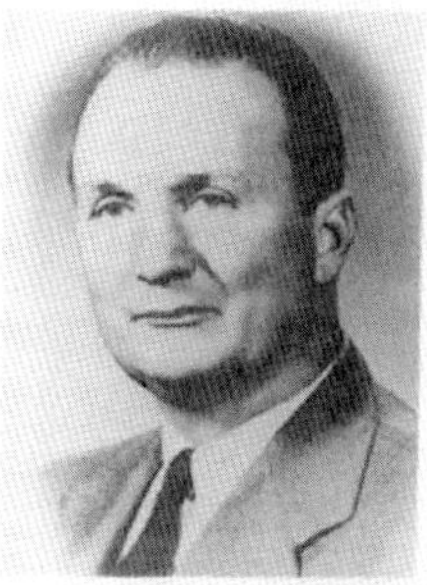

Myron D. Parsons
1950-1951

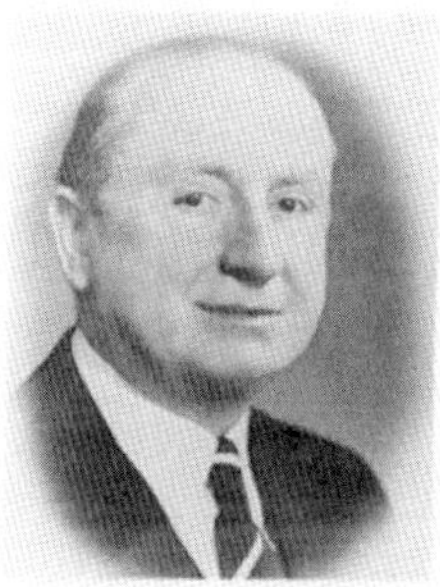

Asher S. Kichline
1951-1952

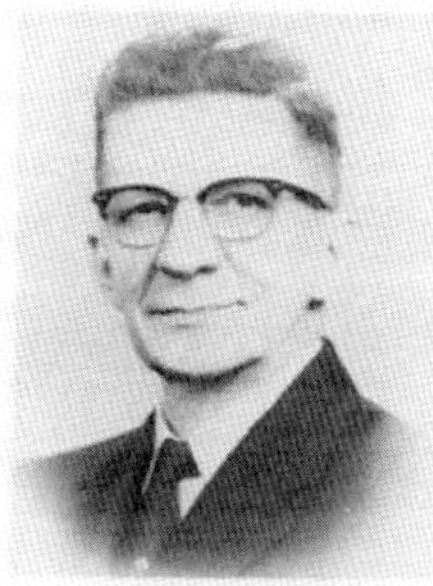

Warren Fritchman
1952-1962

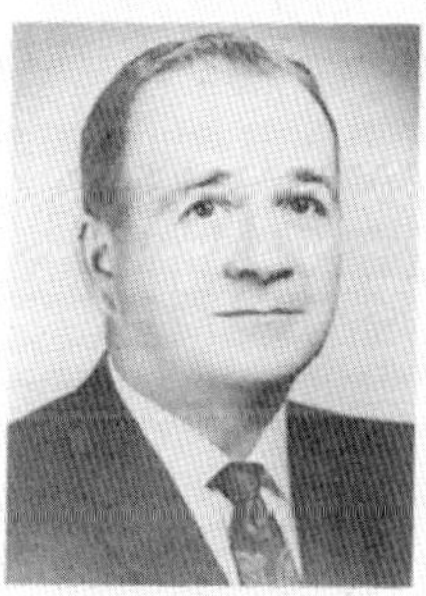

Howard R. Strohl
1962-1966

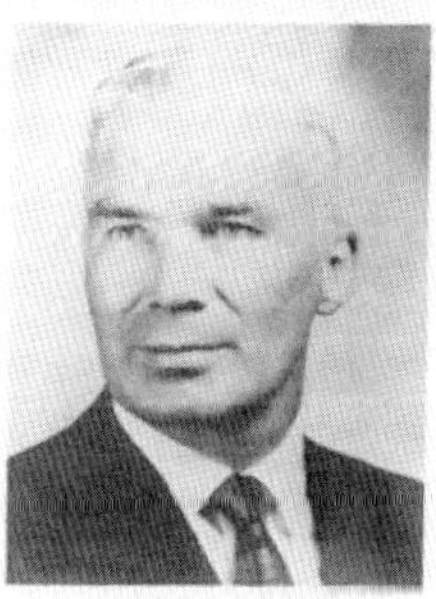

John O. Williams
1966-1969

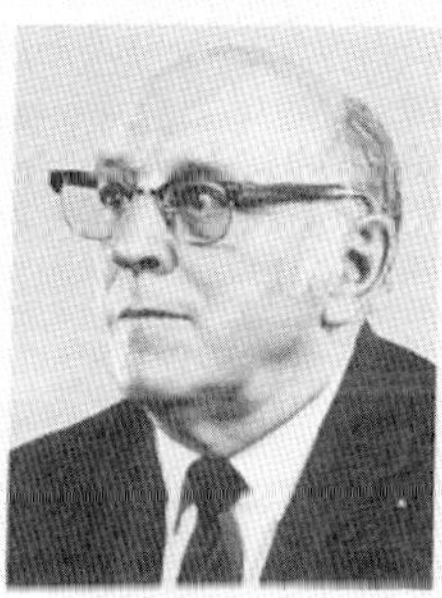

Albert M. Beneck
1969-1970

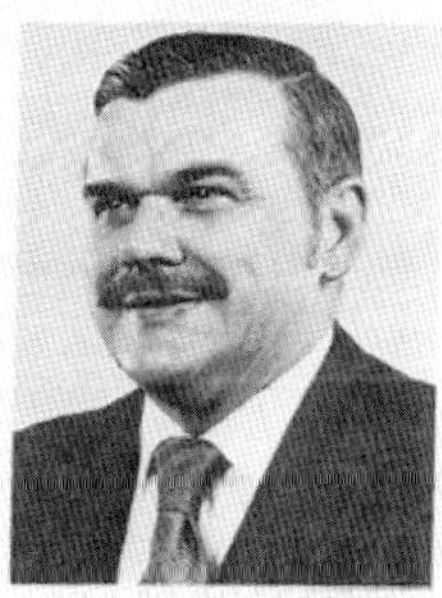

Emerson J. Mills
1970-

first chief burgess following incorporation was Thomas R. Laubach. He was president of Saucon Savings Bank and trustee of the Reformed and Lutheran Evangelical Church. Today, Richard T. Fluck serves the borough as mayor. He is currently in his fourth term.

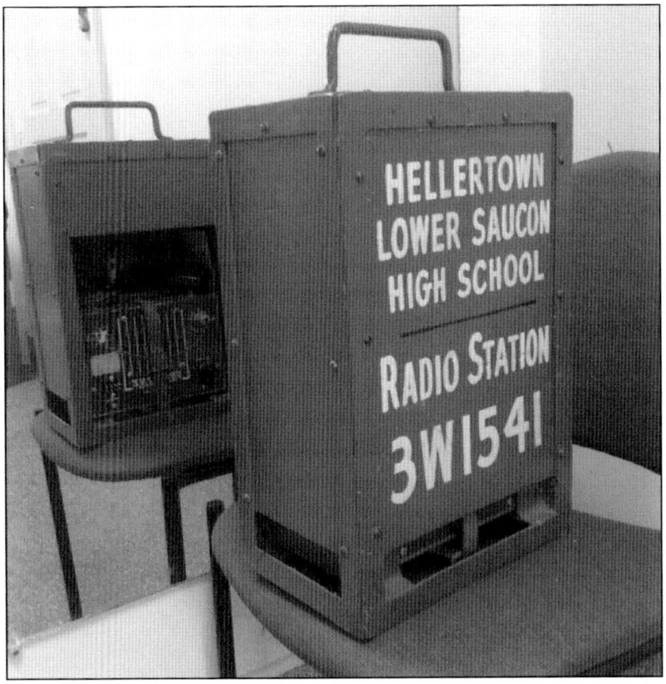

In the late 1950s, schools held frequent drills to make sure their students were prepared for a possible World War III. Radio networks were established to conduct regular "nets" (gathering of on-air radio personnel) to practice proper protocol to ensure that orderly communications take place in the event of an attack. Here is an example of a well-constructed unit containing a one-channel Vocaline Citizen Band (CB) radio set. The labeling indicates that it was housed within the high school.

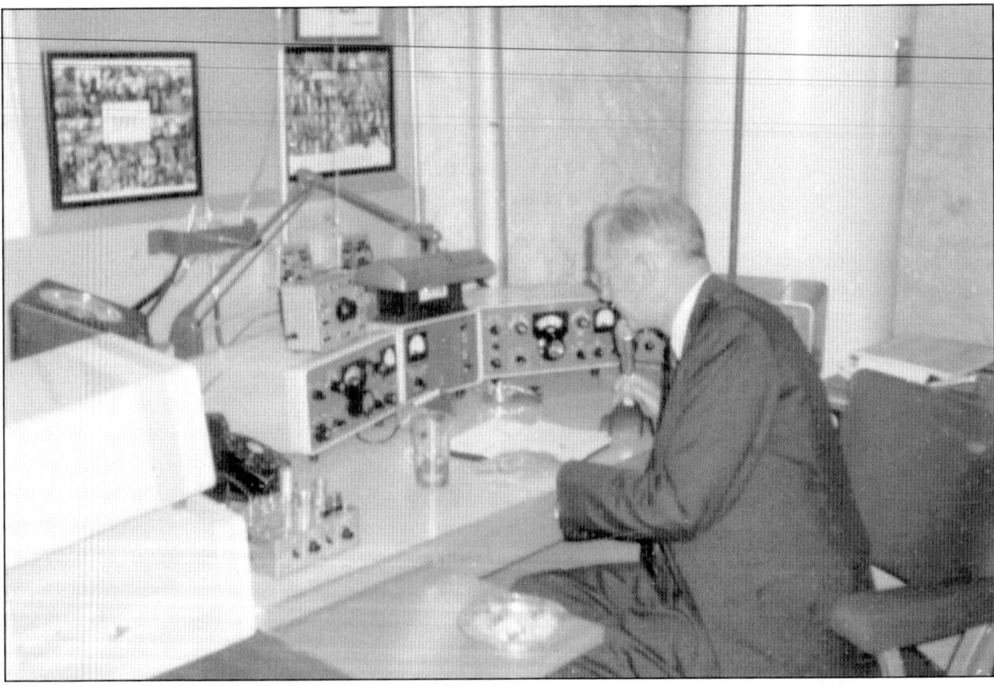

John Marsh was the manager of research at Bethlehem Steel until 1963. His hobby was amateur (ham) radio. He is pictured here in his home's basement station on Stonesthrow Road. His wife taught home economics at Hellertown Lower Saucon High School and was also an amateur radio operator (K3WJG). Under a vanity callsign program of the Federal Communications Commission, John's callsign (W3ZF) has been assigned to Daniel Ruth as an endearing token of their friendship.

Ethel Helms (1899–1987), Lower Saucon Township historian, wrote a play for the Wassergass Bushmen to perform, reenacting the Walking Purchase Treaty of September 19 and 20, 1737. It was performed during the Lower Saucon bicentennial celebration in June 1976. At the event, Helms took this photograph of a reproduction of a Conestoga wagon.

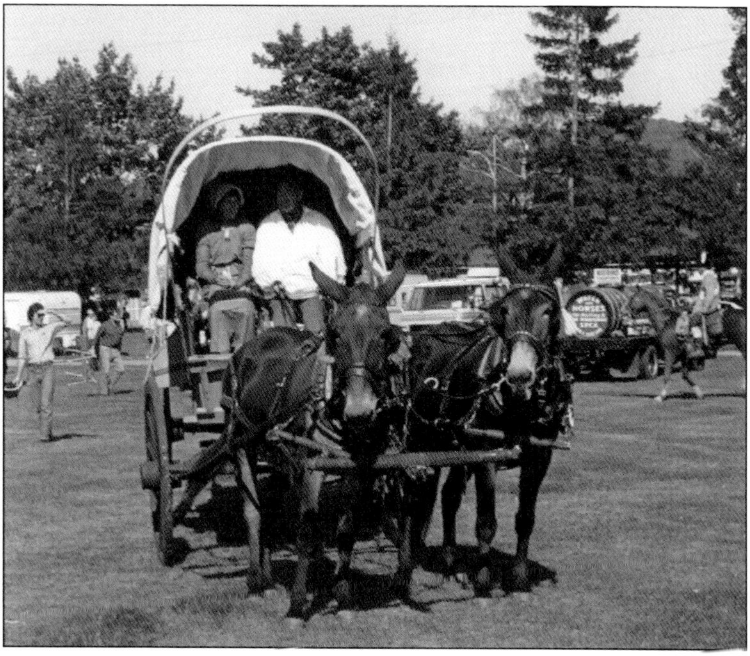

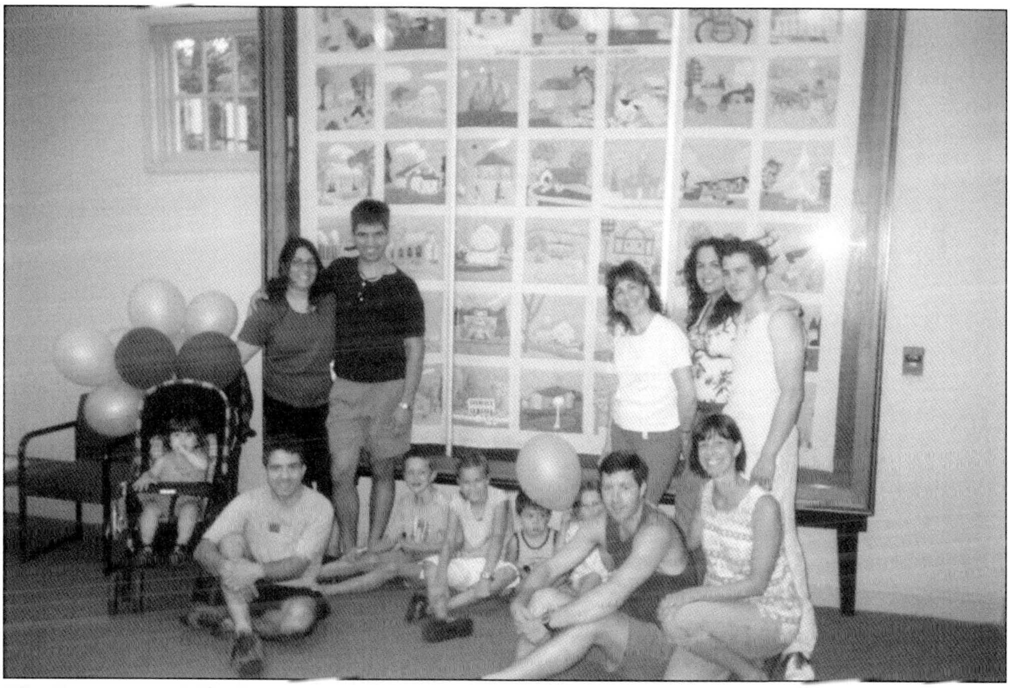

The Bicentennial Quilt Committee worked hard to celebrate local history during the country's bicentennial celebration in 1976. Many quilters individualized Hellertown and Lower Saucon historic sites. Today, the quilt is on display upstairs in Hellertown Borough Hall. This photograph was taken on Hellertown's first Community Day in 2001. The quilt frame was made from wood taken from the Weisel Harness Shop counter by Hellertown Historical Society members.

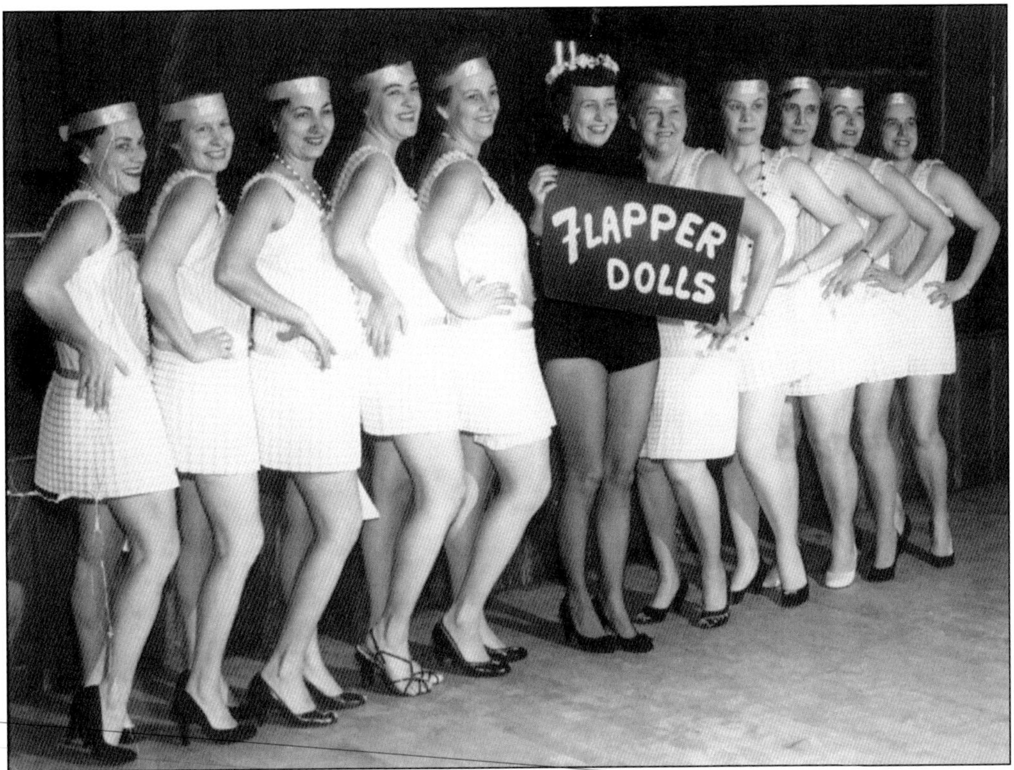

Posing here are, from left to right, Lucille Williams, Margaret Christian, Dorothy Hartman, Dorothy Halloway, Arlene Mills, unidentified, Ruth Werkheiser, Rita Ruth, Corinne Crook, unidentified, and Elaine McCarthy. They are ready to dance at a fundraiser for the Hellertown Women's Club.

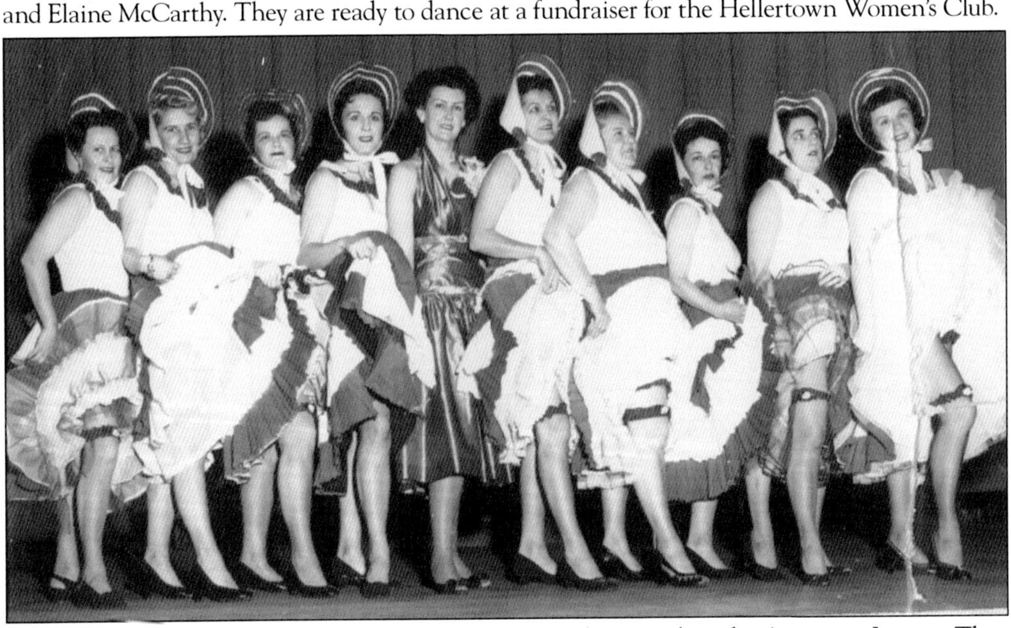

Members of the Women's Club of Hellertown pose for a photograph at the American Legion. They are, from left to right, Margaret Christian, Marion Nicholas, Jane Fehr, Dorothy Spangenberg, Mrs. Gross, Wyn Goldberg, Ruth Werkheiser, Mrs. Panick, Elaine McCarthy, and Rita Ruth.

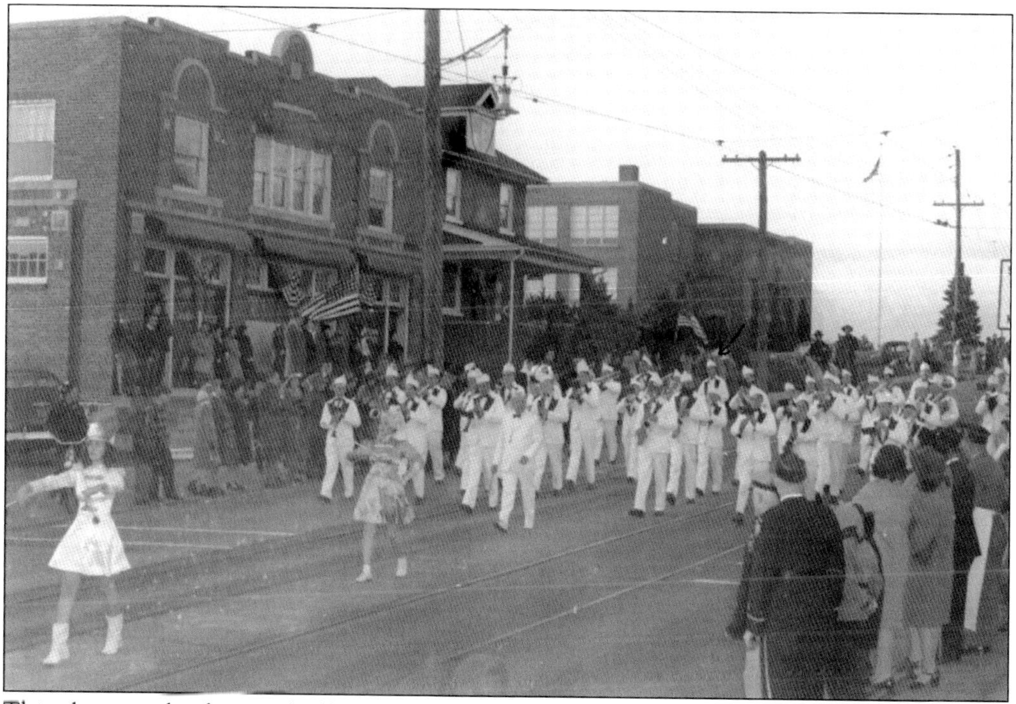

This photograph of a parade illustrates a warm memory for Hellertonians. Parades were greatly enjoyed by the town's residents. This one passes the Hellertown post office at 1000 Main Street. It had just passed Dr. Walter M. Brenholtz's office and, before that, Hellertown High School. The crowd is lined up on both sides of Main Street to enjoy the American Legion Band. The white uniforms and Garrison caps were typical of the time. (Courtesy of the Hellertown Historical Society.)

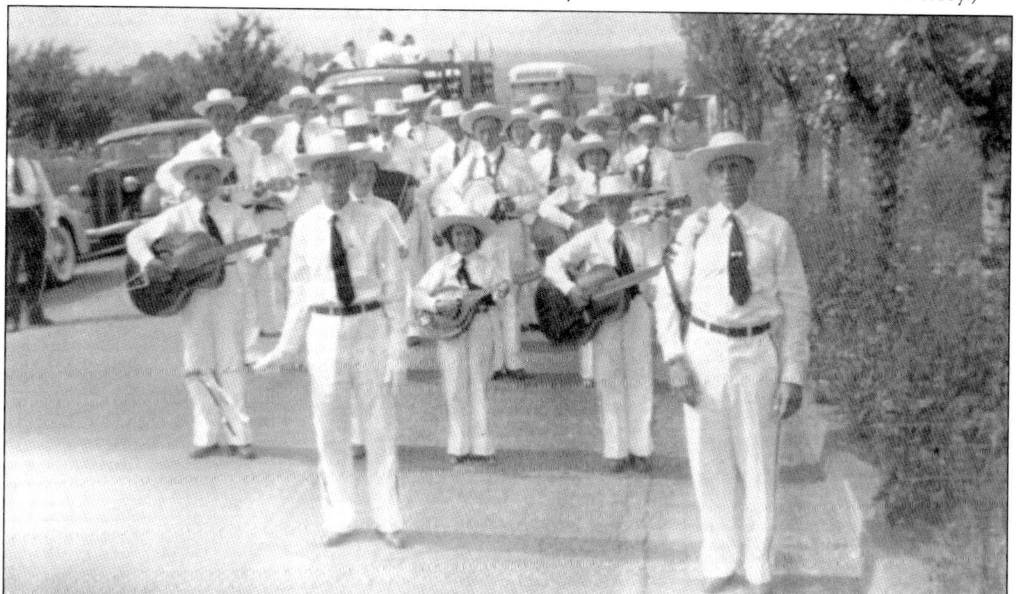

Here are members of the Kish family playing in the Easton Marching String Band. The musically gifted family members played all over the Lehigh Valley. The Kish family farm was located behind a large hill and out of view from Lower Saucon Road. (Courtesy of Lawrence Kish.).

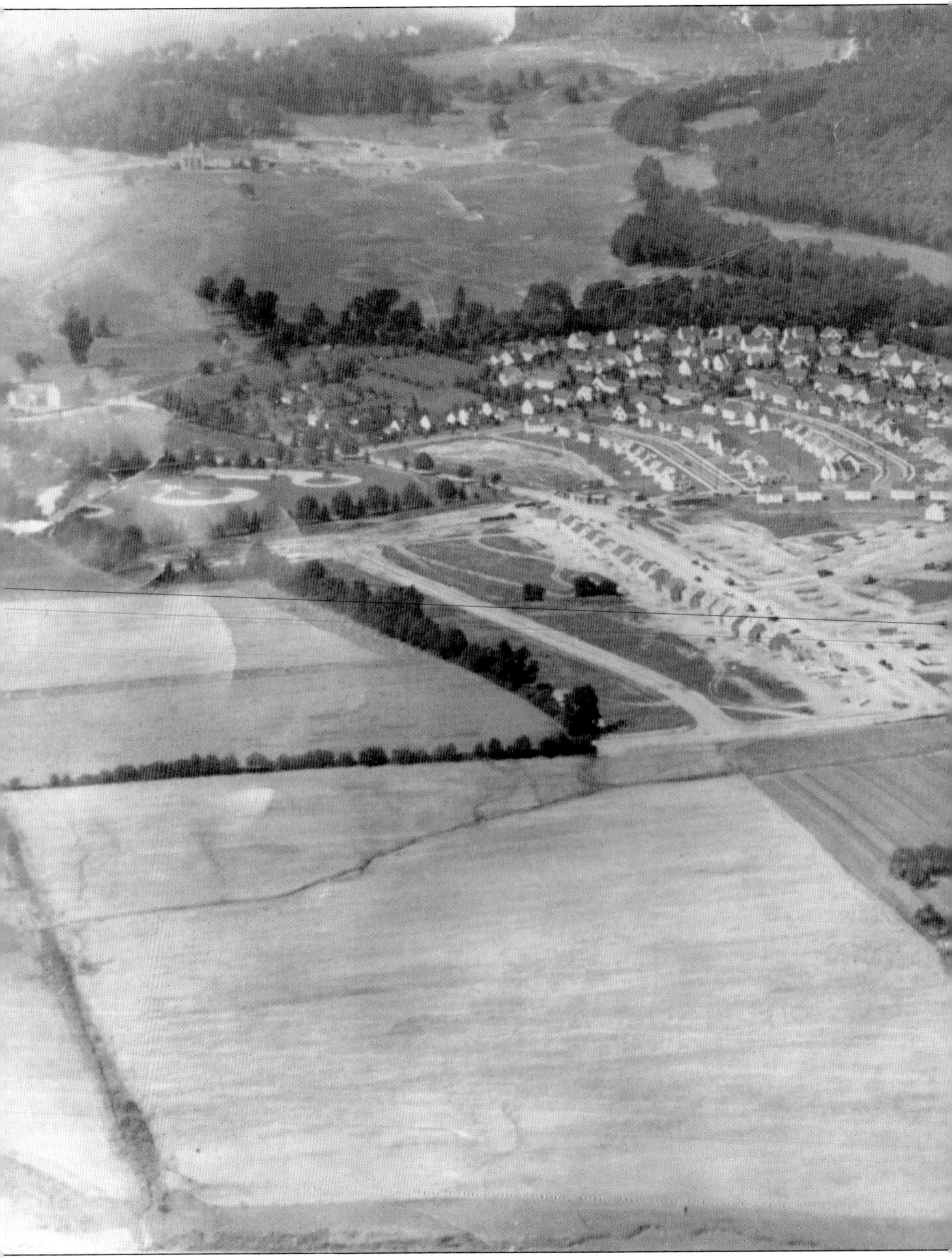

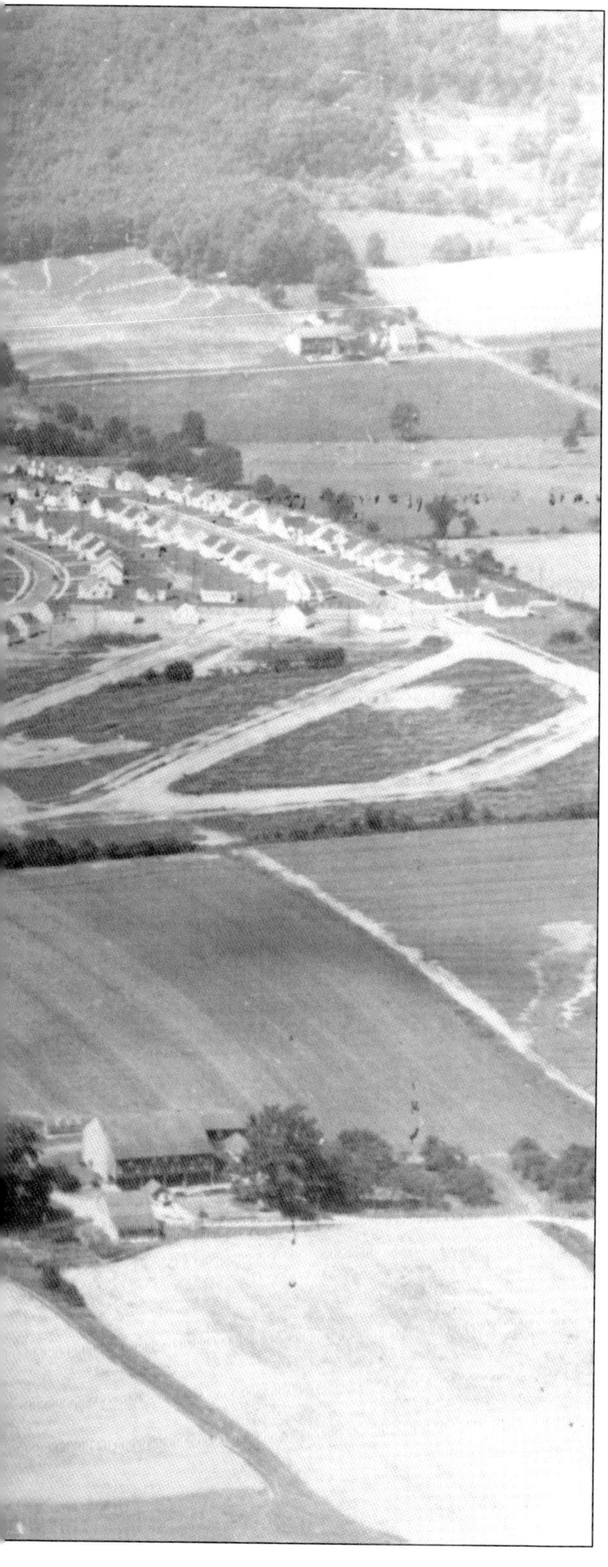

This aerial photograph of developing Mountainview shows the complete formation of Constitution Avenue. What an exciting time it was for the building trades, with the boom in home construction. The farm at lower right would eventually be the site of the current high school complex. The Mountainview development was built in the 1940s and 1950s on the old Rentzheimer farm in Hellertown. The homes were typically one-and-a-half stories, in the Cape Cod style. The GI Bill, passed by Congress in 1944, provided low-interest, zero-down-payment home loans for servicemen. The lots were quickly sold to Bethlehem Steel Corporation workers. (Courtesy of the Hellertown Historical Society.)

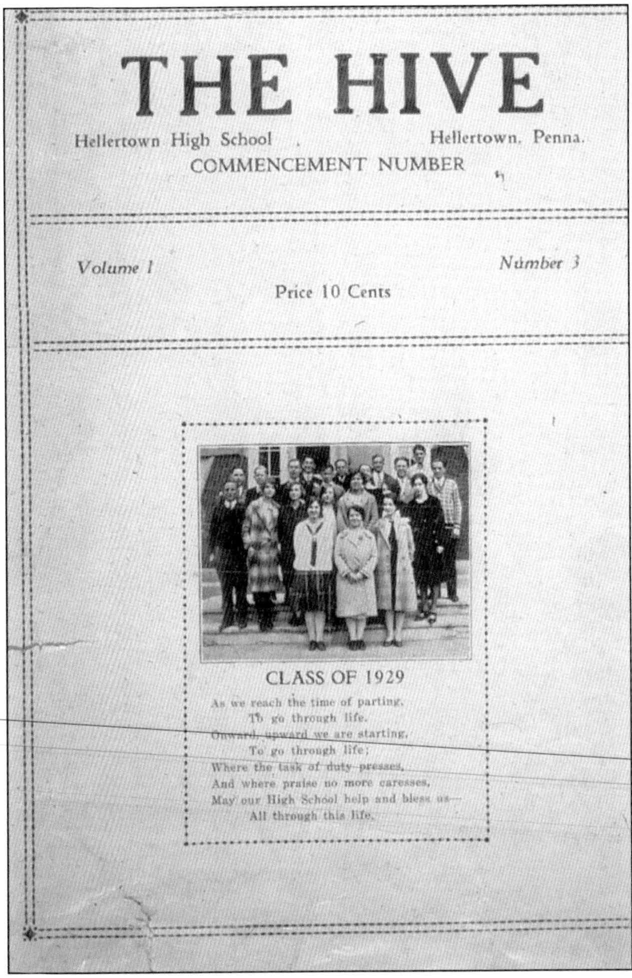
THE HIVE

Hellertown High School   Hellertown, Penna.

COMMENCEMENT NUMBER

Volume I   Number 3

Price 10 Cents

CLASS OF 1929

As we reach the time of parting,
To go through life.
Onward, upward we are starting,
To go through life;
Where the task of duty presses,
And where praise no more caresses,
May our High School help and bless us—
All through this life.

In 1929, the first issue of the *Hive* was printed. It remained the student newspaper of Saucon Valley High School for over 70 years before it went out of publication due to politics within the administration.

This is the June 1966 issue of the *Hive*. The publication gave high school students experience in newspaper categories such as sports, editorials, news, and features, along with photography and illustration. The illustration at the top depicts Hellertown High School, on Main Street between Thomas Avenue and Sycamore Street.

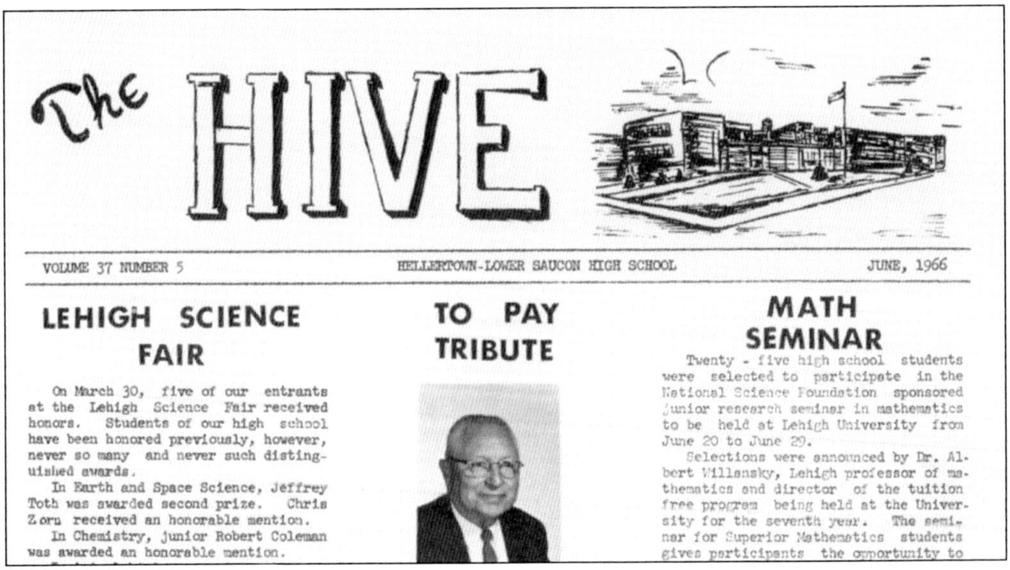
The HIVE

VOLUME 37 NUMBER 5   HELLERTOWN-LOWER SAUCON HIGH SCHOOL   JUNE, 1966

LEHIGH SCIENCE FAIR

On March 30, five of our entrants at the Lehigh Science Fair received honors. Students of our high school have been honored previously, however, never so many and never such distinguished awards.

In Earth and Space Science, Jeffrey Toth was awarded second prize. Chris Zorn received an honorable mention.

In Chemistry, junior Robert Coleman was awarded an honorable mention.

TO PAY TRIBUTE

MATH SEMINAR

Twenty - five high school students were selected to participate in the National Science Foundation sponsored junior research seminar in mathematics to be held at Lehigh University from June 20 to June 29.

Selections were announced by Dr. Albert Willansky, Lehigh professor of mathematics and director of the tuition free program being held at the University for the seventh year. The seminar for Superior Mathematics students gives participants the opportunity to

THE FREE PRESS FINAL EDITION

STATEMENT DISSOLVING THE FREE PRESS

We, the editors of The Free [illegible], [illegible]authorized newspaper intended for the school community of Hellertown [illegible] make this statement concerning it. As [illegible] of us are leaving [illegible] do not want our stigma attached to any paper other than The Free Press, we now dissolve this publication. We in no way have any influence over any paper which may evolve in the future, nor do we endorse any circular with the title of "The Free Press". However, we do feel that Hellertown needs a paper along the outline of The Free Press, and hope to see some group of involved person carry out this idea, and wish anyone undertaking this project the best of luck.

First published in January, 1969, having a circulation of nearly 1,000, and creating an open forum as Hellertown has never had, we are now regretfully disbanding. The Free Press - disolved as of this date - June 1rst, 1970.

The *Free Press* was an underground school newspaper that made its mark in the late 1960s. It was assembled by a group of articulate, outspoken students who took the administration to task on issues with which they disagreed. One of their goals was to provide an open (and frequently rebellious) forum for students to voice their frustrations and opinions.

The Panther Press

Volume I, Number I | Saucon Valley High School, Hellertown, Pa. 18055 | November, 1992

SGA FACES BLEAK FINANCIAL YEAR

By CHRIS FOWLER

At the start of the 1992-93 school year, the Student Government Association treasury had just under $2,000 of start-up money. That is over $8,000 less than the $10,000 available for the start of the '91-'92 school year.

The two chief causes of the low funds this year are higher than normal spending last year and lower than normal income so far this year.

The SGA's three biggest expenditures in '91-'92 were homecoming (about $2,500), yearbook subsidization and prom subsidization (about $1,500). In all, the SGA spent about $3,000 more than normal. The Homecoming expenses included $1,500 to protect the gym floor for traditionally lucrative football concession stand is down 60 percent from last year.

The SGA cut spending for homecoming in half this year, and the SGA also expects to break even on the second annual Christmas dance. But only a strong fall fundraiser can save the SGA treasury

Without SGA subsidies, students could very well be paying $50 or more for the 1993 Reflector yearbook, and $100 or more per couple for prom tickets. Unfortunately, the means of raising money for the Reflector are limited. "Because we are a relatively small school and publishing costs continue to rise, we have very few ways of increasing the money we can take in through book sales and advertising," Mr. Dale

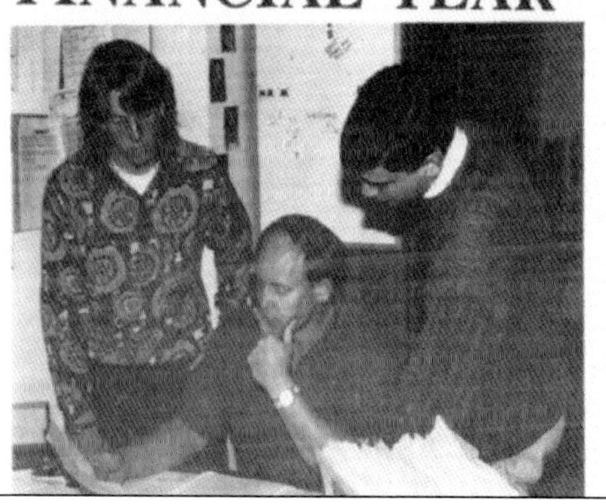

After a hiatus of three years, a collection of students, school advisers, and even a newspaper editorial writer got the school board to allocate enough funds to kick-start the student newspaper back into gear.

BETHLEHEM BULLETIN

Merged with the HELLERTOWN TRIBUNE

ALEXANDER FETSKO, Founder

AN INDEPENDENT LIBERAL NEWSPAPER
ESTABLISHED NOVEMBER 19, 1926

Published Every Thursday by
The Peerless Publishing Co.
Executive and Editorial Office
4th and Polk Streets Bethlehem, Pa. 18016
Telephone 866-3000 and 797-1945

Bernard J. Fetsko....................Publisher
Virginia Peters........Advertising Counsellor

We are not responsible for any manuscript sent us.

Advertising rates given on application. The right to decline or discontinue any advertisement is reserved.

Entered as second-class matter February 19, 1929 at the Post Office at Bethlehem, Pa., under the act of March 3, 1879.

Subscription rates: United States $3.00 per year; Europe, Canada and other foreign countries $4.00 per year. Delivered by mail or carrier.

This is a notification of the merging of the *Hellertown Tribune* with the *Bethlehem Bulletin* newspaper in 1968. The *Hellertown Tribune* began in 1933 with Myron Krivits as the editor and Alexander Fetsko as the publisher. Fetsko was also the publisher of the *Bethlehem Bulletin*. His company was located on East Fourth Street in Bethlehem. The office was known as a place to socialize and catch a few games of poker.

JULY 28, 1976 (687th ISSUE)

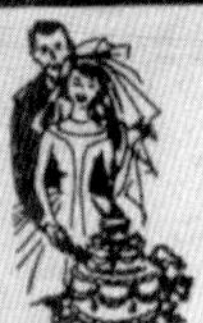

WE'RE READY TO GIVE YOU PROMPT SERVICE!
WEDDING & BIRTHDAY CAKES
All Baking Done On Premises
WE CAN SUPPLY BAKED NEEDS FOR ANY SPECIAL OCCASION!
TRAVISANO'S
RESTAURANT and BAKERY
620 Main St. Phone 838-0461 Hellertown, Pa.

MRS. MARY PUSKAS BIRTHDAY JULY 11

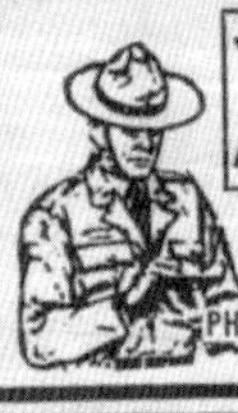

TIME FOR CAR INSPECTION!
IT'S TIME TO CHANGE FROM NO. 1 STICKER TO NO. 3 STICKER
YOU MUST REPLACE BETWEEN AUGUST 1 & NOV. 1
SKRABAN'S GARAGE
PHONE 838-8033 HELLERTOWN, PA.
139 Main Street

KILES

AT OLYMPIC GAMES

Mr. and Mrs. "Kelly" Gutshall are attending the Olympic games in Montreal, Canada . . . Anthony Travisano greeted Mr. and Mrs. Edw. Fluck at Legion Dance . . . "Ronnie" Freudenberger in Princeton, N. J. . . . "Monk" Rice, "Jake" Mowrey and John Molnar saw major league baseball game in N. Y. City . . . "Ed" Gawlikowski greeted Mr. and Mrs. "Tom" Forest in Hellertown . . . (See SEWYCO Circus ad on page 2) . . . "Jake" Fritchman is a "Jimmy" Carter booster for president

MR. & MRS. WM. STRAWN MARRIED 34 YRS. AUG. 16

BAUDERS SHOPPING JOURNAL
Post Office Box 71
Hellertown, Pa.
18055

PATRONIZE SHOPPING JOURNAL ADVERTISERS

ANNOUNCING
SE-WY-CO FIRE COMPANY'S
50th ANNIVERSARY CELEBRATION
August 21 To 28, 1976

SUNDAY — AUGUST 22
10:15 A.M. –Church Service — Friedens Lutheran Church
10:30 P.M. –Dedication (Flag-Flag Pole-Memorial Bldg.)

• Entertainment Nightly — 7 to 10 P.M. •

SATURDAY — AUGUST 28
1:00 P.M. — Firemen's Parade
3:00 P.M. — New Truck Dedication

1926–1976 FIRE EQUIPMENT ITEMS AND COLLECTION OF PICTURES WILL BE ON DISPLAY IN SE-WY-CO SOCIAL QUARTERS

Charles "Pokey" Bauder was the reporter covering local events and advertising for Hellertown and Lower Saucon Township businesses in the 1950s. If one's name appeared in the paper, they were expected to tip the reporter.

Two

The General Store

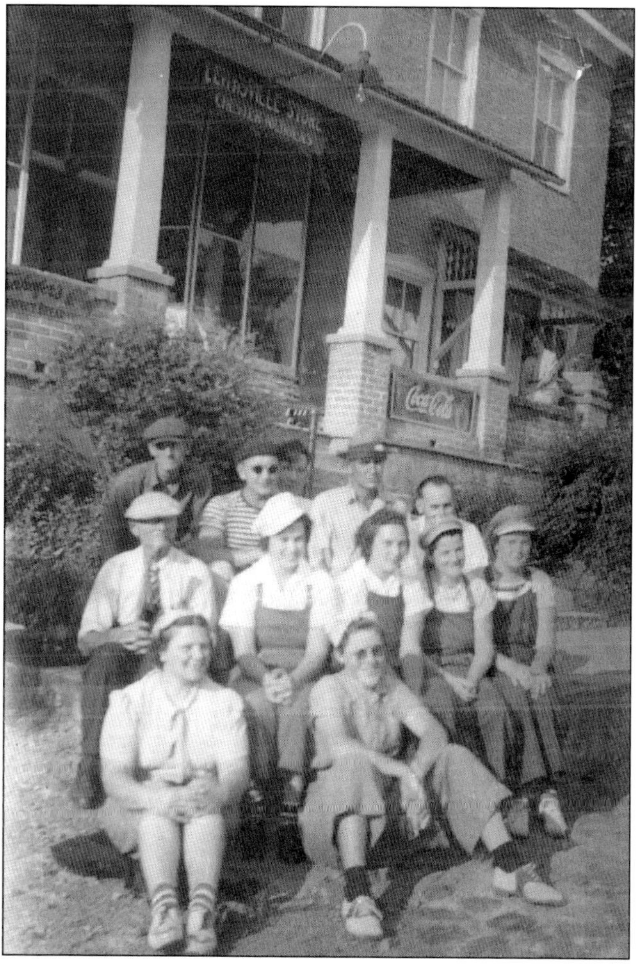

Samuel Leith established this general store in the village of Leithsville in the mid-1800s. Joseph T. Hess purchased the store in 1860 and ran it until his death in 1901. In this 1950s photograph, the sign indicates that Chester B. Nicholas was the proprietor. He learned the business from his father, Richard M. Nicholas, who had a general store on Main Street of Hellertown. Chester's brother, Earl T. Nicholas, operated the Main Street store as a five and dime. It may be Chester's wife, Quedell (Kramer), at far right on the porch. This group of people has gathered before embarking on a trip together.

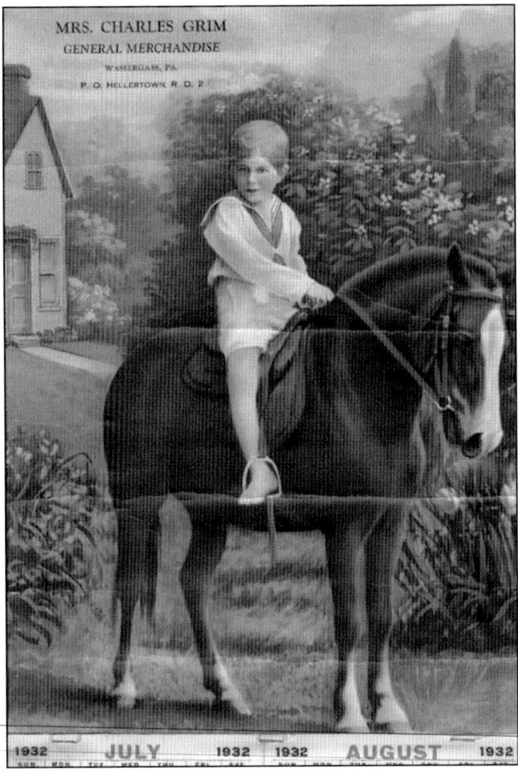

Charles C. Grim and his wife, Rosa, ran the Grim General Store in Wassergass in the 1930s. The Great Depression led to overwhelming hardships in Lower Saucon Township, and business owners like Charles and Rosa felt the crunch. Charles returned to farming as Rosa ran the store. Sadly, the couple had to close up shop before 1940 and move from the area. They had a son, Stewart, and two daughters, Pearl and Dorthea.

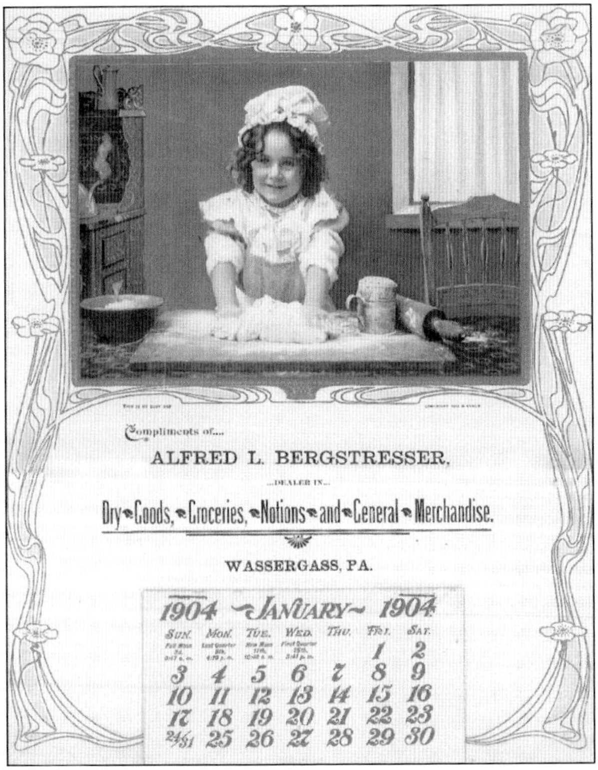

Alfred Linus Bergstresser purchased Jacob C. Wasser's carpentry shop, located in Wassergass, in 1903. Bergstresser established A.L. Bergstresser & Son General Store when he was only 24 years old. The old general store has now been in business for 111 years. Shown here is one of his earliest promotional calendars, dated 1904.

Alfred L. Bergstresser was more than a storeowner. He was a director of the Saucon Valley Trust Company of Hellertown, and he served as trustee of the Ironville Evangelical Church. Bergstresser was one of the founders of the Koch's Iron mine in Lower Saucon Township. He also had a produce stand at the South Side Market, in Bethlehem, Pennsylvania.

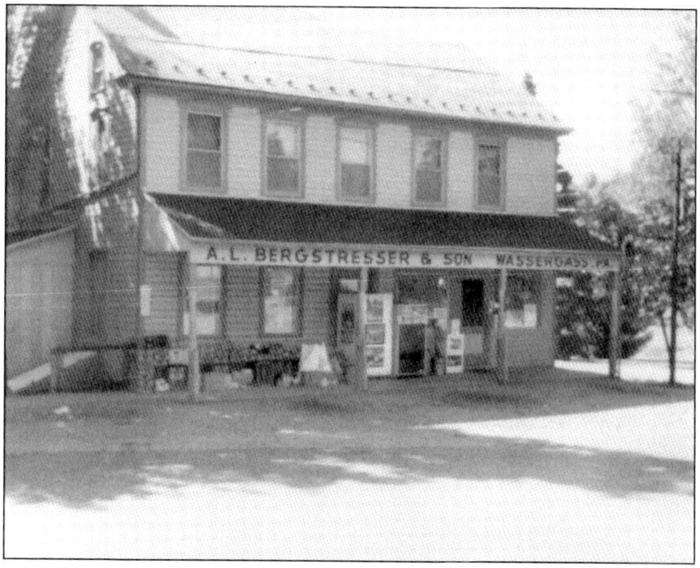

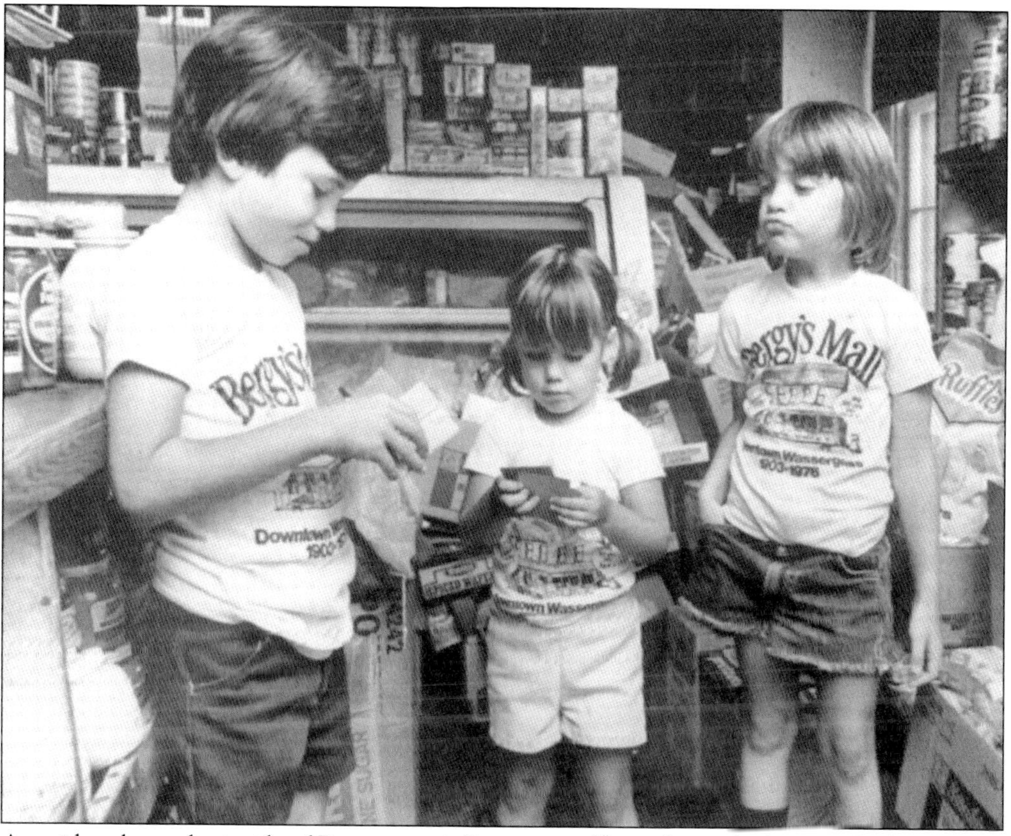

As evident here, the inside of Bergstresser's Store was sufficiently stocked to satisfy the needs of residents, who appreciated the convenience of local shopping. What is not shown are the ready-to-wear clothing and sundries that were stocked on shelves or heaped on counters. Buckets of seed grain lined the center aisle at the entrance, and old-timers discussed politics and swapped tales while sitting on stools.

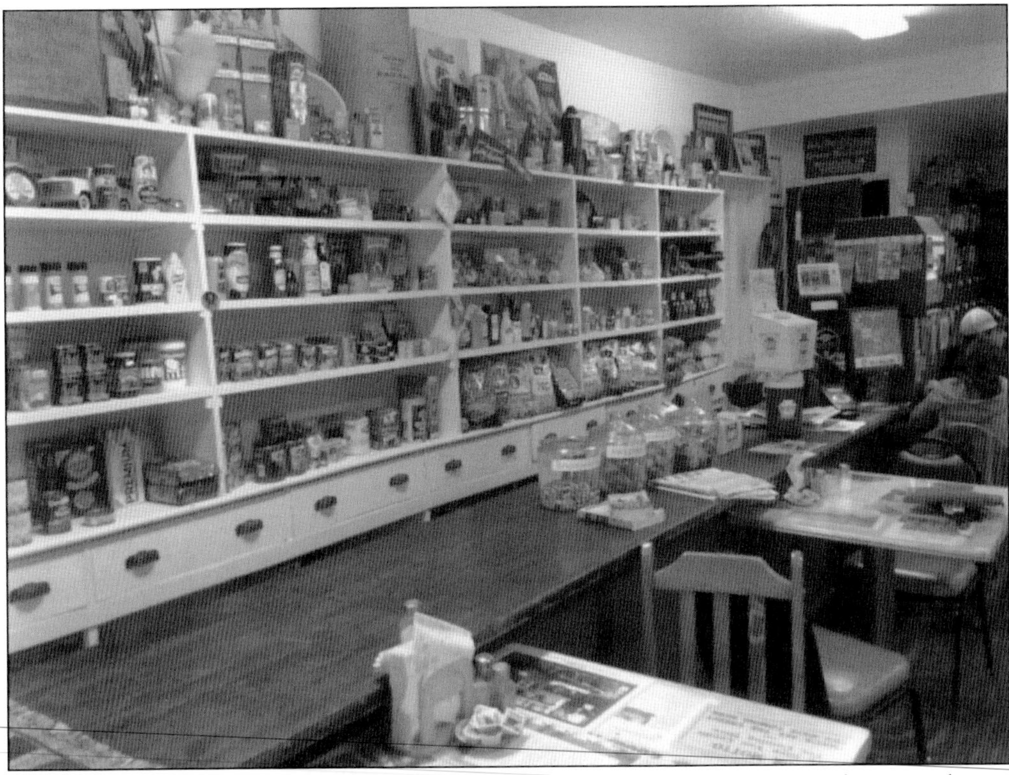

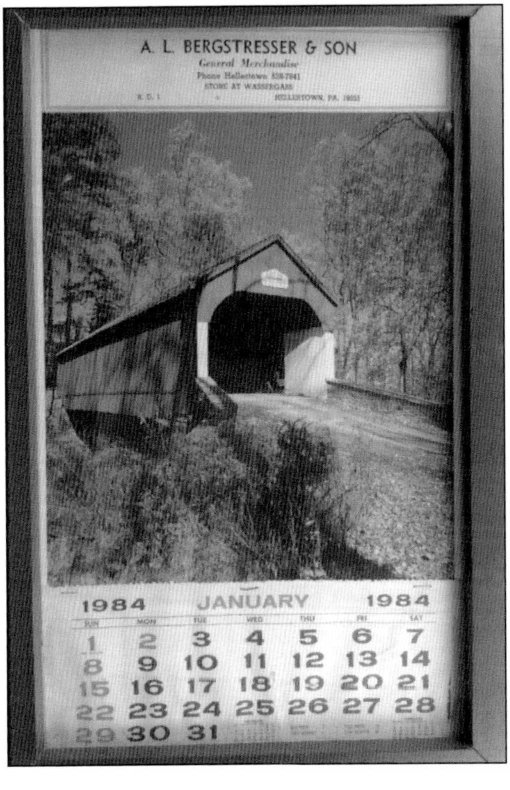

Bergstresser's General Store functioned like a combination department store and grocery, offering everything the community needed. Clothes, shoes, animal feed, hardware, lard, molasses, dairy, vegetables, and candy were stocked on the shelves. The store was a friendly place to pass the time with neighbors.

Promotional gifts from general stores, such as this colorful advertising calendar, were popular with customers. Bergstresser generously gave his customers a calendar each year. This one, dated 1984, was the last such calendar offered. A.J.'s grandson, William Bergstresser, the current owner of the property, printed it to follow his grandfather's tradition.

Toby Clauser's store, like hundreds of others, featured penny candy as well as baseball cards, which attracted children. Customers could always find hardware, fresh produce, butchered meat, bags of peanuts, tobacco products, and canned goods.

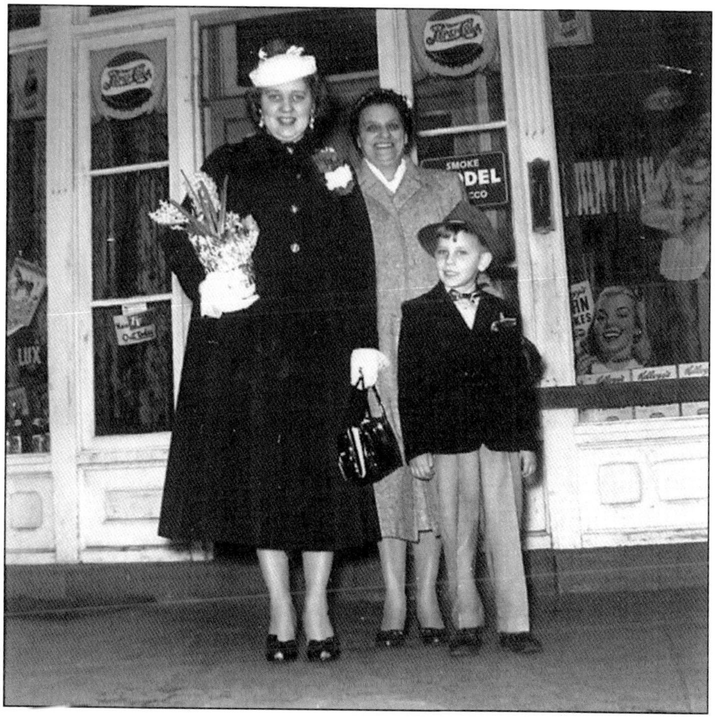

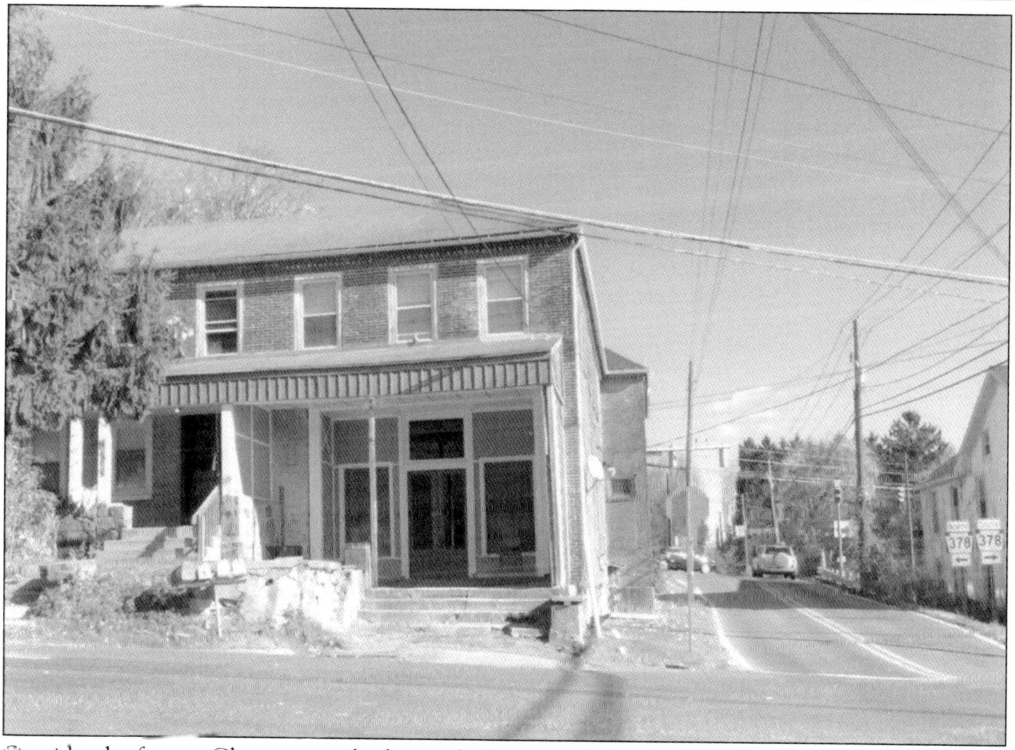

Outside, the former Clauser store looks much the same as the good old days, except it is no longer a retail store for Seidersville folks. It has become a storehouse for furniture and miscellaneous items for the current owner.

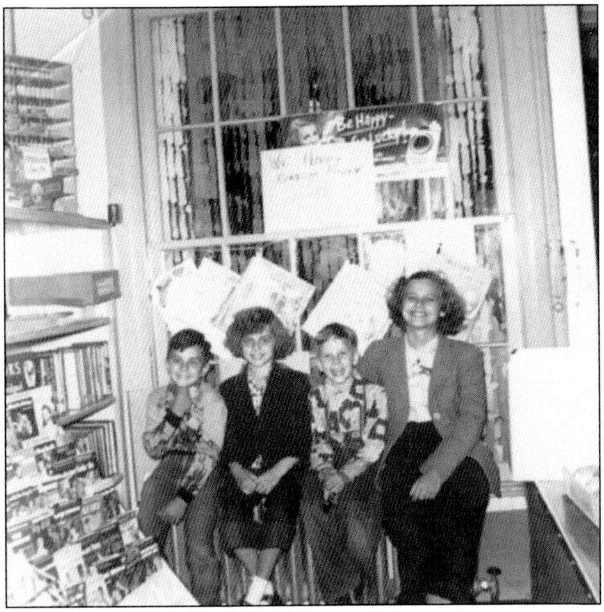

From 1954 to 1961, Helga Dutko (right) and her aunt, Heddy Maetje (second from left), managed Toby Clauser's corner store at Seidersville Road and Old Philadelphia Pike.

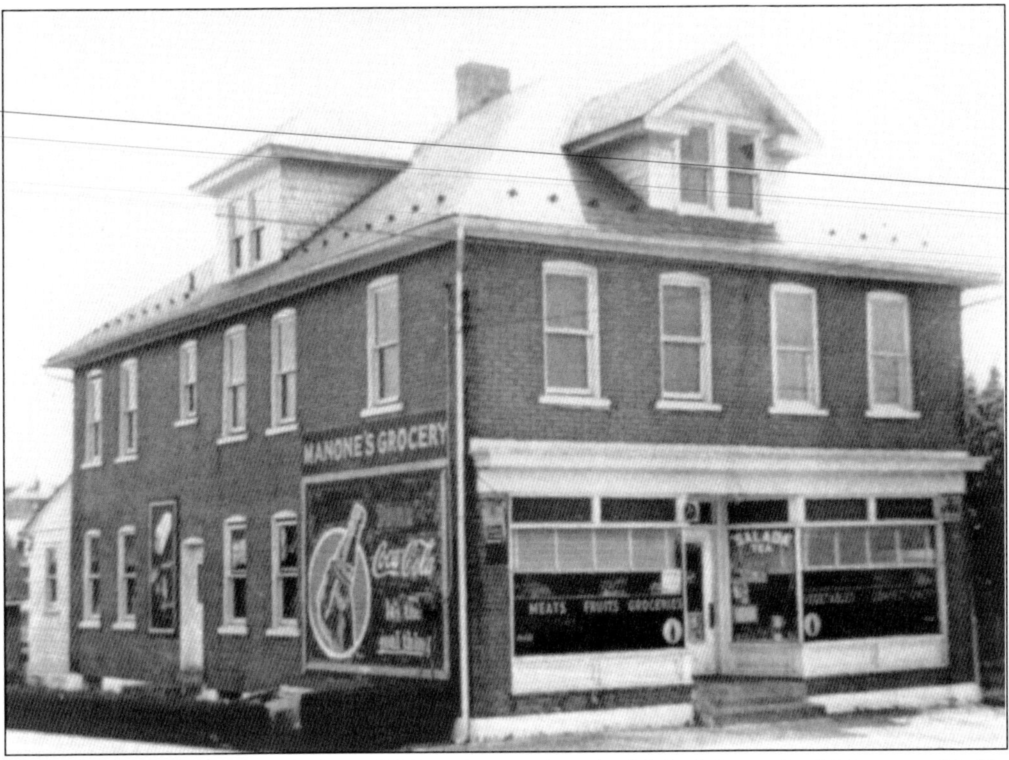

Louis Manone was born in Italy in 1897 and arrived in the United States in 1913, at age 16. He married Frances (Tarsi) in 1919, and they settled down in Hellertown with their four children. Louis was a furnace man for the railroad and then worked for the Pennsylvania Highway Department. On the first floor of the Manone family home at 32 Kichline Avenue, they established a grocery store. It closed in the 1950s, soon after Louis's death in 1952. (Courtesy of the Hellertown Historical Society.)

George and Alice Solomon operated Solomon's Market at 1238 Main Street in Hellertown. The couple worked as local grocers from 1924 to 1957. The store offered a wide variety of meat, displayed on the meat hooks behind the counter. This photograph indicates that their grocery store was a member of the Independent Grocers Alliance (IGA). This location is currently the home of Doggy Dao & Cat's Meow shop, which sells pet supplies. (Courtesy of the Hellertown Historical Society.)

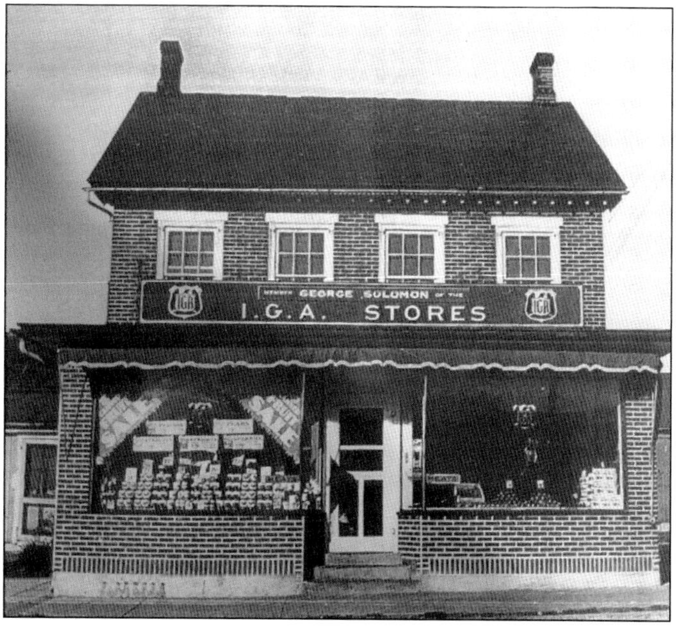

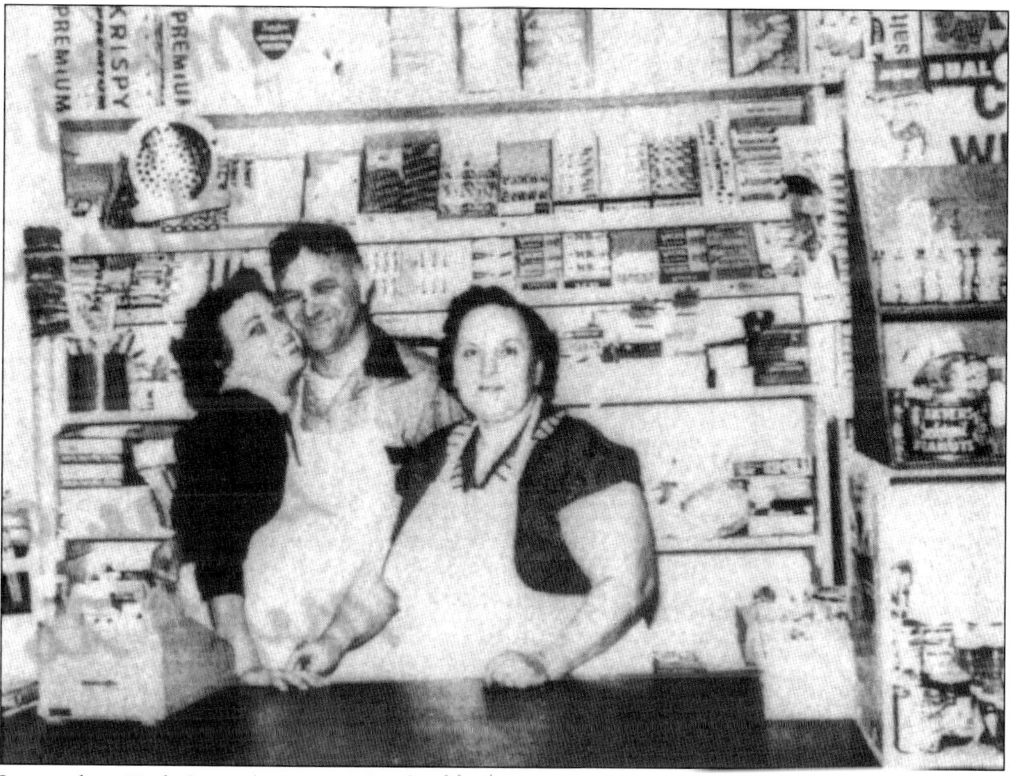

Located on High Street by Wolf School, a block away from St. Theresa's School, Meterko's Store was situated to handle the sweet-tooth needs of all of the schoolchildren. The establishment offered a large selection of penny candy. More important, it was a mom-and-pop grocery store serving the growing number of residents after World War II. Pictured here from left to right are Helen Lippert Hiwizdale, John (Jiggs) Bately, and Mary Meterko.

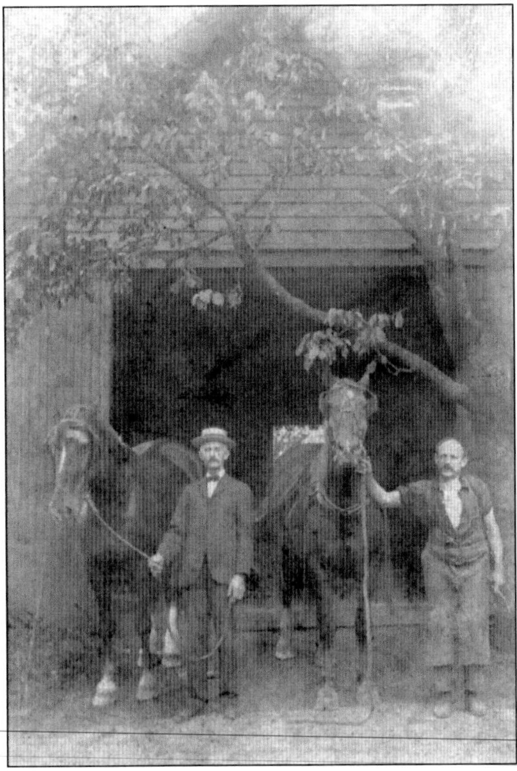

Cyrus O. Weaver (left) and Henry Rothrock pose at the blacksmith shop occupying the land that would later be home to Judd's Superette. Rothrock, owner of the shop, was a blacksmith for the Bethlehem Steel Corporation as well. He learned his trade from his father, Michael Rothrock. (Courtesy of the Hellertown Historical Society.)

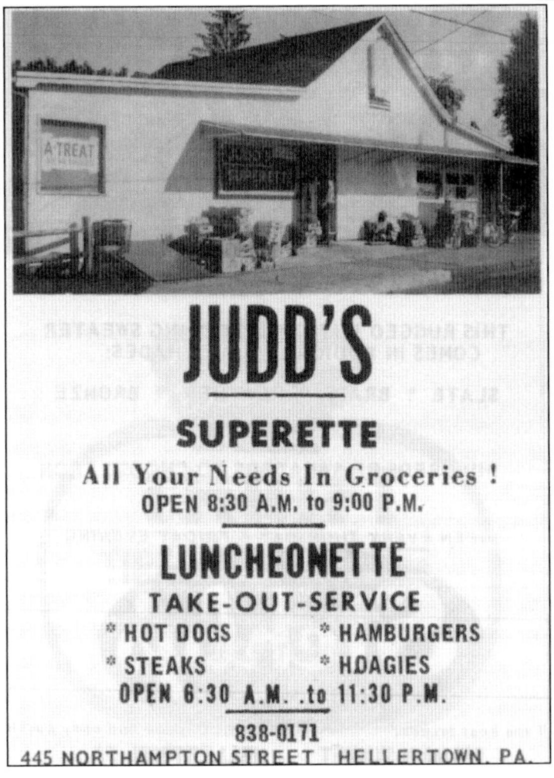

Like Meterko's on High Street, Judd's was another beloved neighborhood market that had penny candy, groceries, and necessary domestic sundries. It was located near Reinhard Elementary School, so it was able to satisfy the candy cravings of the youngsters. During the Fourth of July holiday period, one could stock up on tubes of BANGSITE and flints for the Big Bang cannons.

Three

Wet Your Whistle

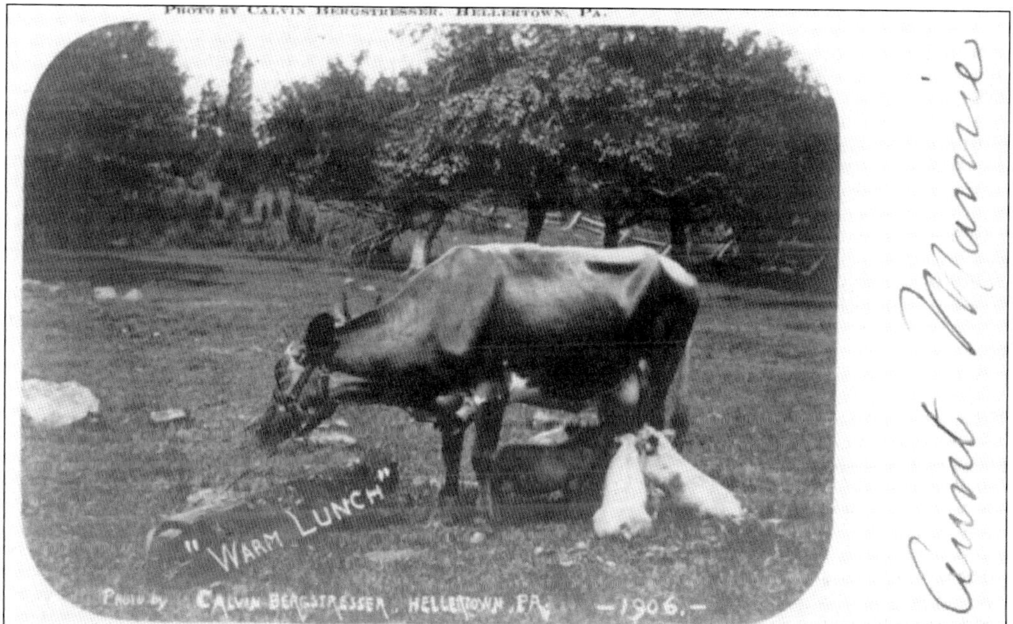

Although not a common occurrence on a farm, a piglet will suckle from a cow if the mother sow has died. This cow was very generous with her milk, as the piglets needed to nurse for at least a month. Prof. Calvin Bergstresser, a Hellertown teacher and photographer, thought this interspecies relationship was unusual enough to be photographed.

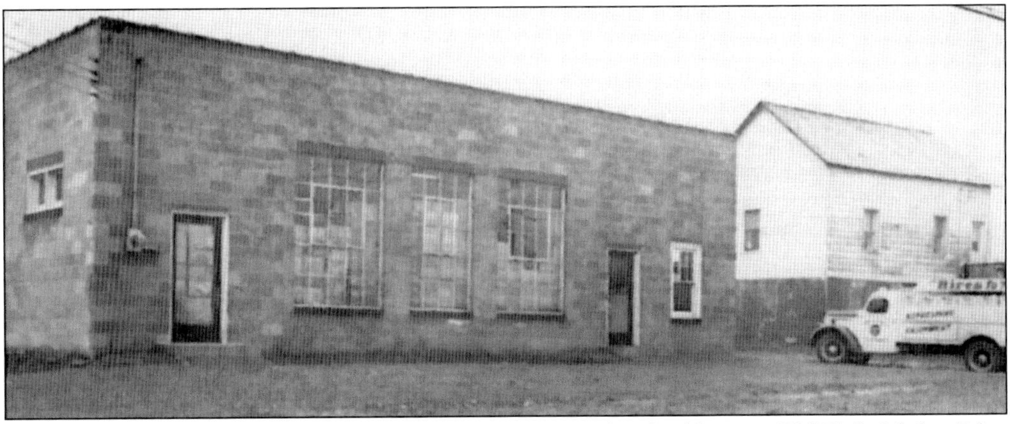

In the 1960s, three brothers-in-law built this 4,000-square-foot building on Old Philadelphia Pike. Pasquale Vigione, Pasquale Tallarico, and John Sewards decided to go into business together and build a bottling manufacturing building for Hires root beer. Following an architect's plan, the men dug the foundation and accomplished all of the cementing and carpentry work themselves.

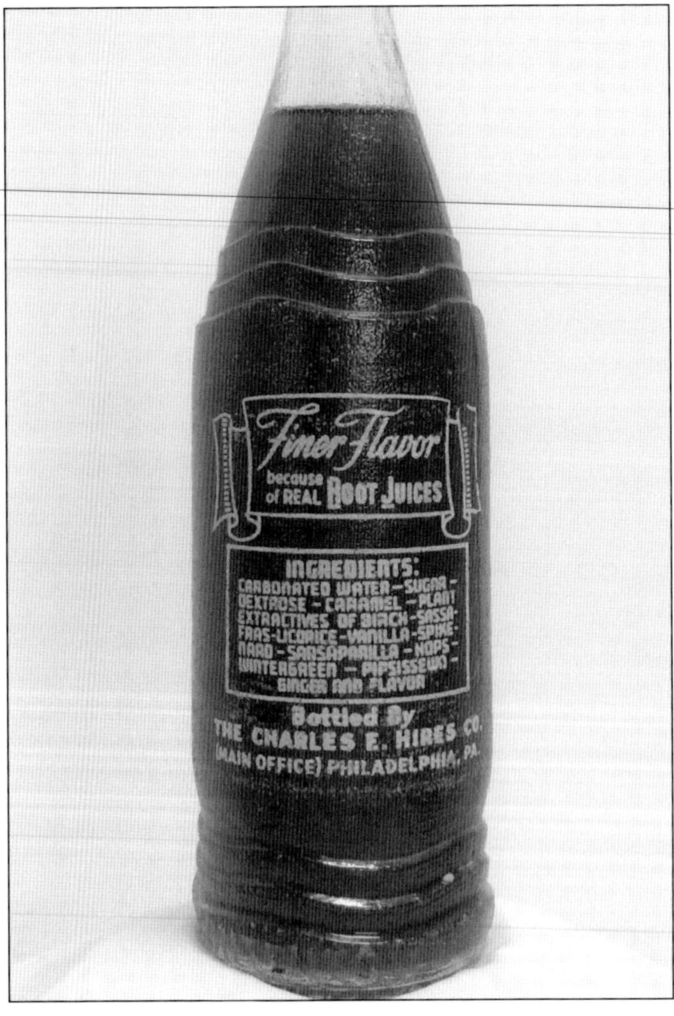

This is a 1940s Hires root beer bottle, which advertises, "Finer flavor because of real root juices." Philadelphia pharmacist Charles Elmer Hires invented his own version of the Colonial-era drink in 1876. The main root juice in root beer is sassafras oil. Hires is difficult to find today, as A&W has taken over the market.

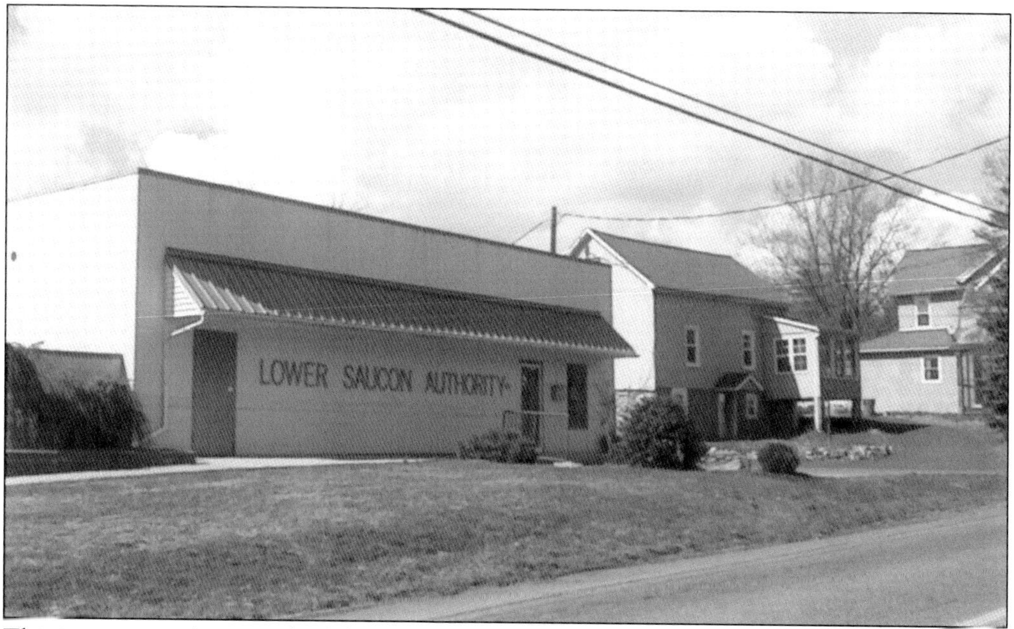

This is a current photograph of the former Hires building (see page 46). It serves as the offices of the Lower Saucon Township Water Authority. The authority was formed in the 1950s with the goal of providing water to the developing area on Black River Road. Today, the water authority is responsible for 2,166 water customers through 41 miles of public water mains.

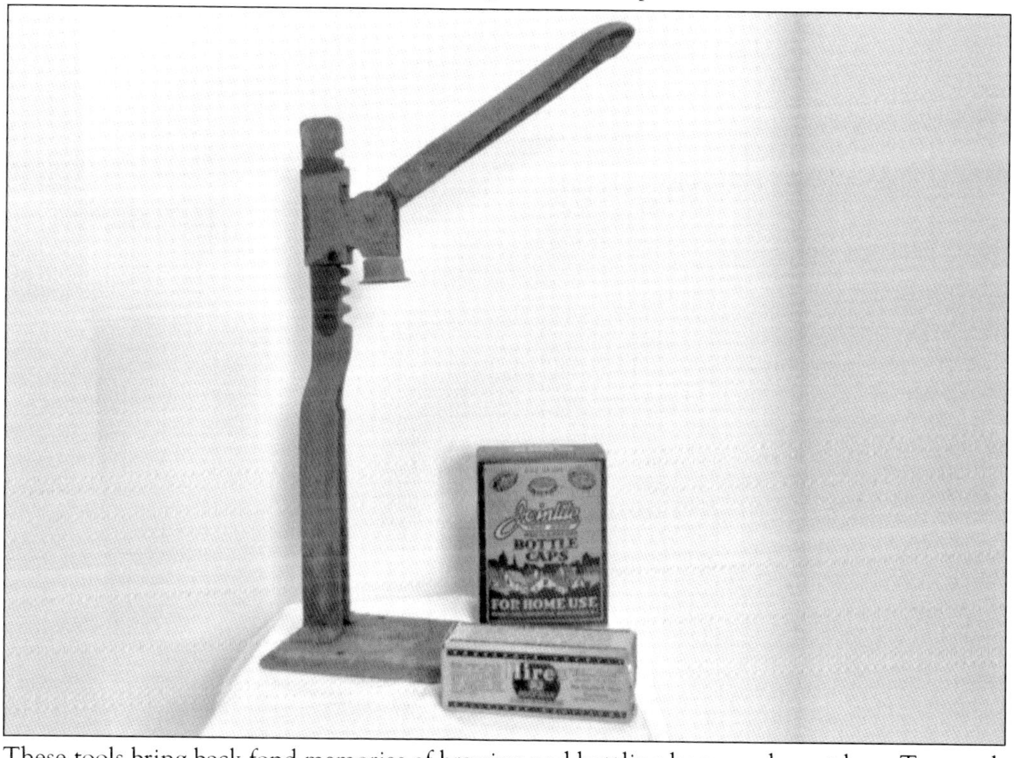

These tools bring back fond memories of brewing and bottling homemade root beer. Too much yeast made opening a bottle of this beverage akin to opening a bottle of champagne.

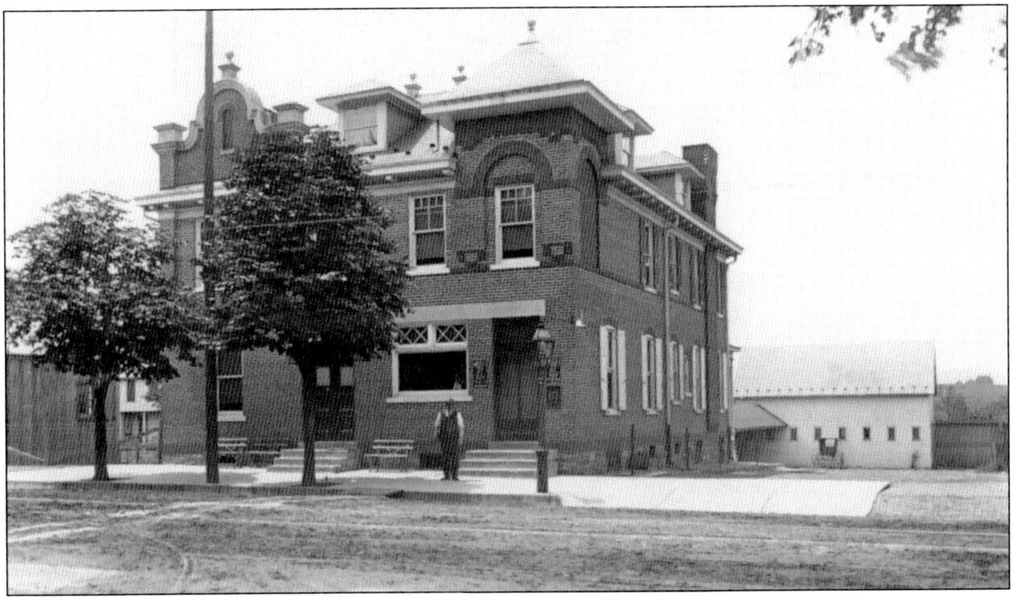

Louie Vargo managed the Eagle Hotel for many years, making this South Main Street watering hole a popular spot. Charles Bartolet's great wrestling teams were treated to pizza there after home matches. In the early 1900s, it featured a hostelry for Lower Saucon farm horses whose owners took the trolley to Bethlehem Steel Corporation.

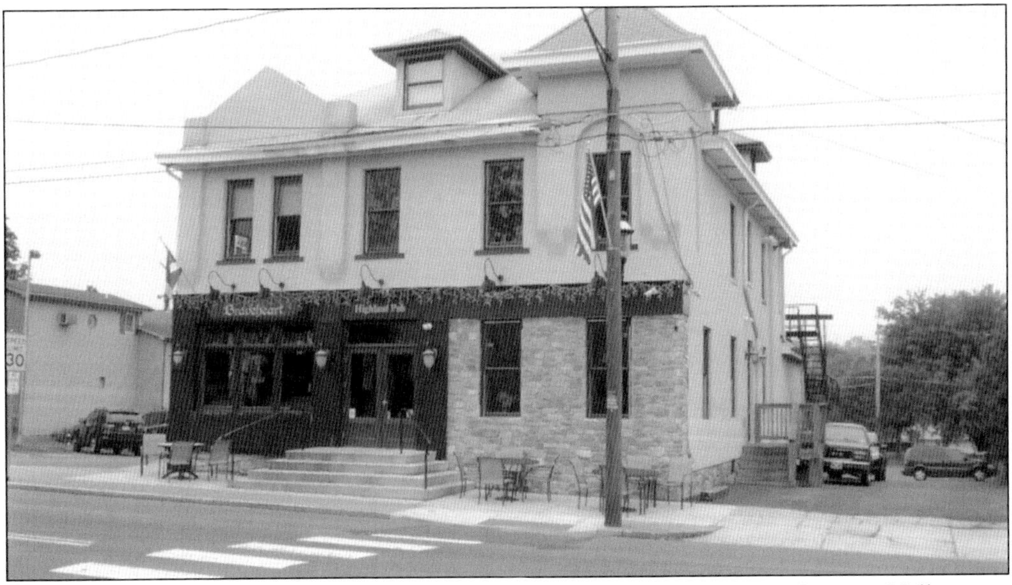

Shown here in 2012 is Braveheart Highland Pub, a popular restaurant on Main Street in Hellertown. Braveheart opened in 2006. Previously known as the Hellertown Hotel, it was purchased in 1979 by Ray Matey and his sons Ray Jr. and Ron. Originally built as the Eagle Hotel in 1907, it was managed by Louis Vargo in the 1950s and 1960s.

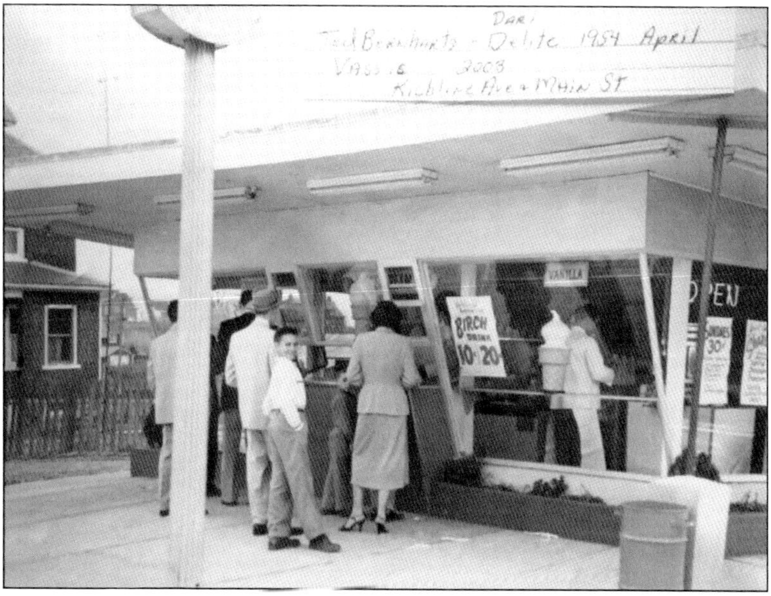

Vassi's Drive-In snack bar has long been a favorite of passersby on Main Street in Hellertown. It is especially known for its delicious gyros. Prior to Vassi's, children lined up for soft ice cream at Dairee Delite in the 1950s.

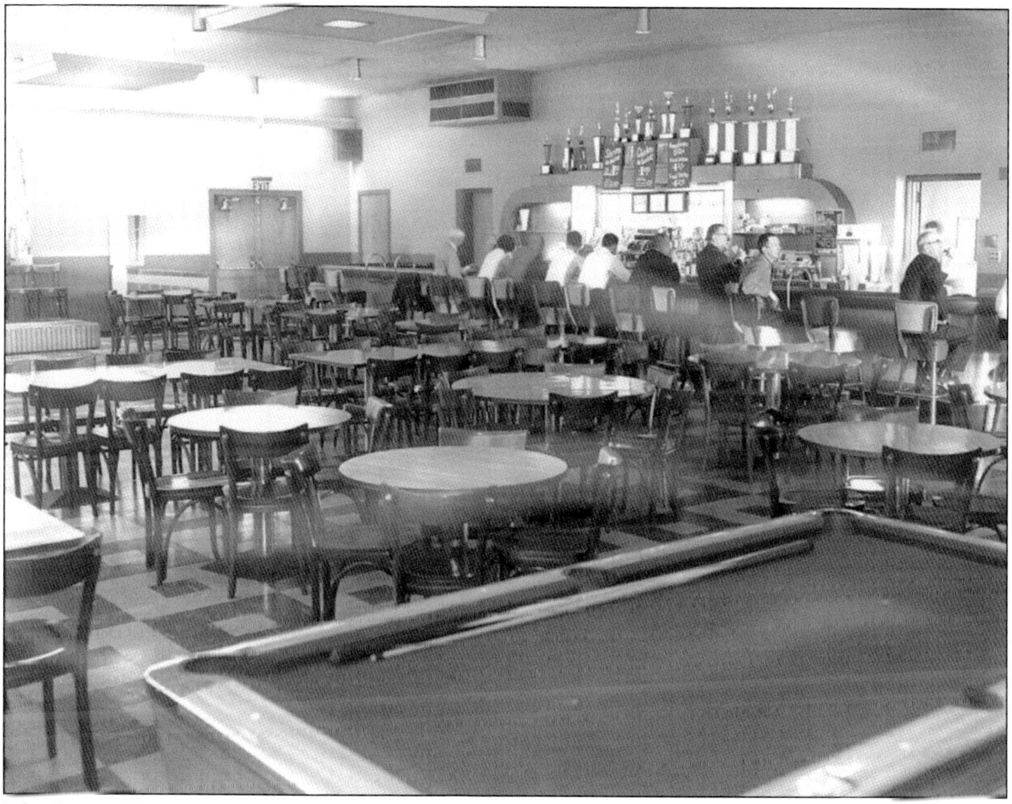

The Dewey Fire Company social hall was a spacious room that had a handsome bar, shuffleboard table, and enough tables and chairs to host large social events. A large kitchen behind the bar was capable of preparing food for these events, and the bar had a decent menu. Eventually, the bar was moved to an area previously used as a lounging and television area. A cardkey was required to access this private facility. (Courtesy of Dewey Fire Company.)

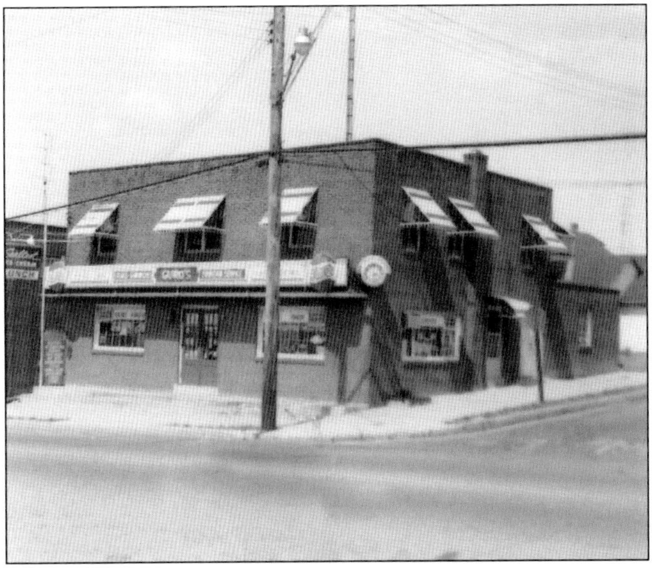

Guro's Luncheonette was a fixture on Main Street for over 40 years. It was a family business of Andrew and Anna, who worked in the luncheonette during operating hours and lived with their family on the second floor. Andrew began working at age 16 in a silk mill and spent a career as a gauge man for Bethlehem Steel Corporation. Anna also worked in the restaurant to make it a successful business. (Courtesy of Edward Guro and Patricia Guro Bendrick.)

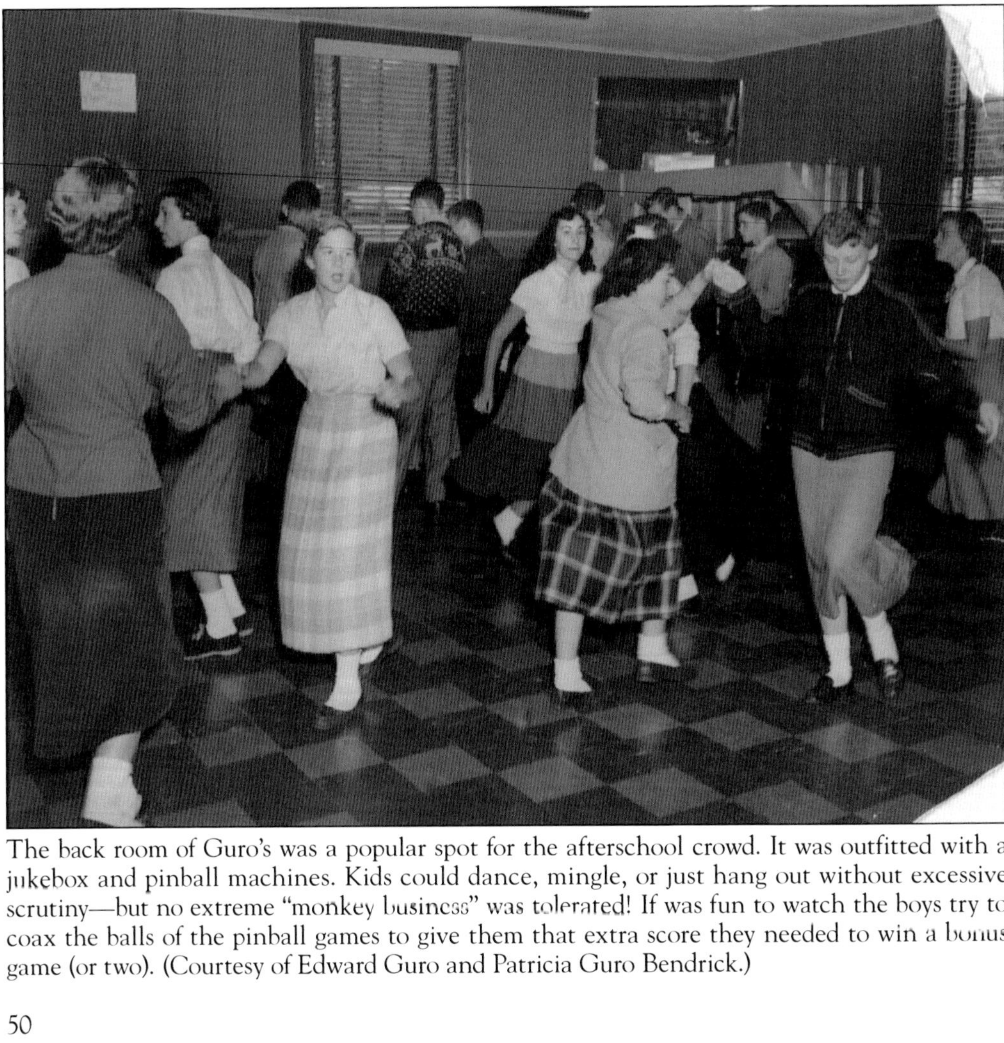

The back room of Guro's was a popular spot for the afterschool crowd. It was outfitted with a jukebox and pinball machines. Kids could dance, mingle, or just hang out without excessive scrutiny—but no extreme "monkey business" was tolerated! If was fun to watch the boys try to coax the balls of the pinball games to give them that extra score they needed to win a bonus game (or two). (Courtesy of Edward Guro and Patricia Guro Bendrick.)

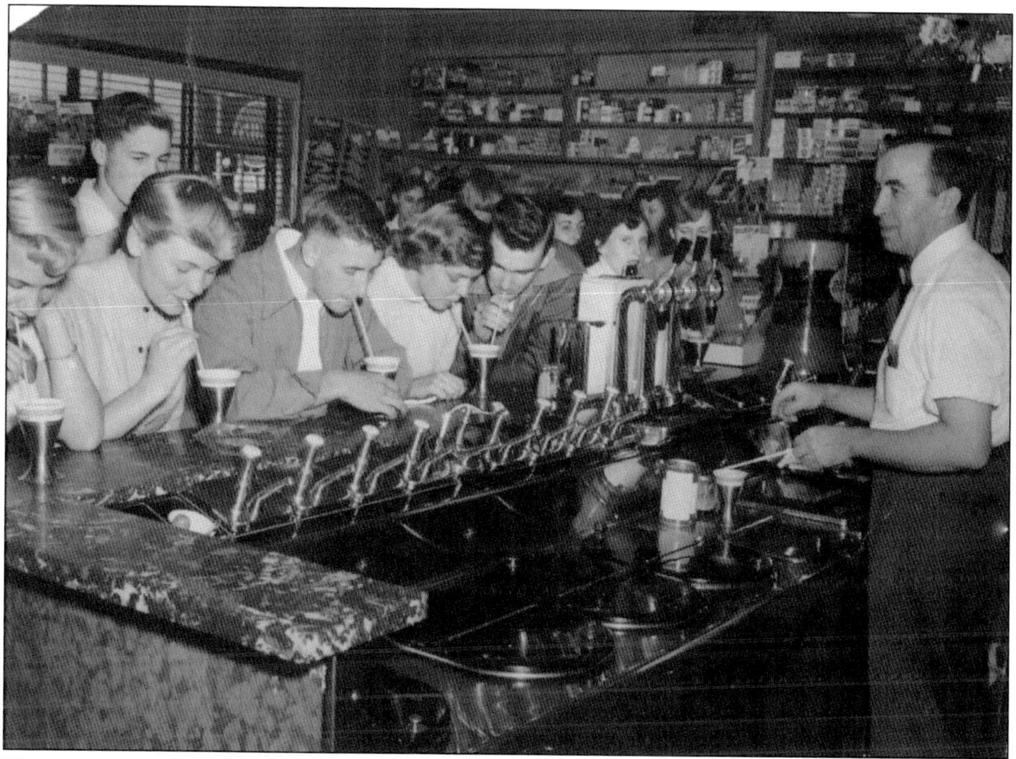

This is a rare 1950s photograph of the inside of Guro's Luncheonette at 1105 Main Street. Brothers Andrew and Walter Guro started the luncheonette around the corner on Thomas Avenue in 1945. In 1949, they moved to the Main Street location, and Walter left the business. Andrew and his wife, Anna (Kozlowski), ran the business for over 30 years, closing in the late 1970s. Andrew Guro is serving drinks on the right. (Courtesy of Edward Guro and Patricia Guro Bendrick.)

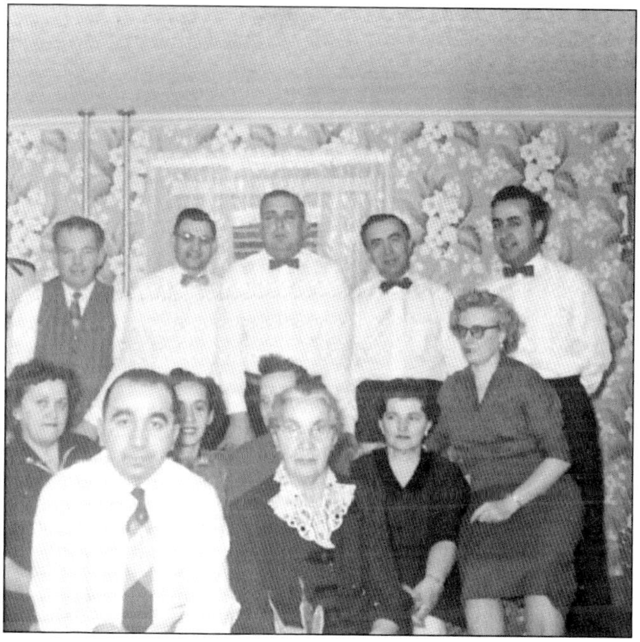

Shown here are two generations of the Guro family. John, the one bachelor, sits next to his mother, Mary, in front. Behind them, wives are seated in front of their respective husbands. Shown are, from left to right, Helen (Guro) and Andy Karch, Agnes (Guro) and Joseph Jamiolkowski, Martha and Frank Guro, Anna and Andrew Guro, and Florence and Walter Guro. The Guro children took up residence on Thomas Avenue in homes that were converted from offices and stables previously belonging to the Thomas Iron Works.

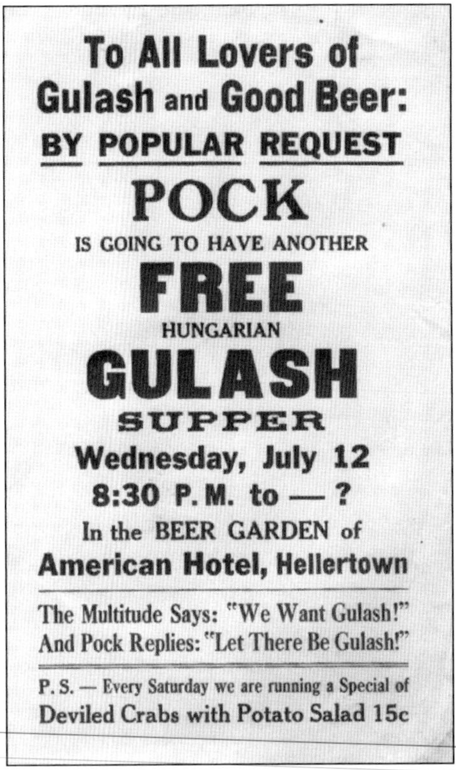
To All Lovers of
Gulash and Good Beer:
BY POPULAR REQUEST
POCK
IS GOING TO HAVE ANOTHER
FREE
HUNGARIAN
GULASH
SUPPER
Wednesday, July 12
8:30 P. M. to — ?
In the BEER GARDEN of
American Hotel, Hellertown

The Multitude Says: "We Want Gulash!"
And Pock Replies: "Let There Be Gulash!"

P. S. — Every Saturday we are running a Special of
Deviled Crabs with Potato Salad 15c

This poster advertised Karl Pock's gulash supper, back "by popular request." His gulash, or goulash, was a local favorite. Karl and Pauline Pock established a restaurant in the American Hotel, on Main Street, in the early 1930s. The Pocks were running the entire hotel by the late 1940s and sold the business in 1950. On Christmas Eve of 1969, a fire destroyed the building. (Courtesy of Fran Robb.)

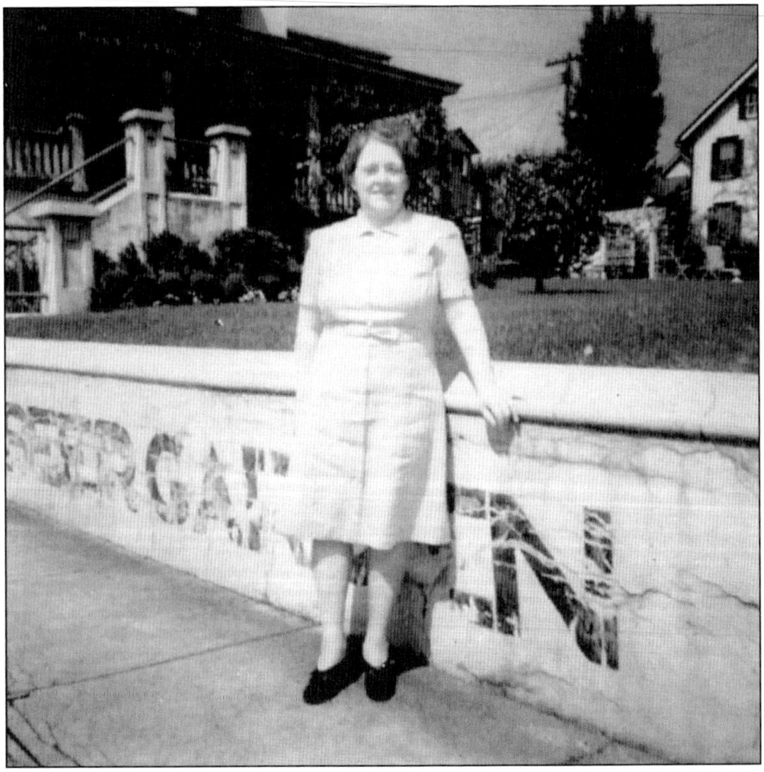

This woman, identified only as Marjorie, poses in front of Pock's Beer Garden. Pock's Hotel is in the background at left. This 1944 photograph shows a lovely garden created by Karl and Pauline Pock. The beer garden, lined with tables and chairs, must have been a pleasant place to spend a warm summer evening. (Courtesy of the Hellertown Historical Society.)

This diner operated under a few different names, including Andy's Diner, Cope's Diner, and, finally, Mom's Diner. It was located at 1333 Main Street, across from the PMP bowling lanes. The right side of the diner (pictured) was once Liberty Bell trolley car No. 810 (see page 22). (Courtesy of the Hellertown Historical Society.)

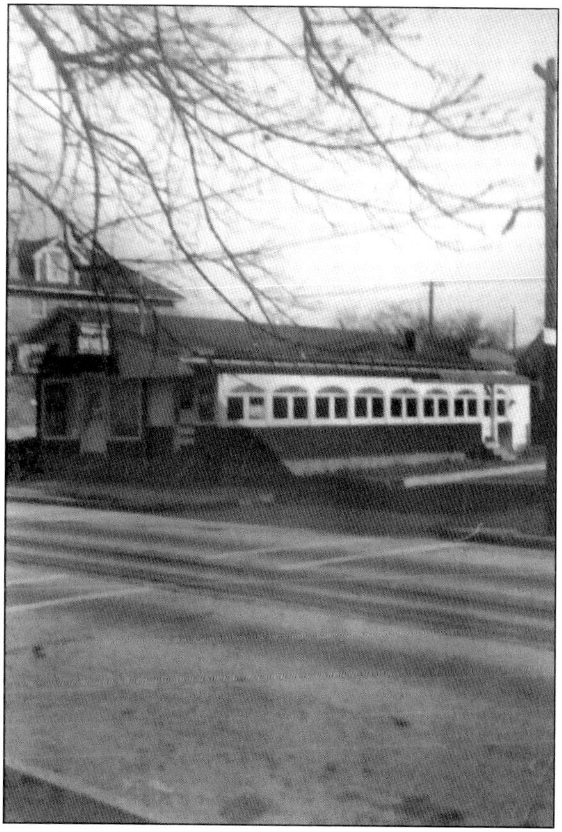

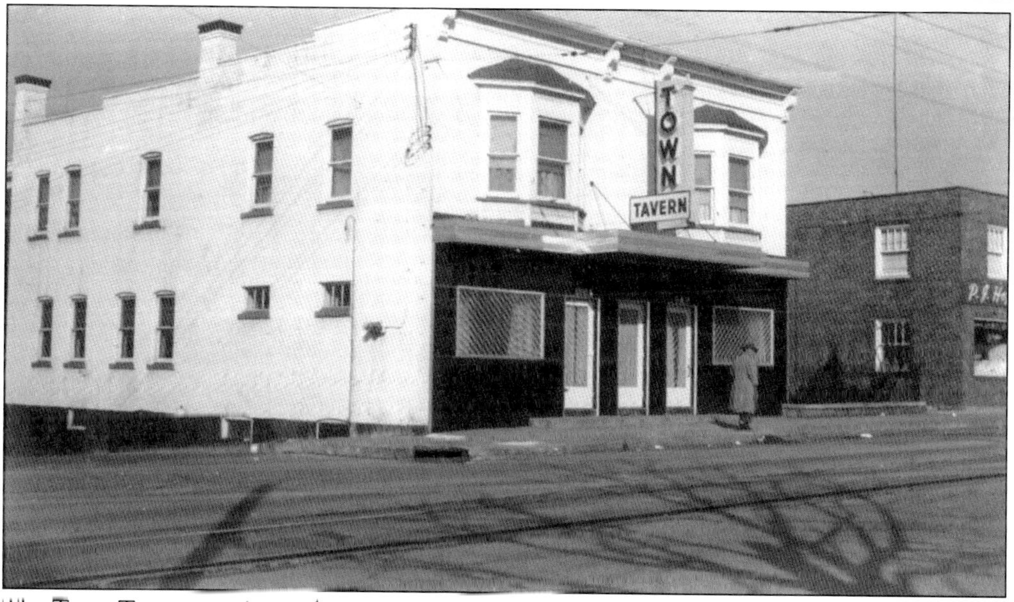

The Town Tavern was located at 1214–1216 Main Street. William Sakovics owned it for over 30 years. When Sakovics retired in 1986, he sold the business to Edward R. Mellon, who changed the name of the bar to The Full Mug. Today, the business that occupies the site is Beer Mussels Bar and Grill.

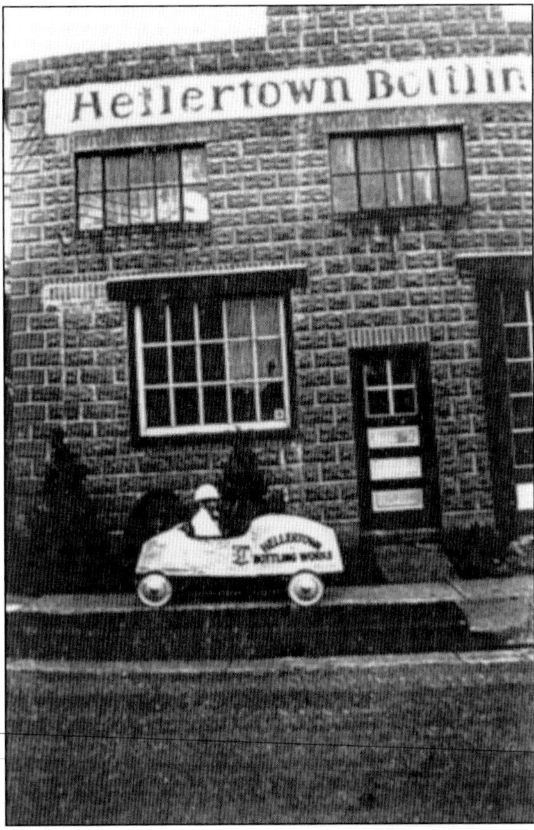

This is a rare glimpse of a metal pedal car, popular with children. Many children could only dream of such a luxurious plaything. The heyday for pedal cars in the United States occurred between World War I and World War II. (Courtesy of the Hellertown Historical Society.)

William A. Siegfried was the longest-serving superintendent of Hellertown Bottling Works. Many children of the 1950s remember his special concoction of chocolate soda. This noncarbonated drink had to be shaken, not stirred, to mix the chocolate that settled to the bottom of the bottle. (Courtesy of the Hellertown Historical Society.)

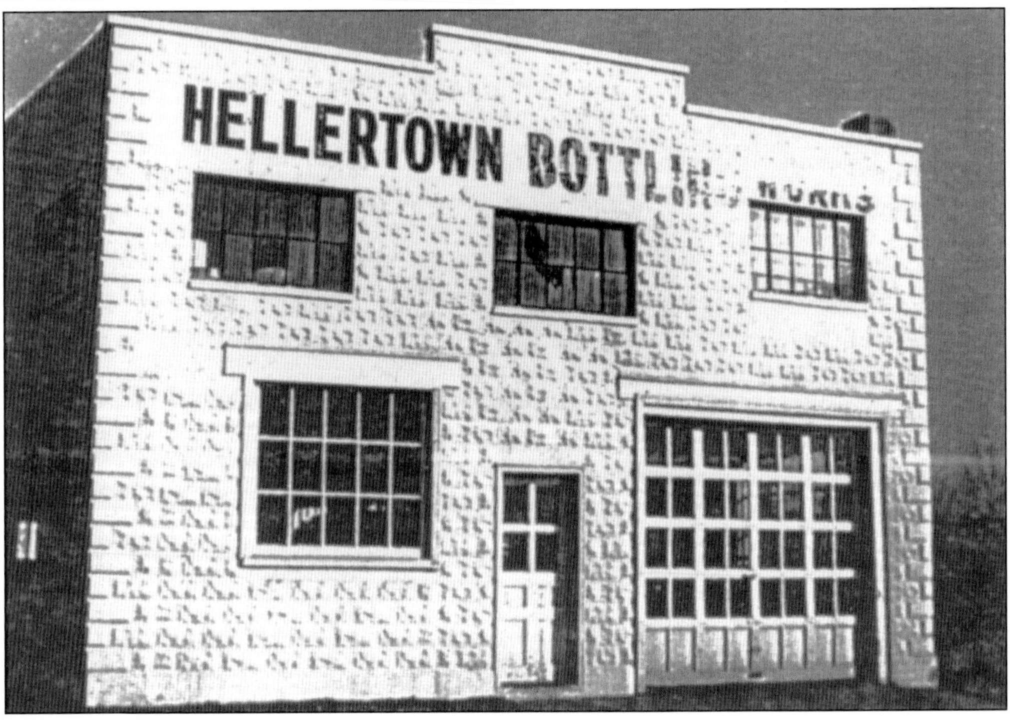

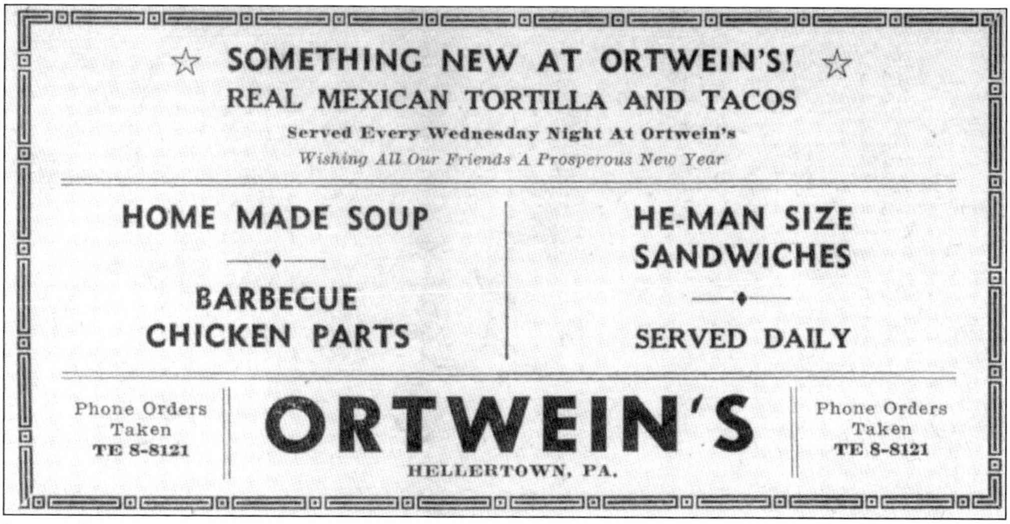

Located at 910 Main Street, Ortwein's tavern was another favorite spot for hungry and thirsty patrons. Centered above the long bar was a sandwich board, which listed the handsome selection of "he-man size sandwiches." Still available here was a Limburger cheese sandwich, an item of declining popularity in society. After preparing one of these sandwiches, Tom Ortwein would wash his hands under an open beer tap in an attempt to eliminate the smell.

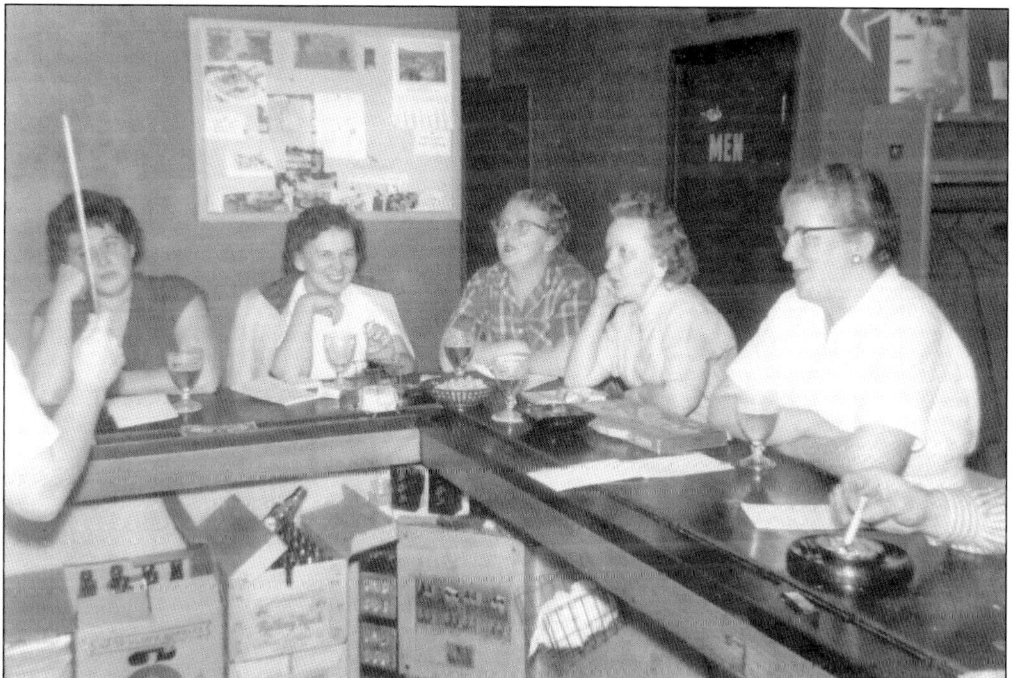

This merry group of women enjoyed some good camaraderie after a night of bowling by attending the Monday night sing-along at Ortwein's. They bowled at the lanes above Raucher's Hardware store. From left to right are Shirley Gad, Grace Williams, Marion Polinchok, Flossie Savitske, and Catherine Ortwein.

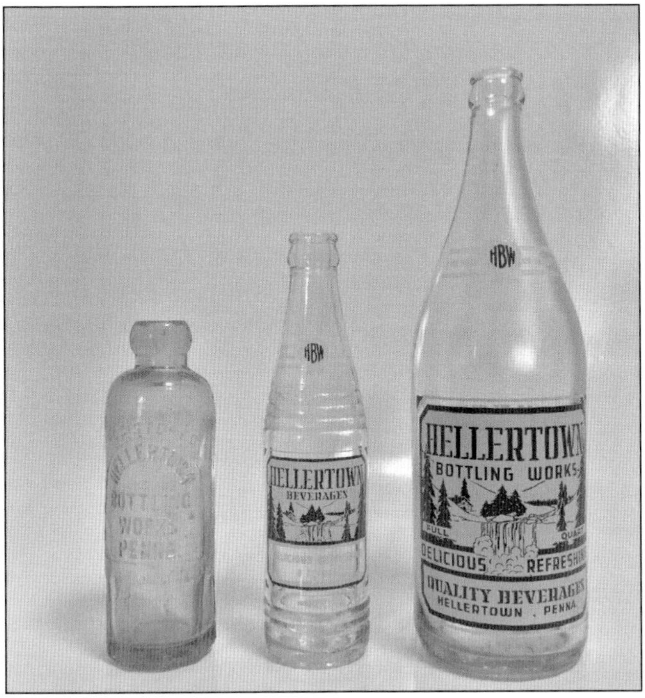

These bottles span decades of Hellertown Bottling Works and are now collectors' items. William A. Seigfried owned the business on Easton Road from 1935 until 1971.

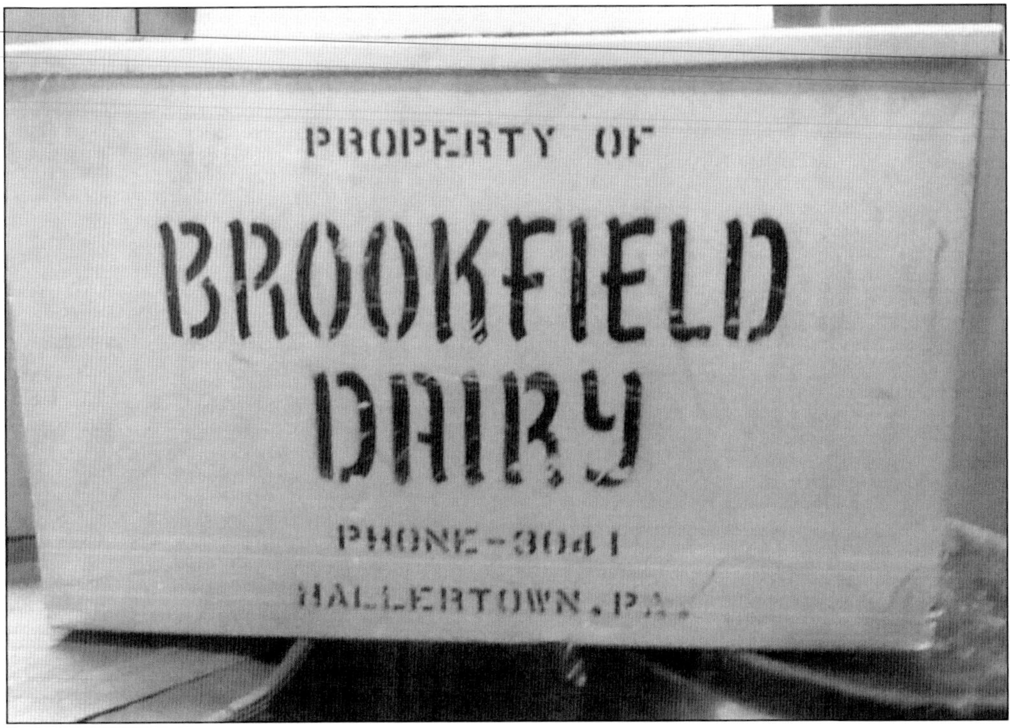

Brookfield Dairy was located at 710 Front Street in Hellertown. The dairy was started in the 1920s as the Lerch Dairy. Howard and Neta Kemp purchased it in 1949 and changed the name to Brookfield Dairy. It has since been torn down, and an apartment building is now at that location. Note the misspelling of Hellertown.

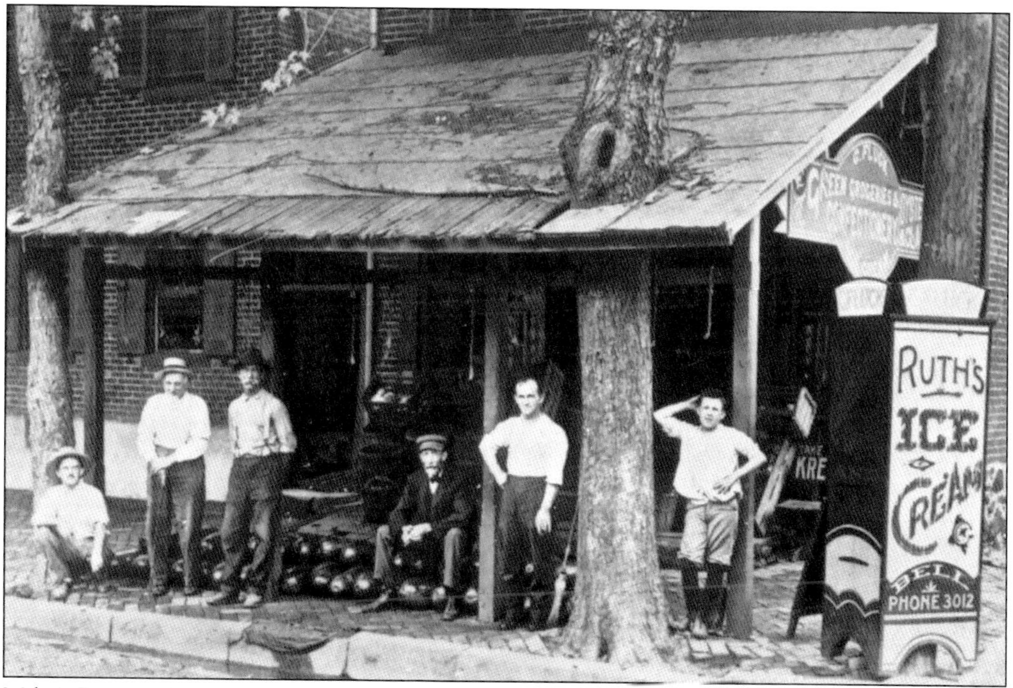

Mike's Doggy Shop now operates out of this building at 501 Main Street. The store shingle in this photograph advertises Green Groceries & Confectionery as well as oysters and clams. From the looks of things, this may have been a hangout for the locals, where they could discuss politics and other civic matters of the day. Calvin Fluck was the owner. (Courtesy of the Hellertown Historical Society.)

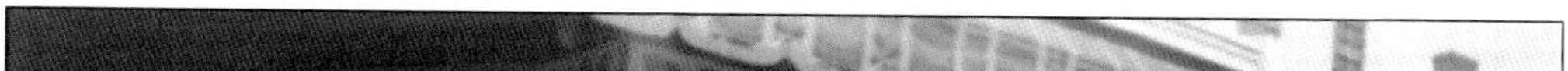

Brothers Harrison W. and Joseph Prosser carried on the family business of Prosser's Drugstore at 834 Main Street. Harrison and his wife, Myrtle, lived above the drugstore. Harrison loved to eat Limburger cheese and crackers as he discussed current events with the men who gathered daily to socialize. In the 1930s, an unidentified young woman stands outside of the store. The first bowling alley in Hellertown was located in the basement of Prosser's.

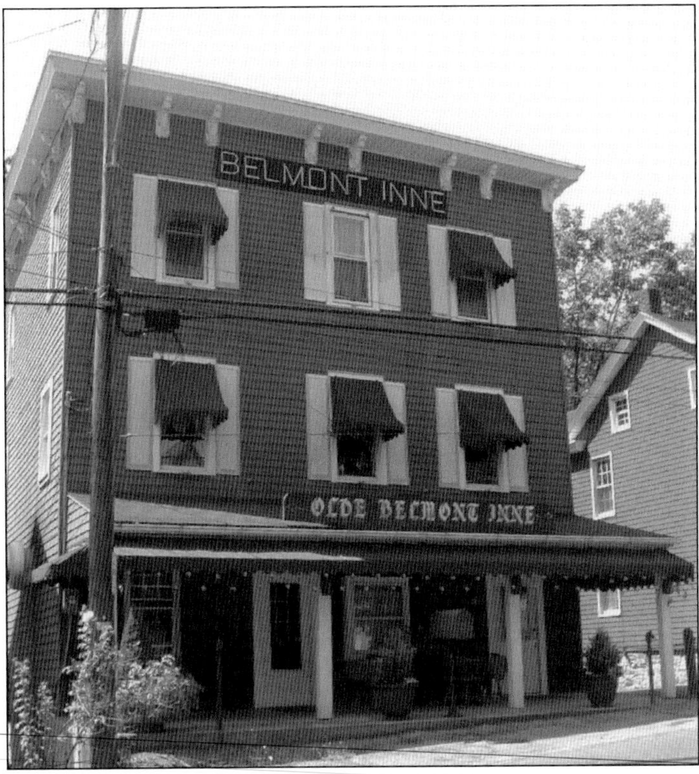

The Olde Belmont Inne, located at 3750 Old Philadelphia Pike, was built in the mid-1800s. It still has the original ornate wooden bar and pressed-tin ceiling. The inn served as an important meeting place for the community in the early 1900s. The Lower Saucon Township Council, school board, and club meetings were held there. Legend has it that, when the zinc mine workers rode by the inn on horseback in the 1850s, "ladies of the evening" would lean out the third-floor windows to wave to the men.

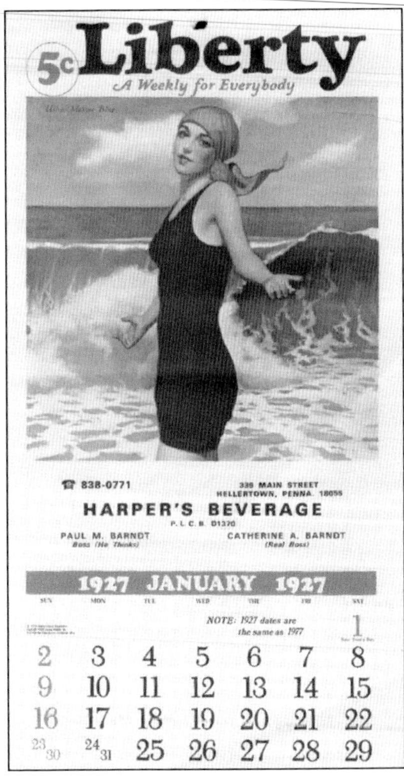

There was not a preponderance of beer distributors in Hellertown. Harper's was nicely positioned close to the only Pennsylvania State Store in town at 339 Main Street. This 1927 calendar is a reminder that this was a long-running business that closed in 1972. (Courtesy of the Hellertown Historical Society.)

Four

LITTLE BUSINESSES

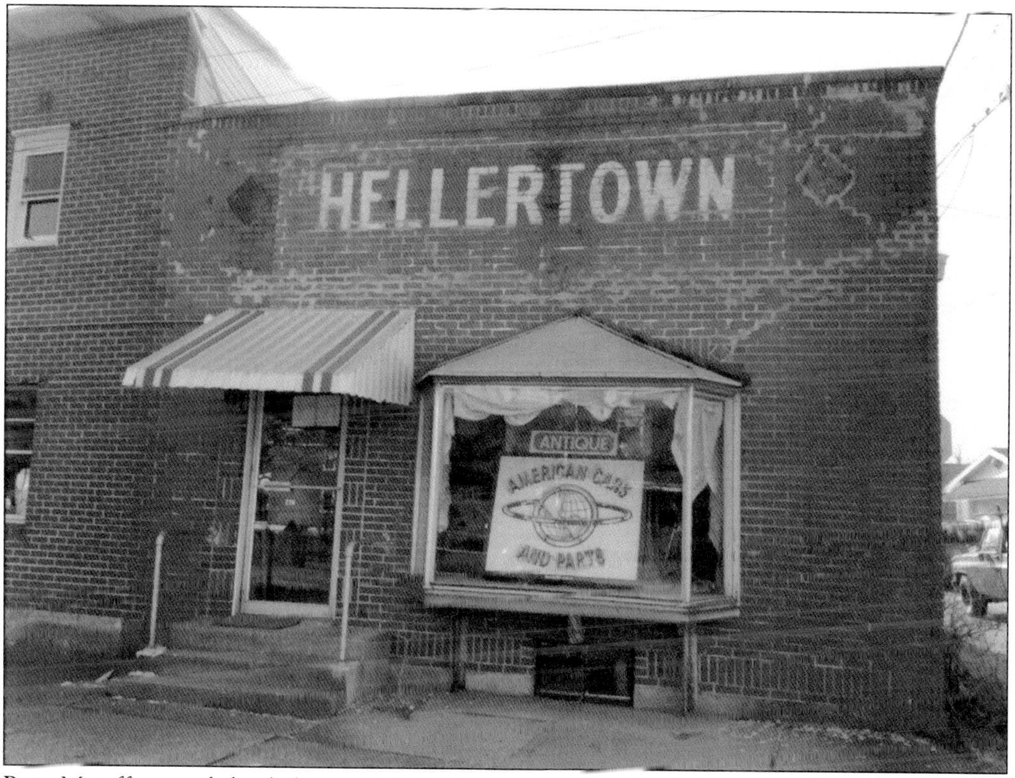

Boin Mateff opened this bakery on Linden Street early in the 20th century; he also had one in Northampton. His son Eugene Mateff Sr. sold them in 1974 to Vendel Csaszar, and the bakery lasted almost into the 21st century. This area of Hellertown was called Koke-le. This photograph shows the new occupants, American Cars and Parts.

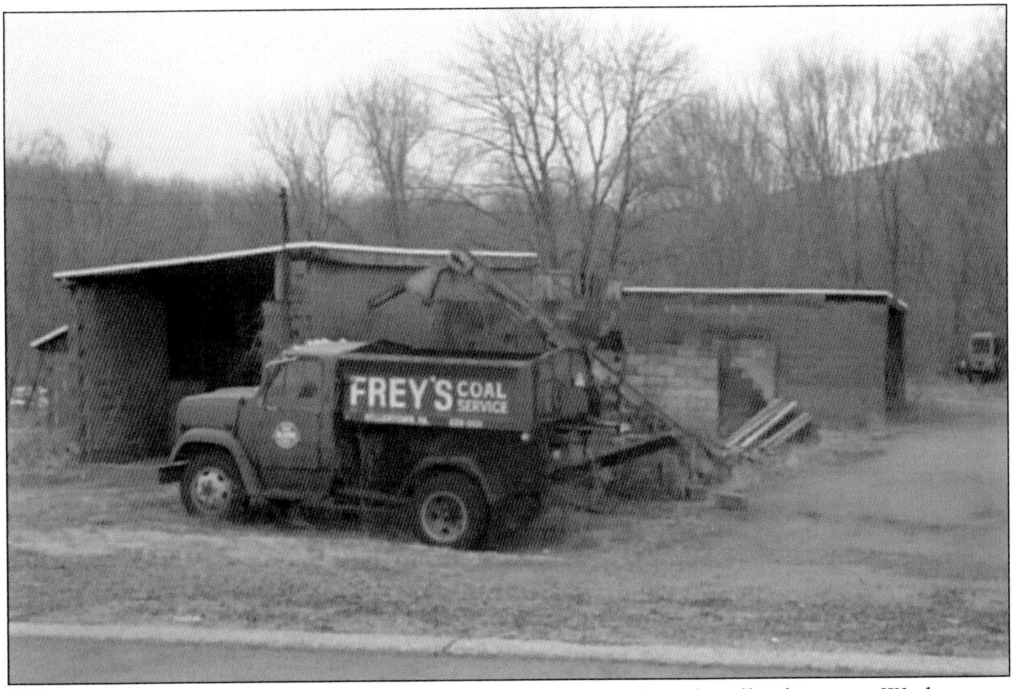

Frey's Coal Service was a small-time delivery service located in the alley between Washington and Jefferson Streets in northwest Hellertown. Coal furnaces supplied heat in homes until oil was widely used.

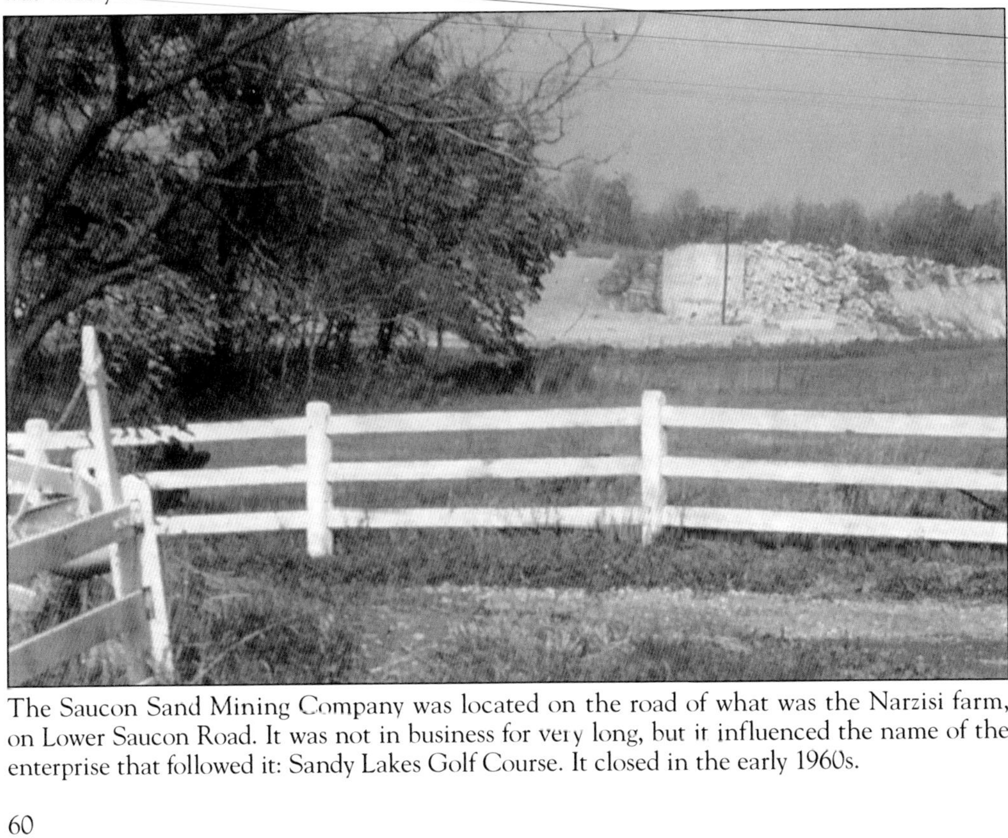

The Saucon Sand Mining Company was located on the road of what was the Narzisi farm, on Lower Saucon Road. It was not in business for very long, but it influenced the name of the enterprise that followed it: Sandy Lakes Golf Course. It closed in the early 1960s.

William Strauss ran the Skate-A-Date Roller Rink in the 1940s. The rink, located at 1804 Leithsville Road in Hellertown, was open every Wednesday, Friday, Saturday, and Sunday night between 7:30 and 11:00. The building was then home to the Dora Lee Dress factory.

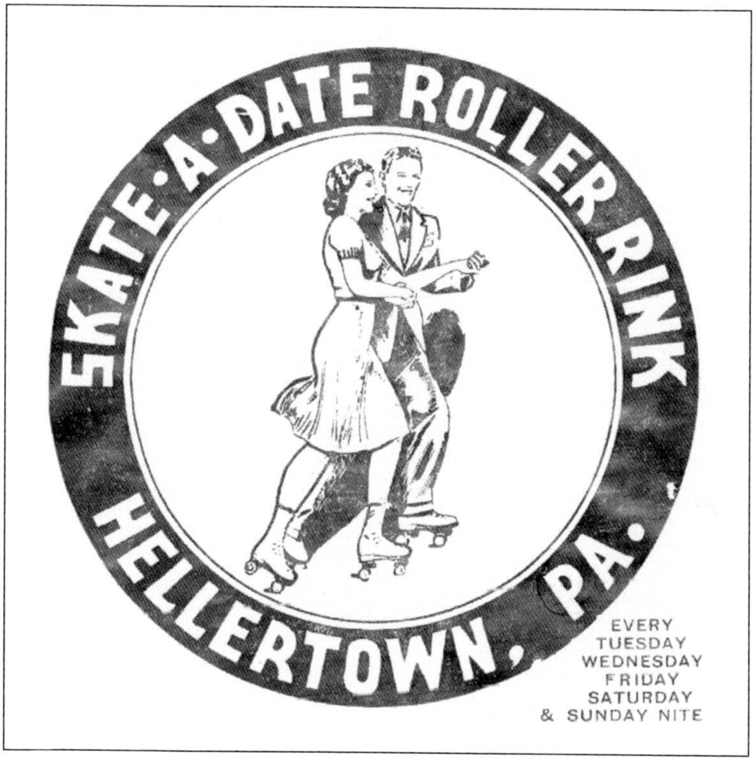

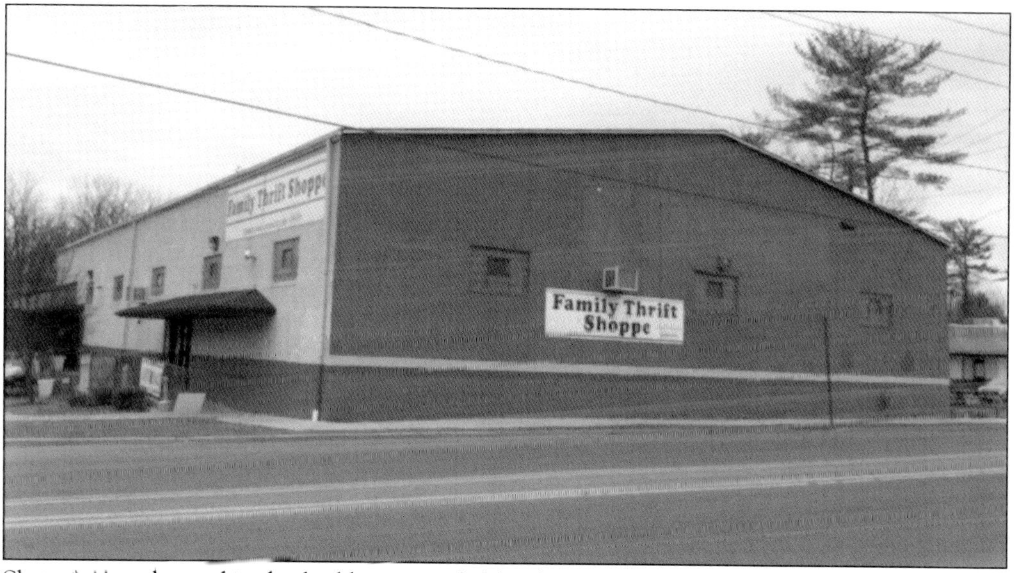

Skate-A-Date, located in this building, provided fun for a mostly younger—and sometimes rowdy—clientele. Although similar activities, such as rollerblading and skateboarding, are still enjoyed today, roller rinks are few and far between. Today, Family Thrift Shoppe occupies the building.

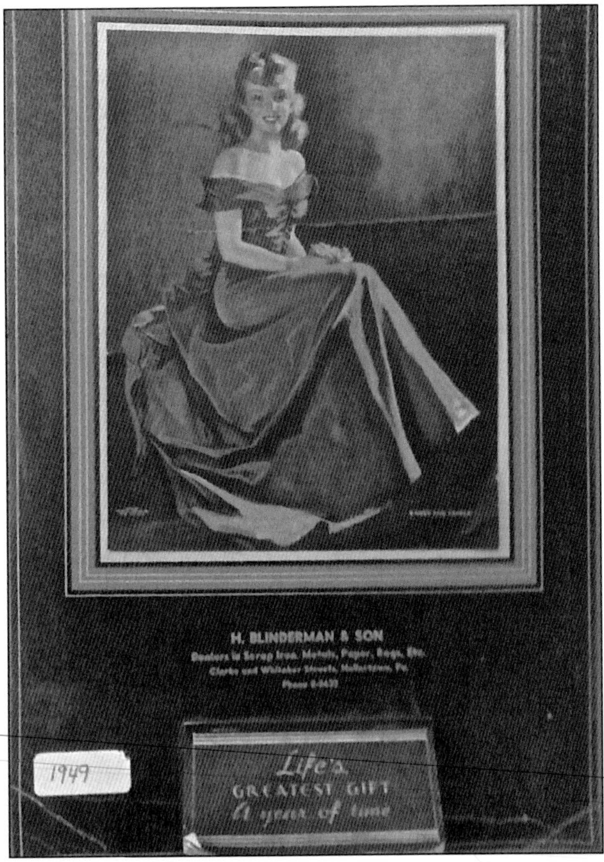

Blinderman Junk Yard, now known as Blinderman Recycling, is remembered by 1950s Hellertown children, who often pulled their wagons from house to house to collect used newspapers. They then sold the paper by the pound to Blindermans for spending money. Shown here is a Blinderman promotional calendar.

Robert G. and Irene S. McKay took ownership of Beckett's Catering Service at 910 Main Street in Hellertown in the 1960s. The McKays ran it for over 40 years before retiring. It was a popular choice for banquets, weddings, and clambakes. (Courtesy of the Hellertown Historical Society.)

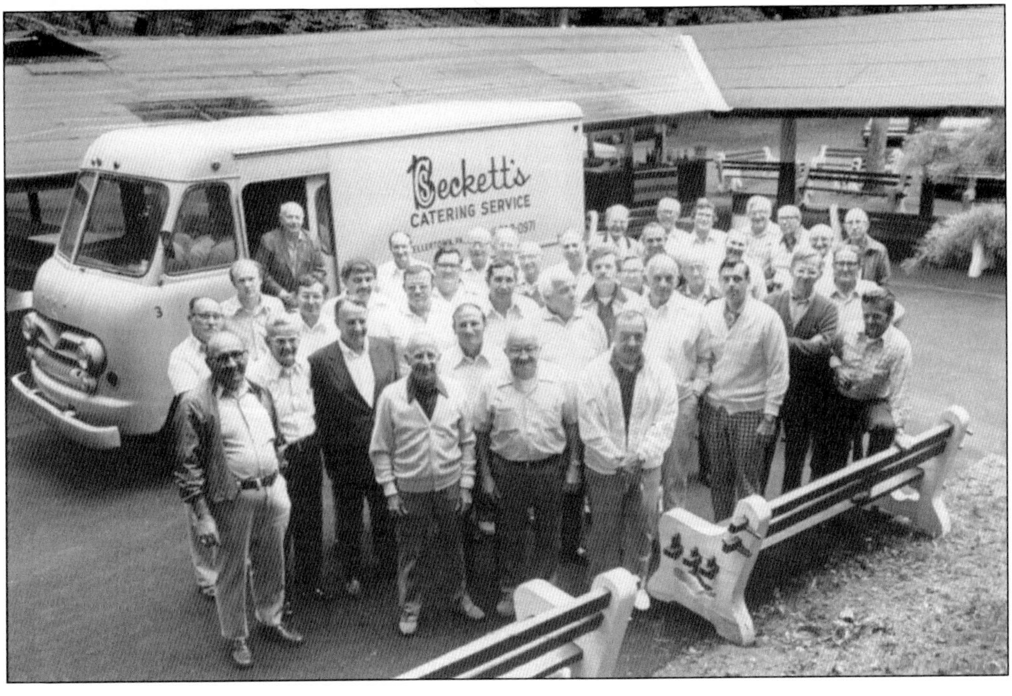

This is the cover of the "Billy and Ruth" 1956 catalog for Horvath's Sporting Goods, 766 Main Street. Joseph J. Horvath, the owner, ordered the catalog and toys through Supplee-Biddle, a toy wholesaler. "Billy" and "Ruth" were the names of the children of William George Steltz, president of Supplee-Biddle. The price of each toy in the catalog averaged about $1.

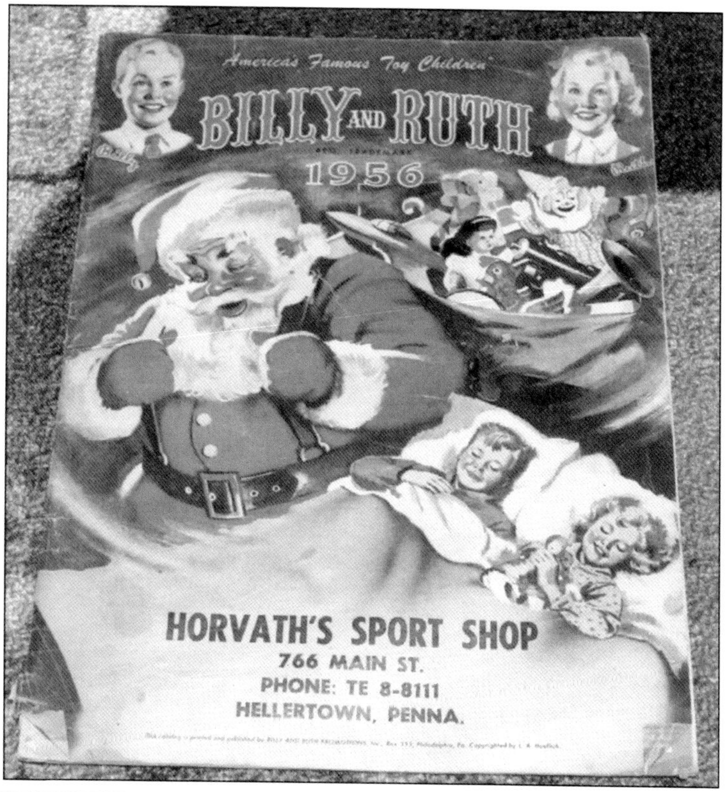

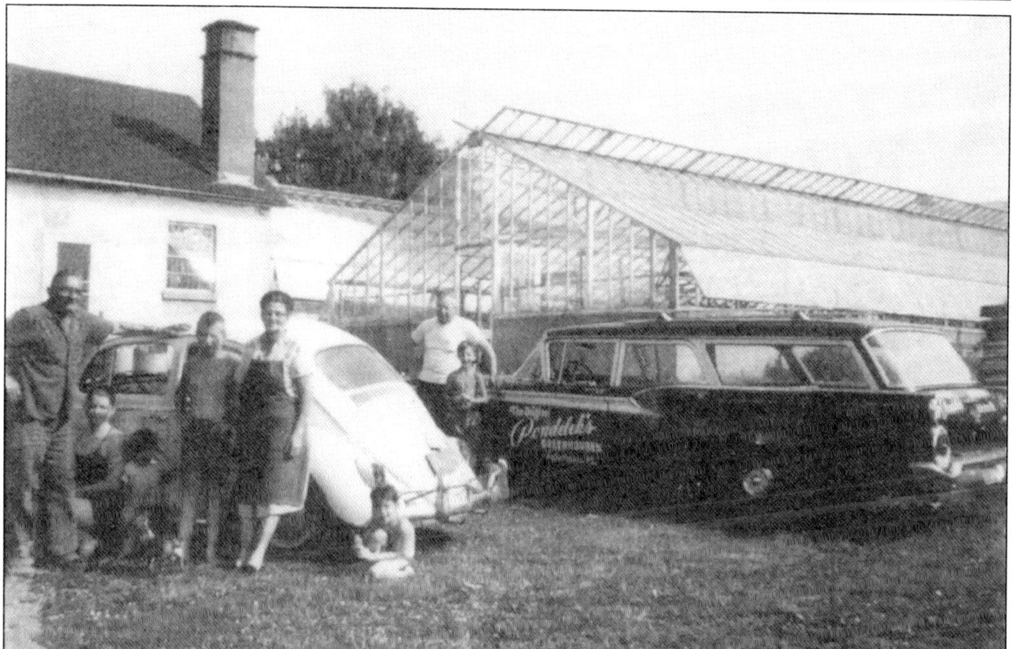

Pictured by the VW are Frank Pondelek, Melody, Robin, Frank Bodor, Elisabeth Pondelek. By the station wagon are Andy and Jamie Bodor. This photograph was taken before the new addition was built, most likely 1962 or 1963. (Courtesy of Pearl Boder.)

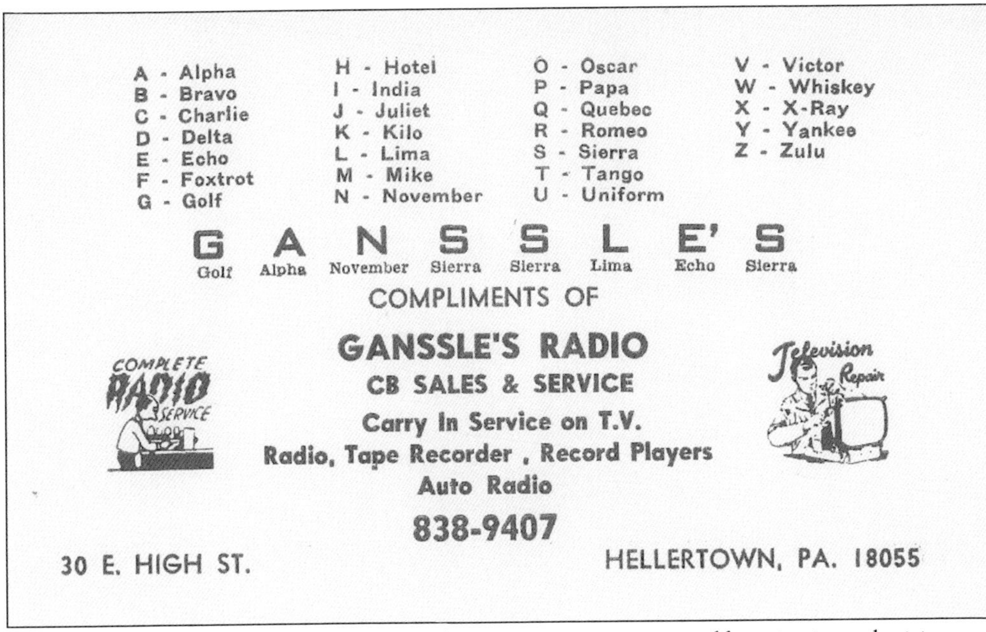

It was always nice to have a neighborhood repairman to service malfunctioning televisions and radios. Ralph Ganssle was one of those individuals. His repair facilities were in the basement of his High Street home. He also had a modest display of equipment and accessories to satisfy the growing demand for the new Citizens Band Radio Service, which came to be known as CB radio.

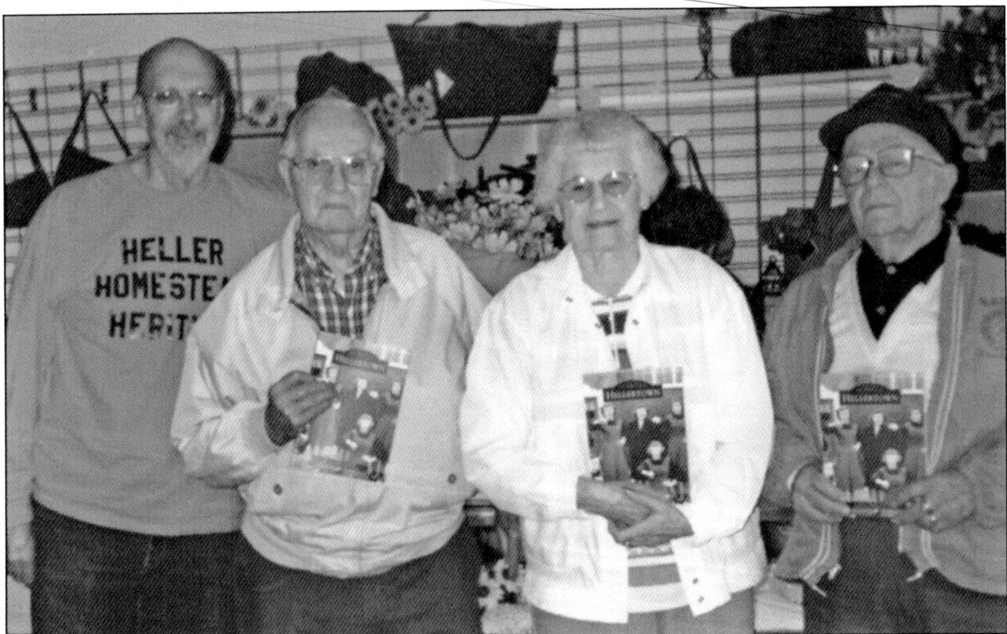

Proficient historical writer Lee Weidner (far left) attends a book signing upon the completion of his first Arcadia book on Hellertown. Ralph Ganssle stands next to Weidner. The other two people are unidentified. (Courtesy of the Hellertown Historical Society.)

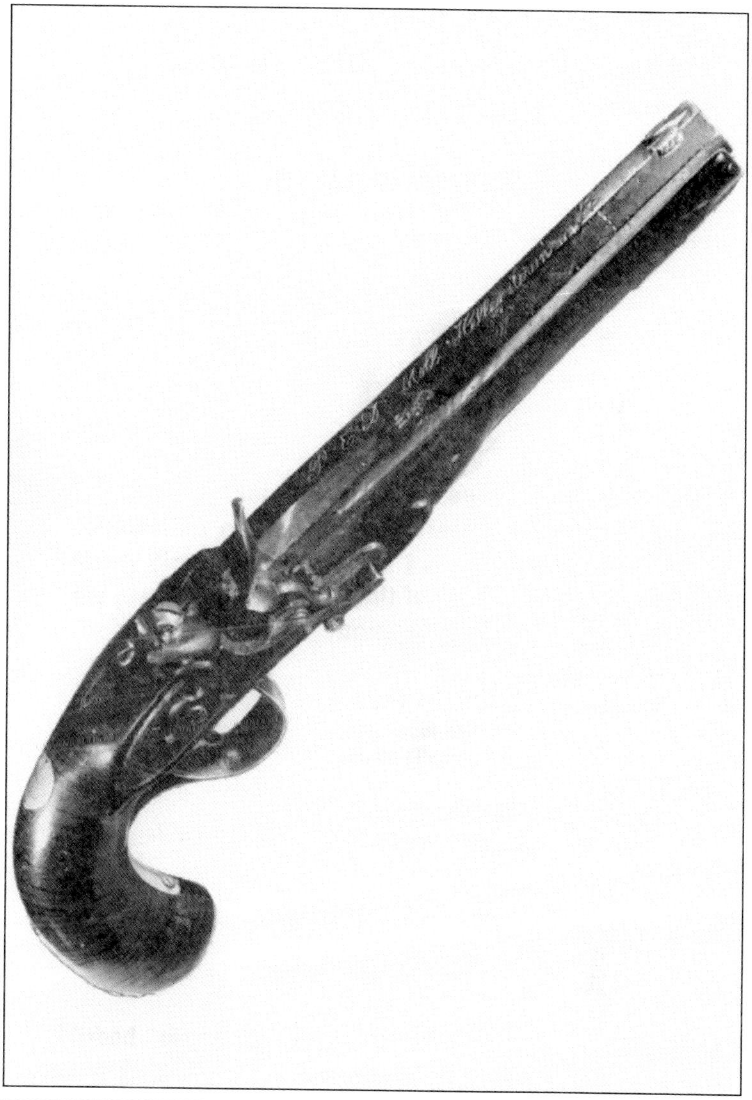

Shown on the right is a rare Moll pistol. Antique gun collectors scrutinize the inscribed company name on Moll rifles, as shown below. The Moll rifles frequently had "Hellerstown" inscribed on the barrel. As the Hellers were the founders of Hellertown, locals called the area Heller's Town.

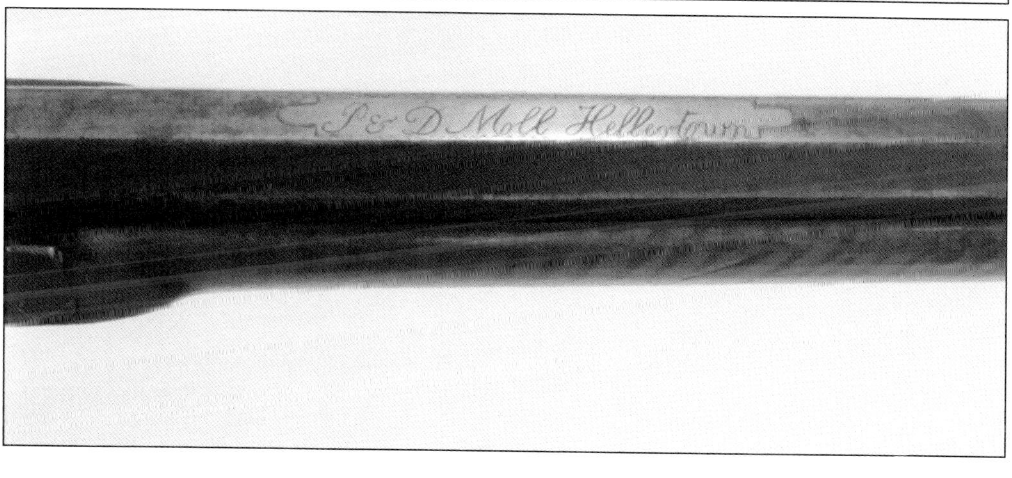

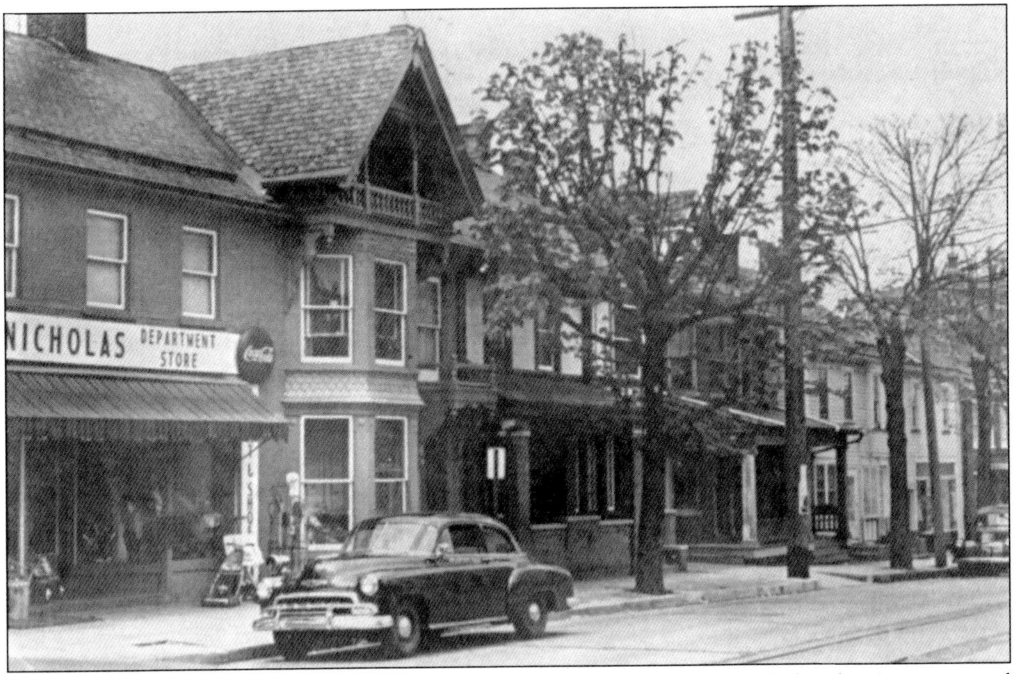

Historically, this block of properties was the home base of the Moll gunsmith family. Now occupied by Hero's Electric, the Nicholas five-and-dime shown here carried a variety of merchandise that attracted young and old alike! (Courtesy of the Hellertown Historical Society.)

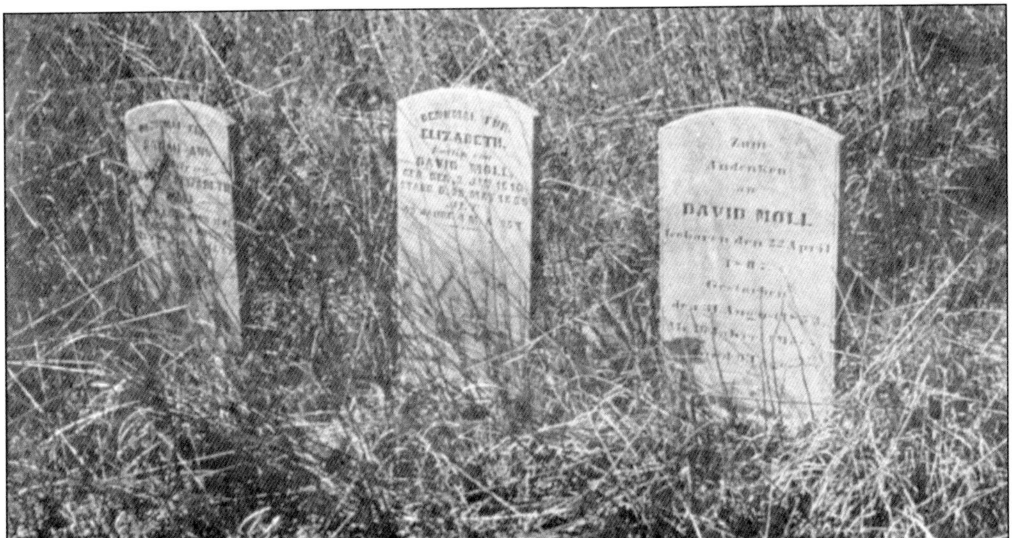

Peter and David Moll were gunsmiths on the western side of the 600 block of Main Street. Interestingly, they were more known for their pistols than their rifles. David is buried in New Jerusalem Cemetery (shown), south of Hellertown on Route 412. Peter's doctor was Henry Detweller.

A few businesses in Hellertown evoke fond memories, and Stehly's Mens & Boys Wear is no doubt one of them. It was a place where fathers could go to get that special suit and mothers could shop for their male offspring. Burton Stehly knew the families that he served, and this made for a special shopping experience.

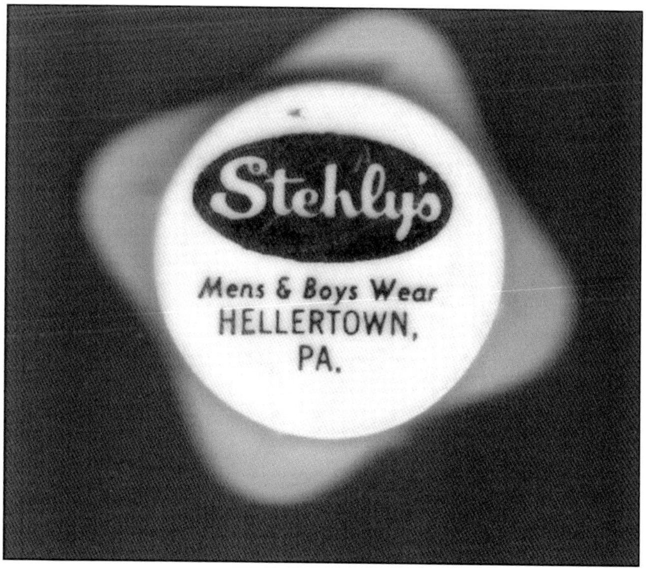

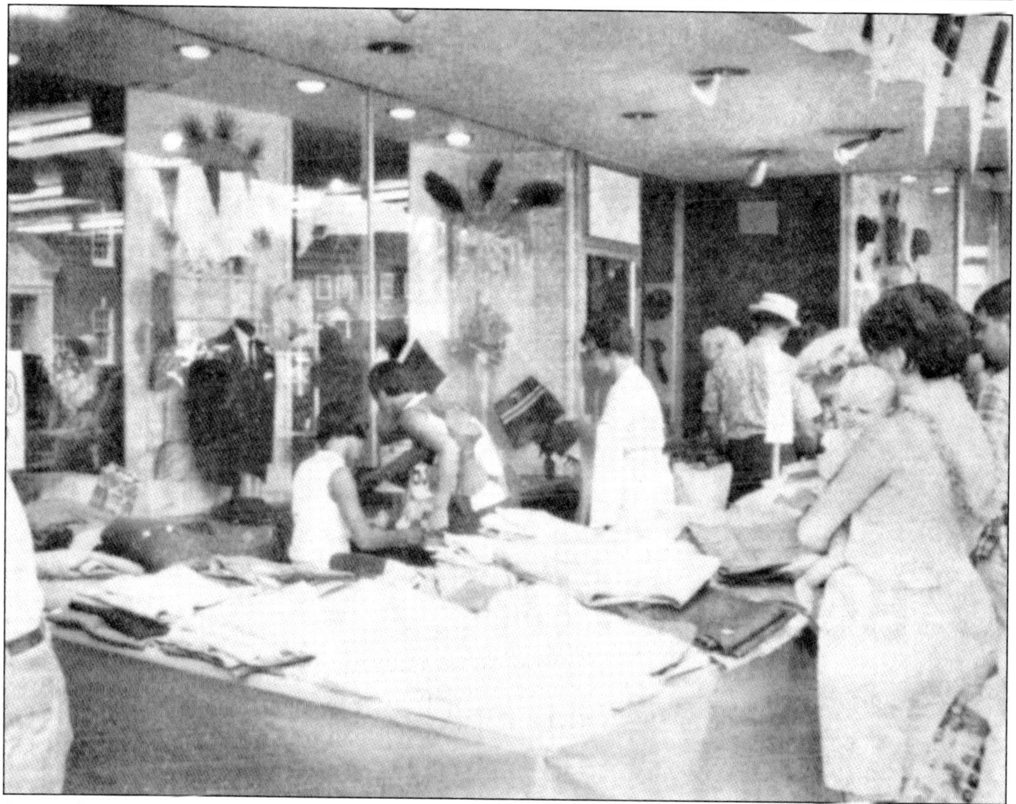

Started in 1965, the Sidewalk Sale was the last hurrah before school started and became a beloved annual event. Merchants along Main Street set up tables on the sidewalks in front of their businesses. While Main Street was never really closed, pedestrian shoppers had little worry about traffic. It was stopped in the mid-1980s with the enforcement of regulations forbidding closing a state highway (Main Street was Route 412). This photograph was taken in front of Stehly's and Yeager's.

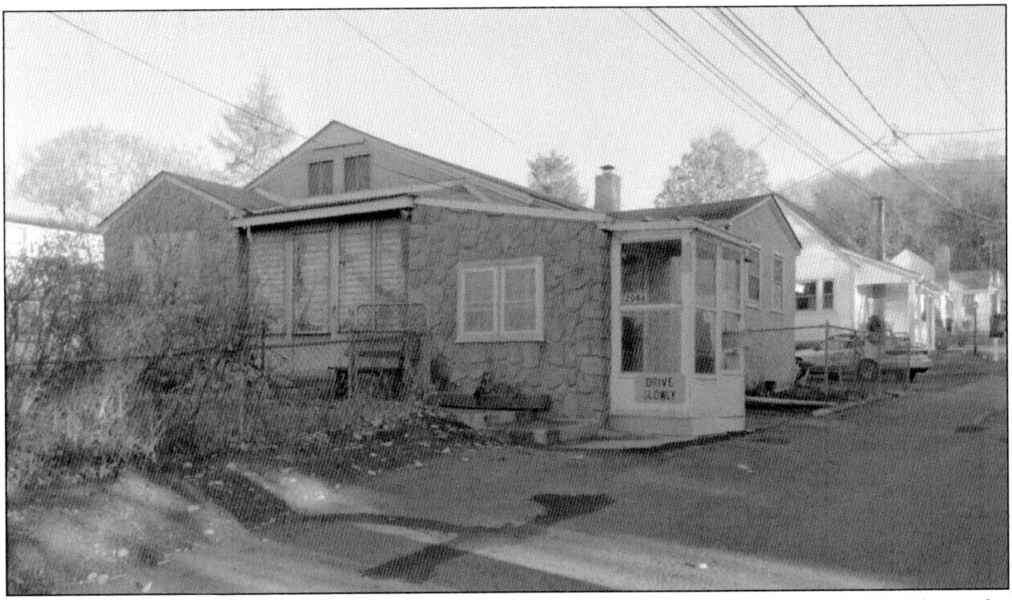

Washburn Printery was a modest business conducted in the home of Robert J. Washburn for 50 years, until his retirement in 1987. It was located on what is now Washburn Lane, near the intersection of Easton Road and Cherry Lane.

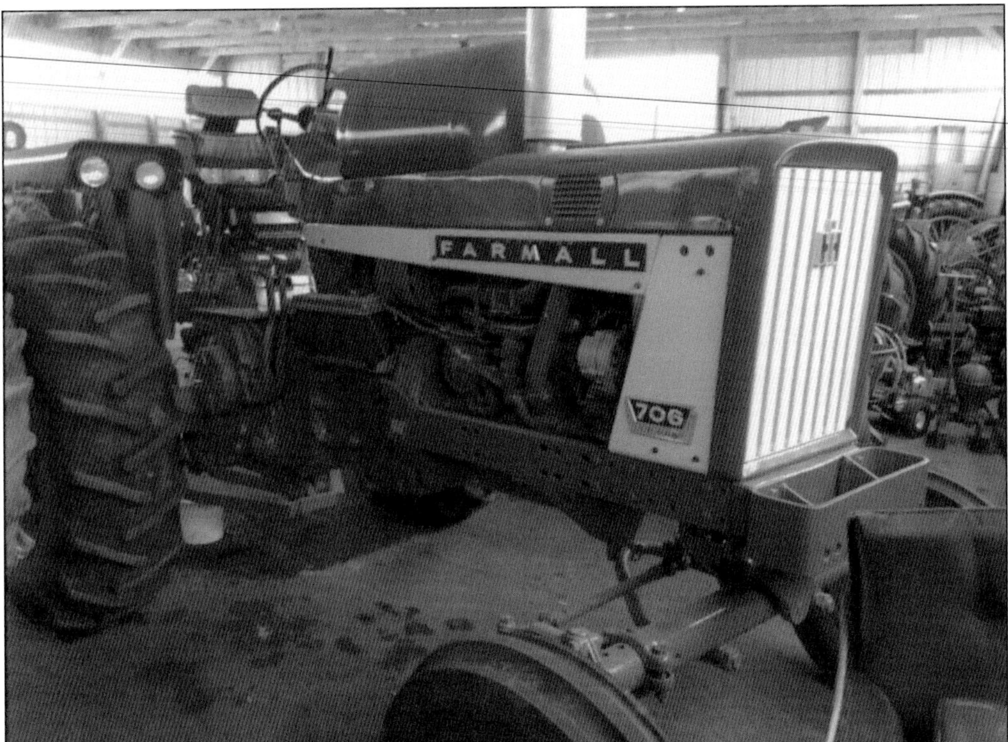

In the Saucon Valley area, the Pichels had been a noteworthy farming family in the latter part of the 20th century. To this day, Raymond Pichel maintains an impressive collection of farm tractors. Here is an unusual Farmall model, powered by propane gas.

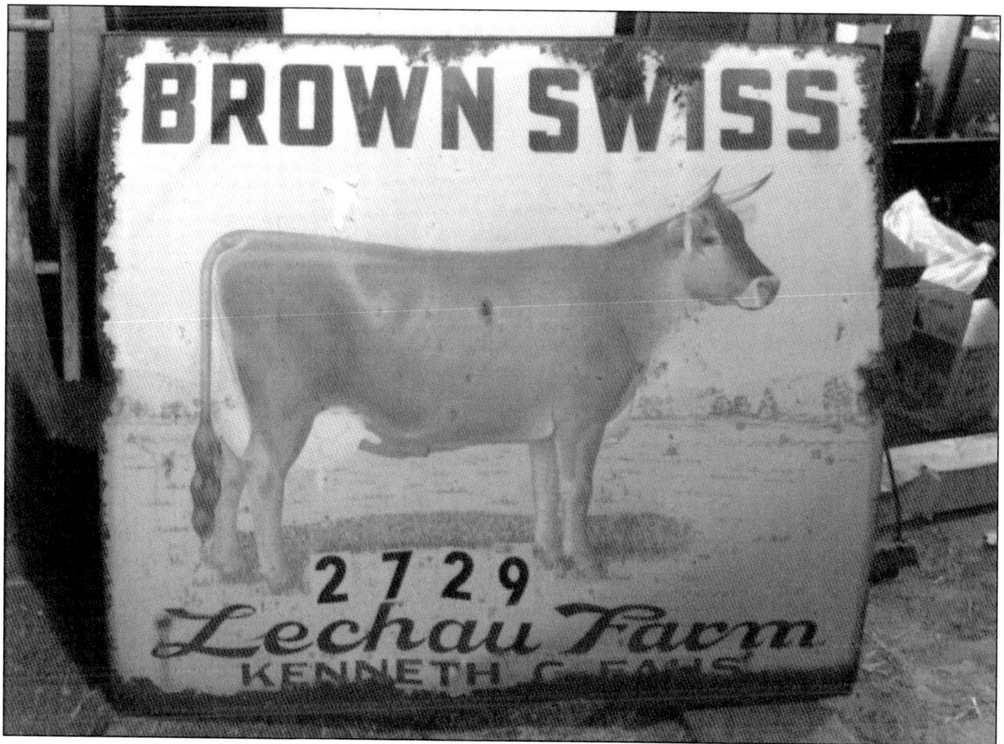

Kenneth and Marion Fahs maintained an efficient farming operation on the road to Redington and supplied milk to the local cooperative. Their livestock of choice was the Brown Swiss breed of dairy cow. In their senior years, their son David continued maintaining the farm, which had been greatly intruded upon by Interstate 78. The Fahs named their farm for the Delaware Indian name for the Lehigh River "Lechau."

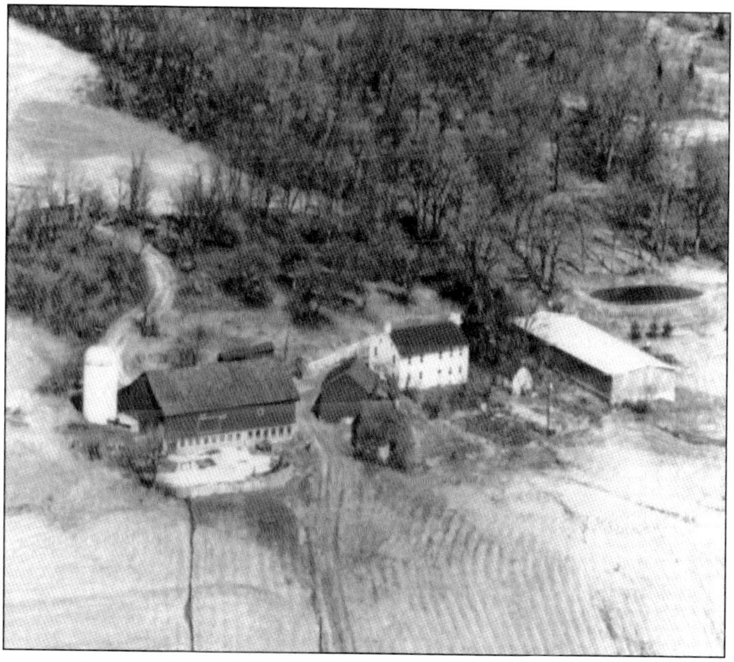

Located just west of Kunsman's Crossing, the Gardner family operated two farms in Lower Saucon. This farm is set back behind other homes along the road and therefore somewhat hidden from view. (Courtesy of Ray Shook.)

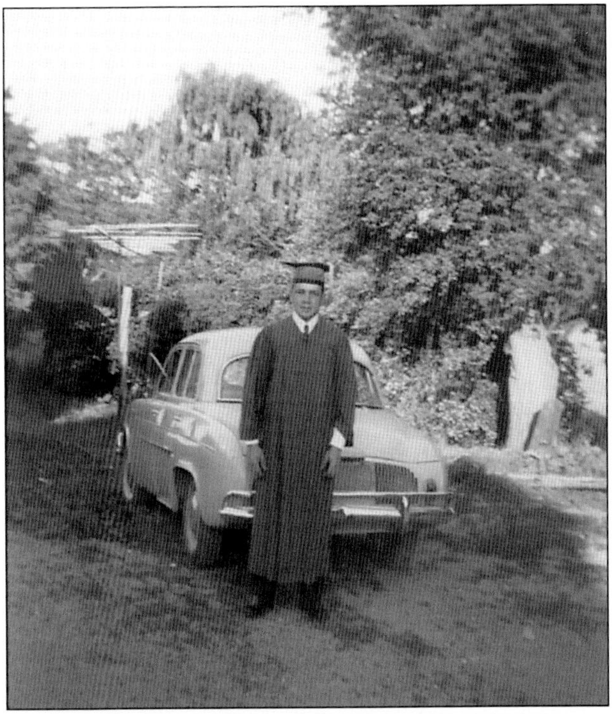

Ray Shook was one of many kids taken in by Howard and Stella Gardner. Like other farm kids, he had to balance chores around the farm with schoolwork. The Gardners were married for 50 years. (Courtesy of Ray Shook.)

The Gardners took in many foster children, and this made for enough hands to operate their farm. The farm provided these kids with a good environment of work and family. Howard Gardner worked at Bethlehem Steel Corporation for 42 years. Pictured from left to right are (first row) Thomas Huff and Gus Tonn; (second row) Ray Shook Jr., Flora Gardner Cathers, Howard Gardner Jr., and Anna May Saylor. (Courtesy of Ray Shook.)

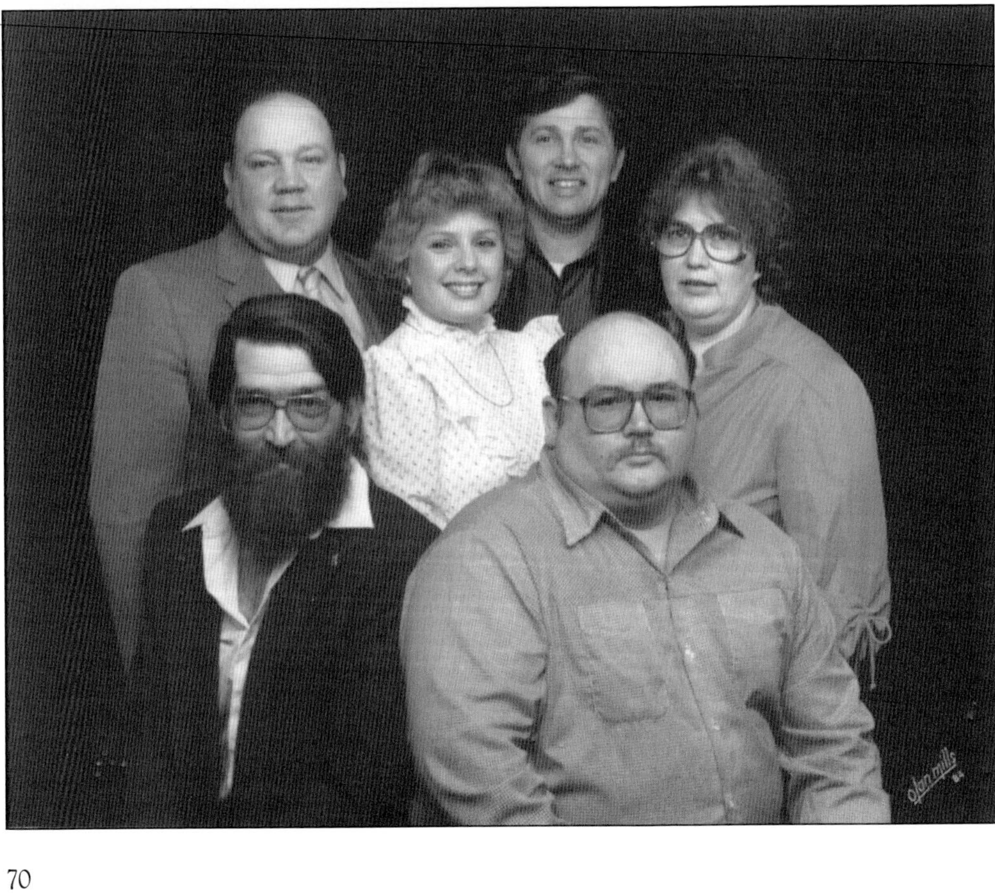

John Kofler opened the doors of the Sauconia Theatre on the evening of Friday, September 13, 1940. He previously had managed The Movies, shown at the American Legion.

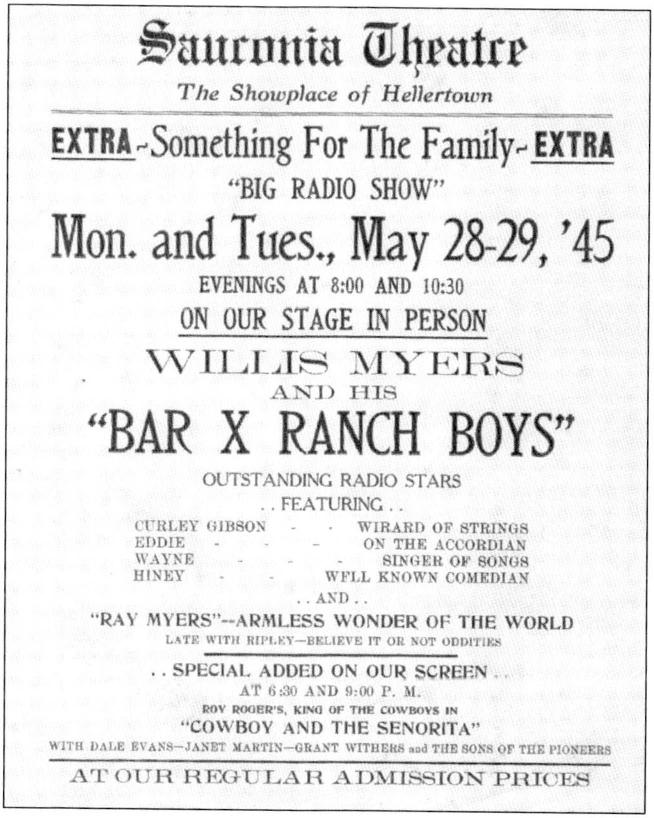

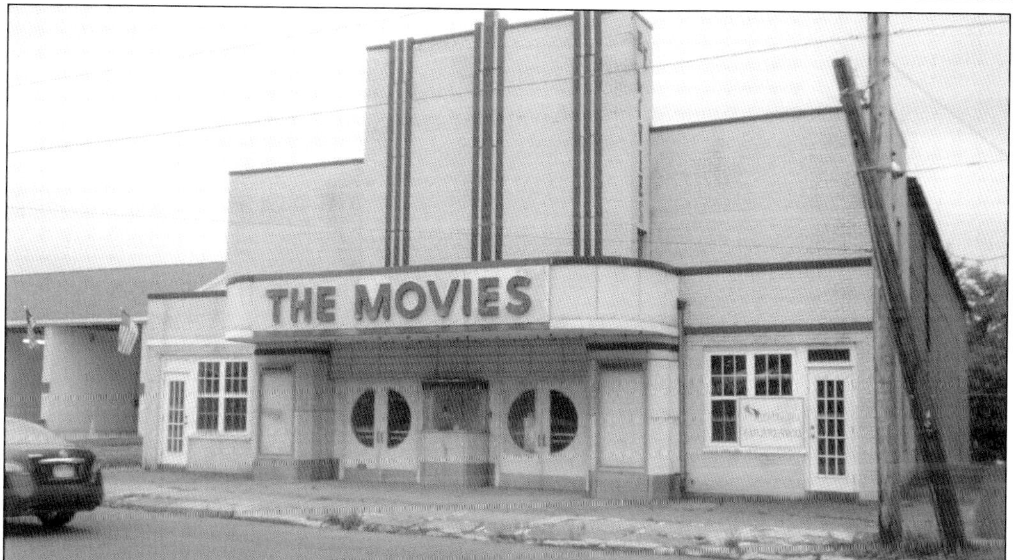

The Sauconia Theater was known as the "Showplace of Hellertown." The first film shown in this luxurious setting was *Maryland*, starring Walter Brennan, Fay Bainter, and Brenda Joyce. For Saturday matinees, it was the place for children of the 1950s. It was renamed The Movies, as shown here, when John Kofler's daughter Ellie Kofler refurbished and reopened it in 1968. Today, a dentist office and day spa occupy the building.

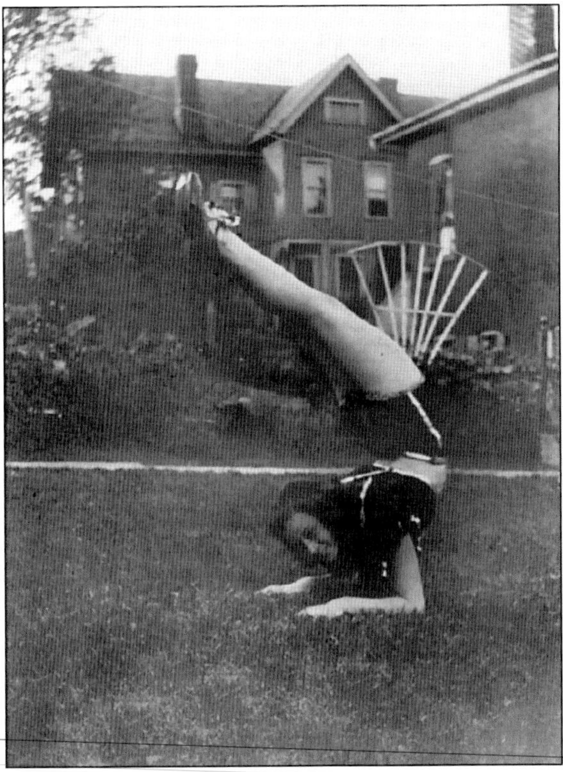

Rita A. Ruth was an orphan who found refuge in dancing at an early age. She is shown here in the backyard of Susan Crilly, her foster mother, on First Avenue in Bethlehem. Ruth was a renowned dance teacher who taught from the 1930s until retiring in 1994. She operated dance schools in Bethlehem, Lower Saucon Township, Hellertown, and Easton. She also participated in the Lehigh Valley Dance Teachers Cooperative and the Ballet Guild of the Lehigh Valley.

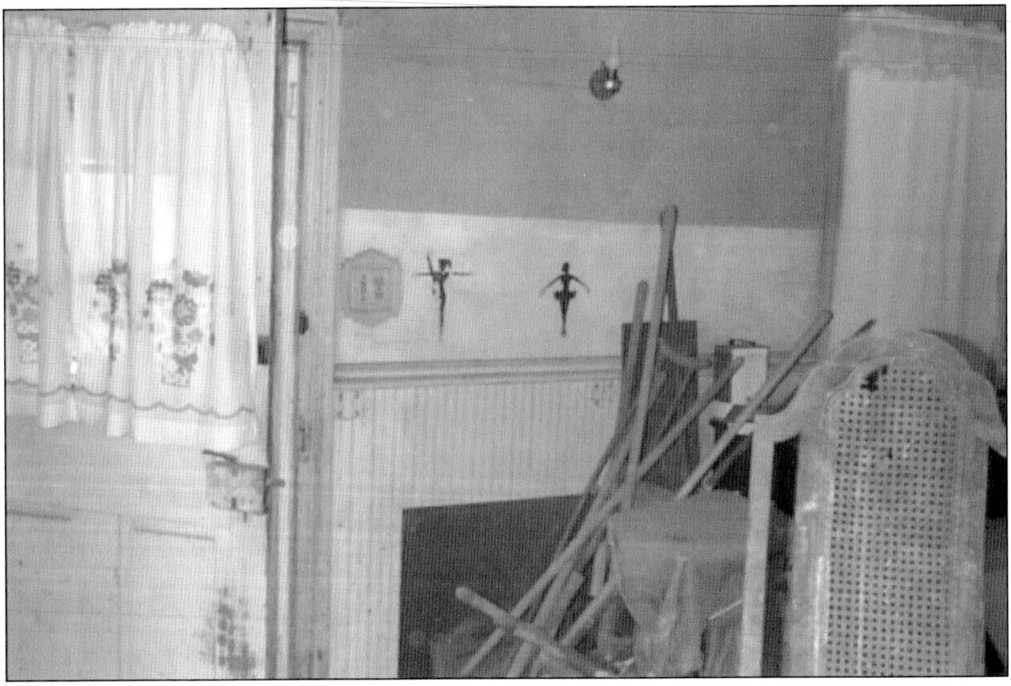

When William and Rita (White) Ruth moved to a farm in Lower Saucon, Rita set up a studio in an adjoining summer kitchen. Remnants of the ballet bar fixtures and dance silhouettes are silent reminders of activities that took place here in the 1950s.

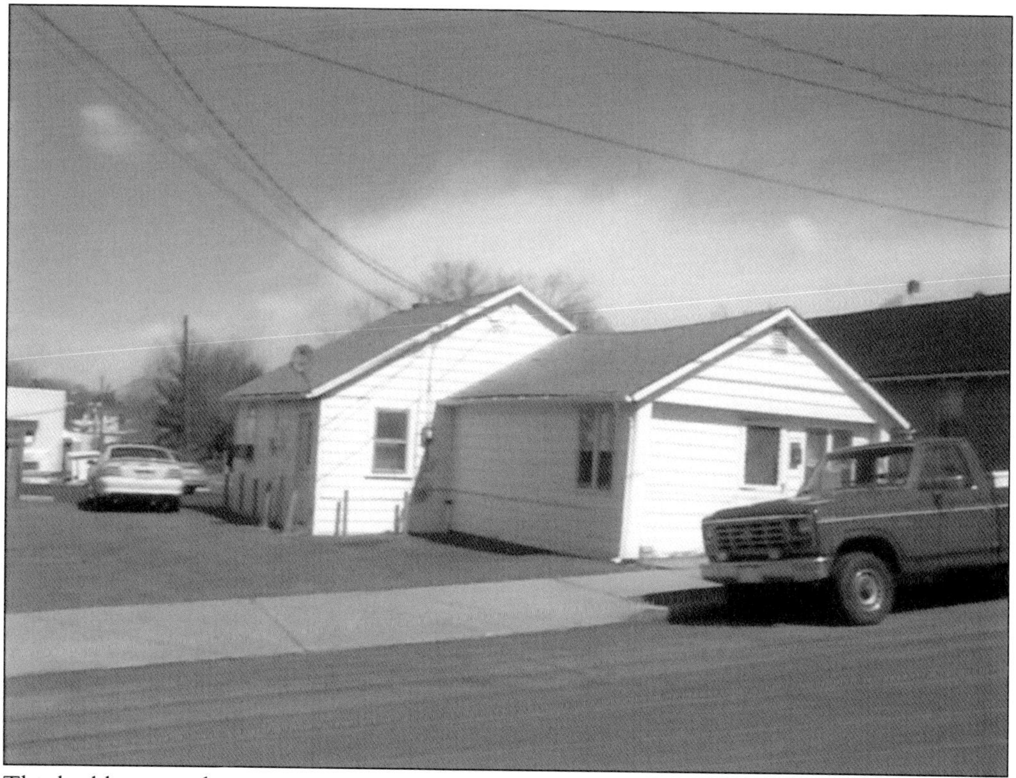

This building was the original Guro's luncheonette. Opened in 1945, it quickly became a popular spot to watch "the fights," as it contained one of only three televisions in the area. Even Max Hess was known to visit here. The back room, which later became a dancing studio, was where the television was located. A large glass magnification piece placed in front of the screen allowed everyone to enjoy the view. This building was razed to make room for a larger parking lot around 2006.

Ruth's "Country Club Dance Studio" then moved to the Masonic Temple. Here, there were two dancing rooms plus a waiting and dressing room. The first floor of the Masonic Temple was home to a few businesses before it became a dancing school. The Foster Eisenhart Apothecary was replaced by Yeager's Ice Cream in 1940 and later became Yeager's Pharmacy. Blew's Bakery then located here from 1957 to 1962.

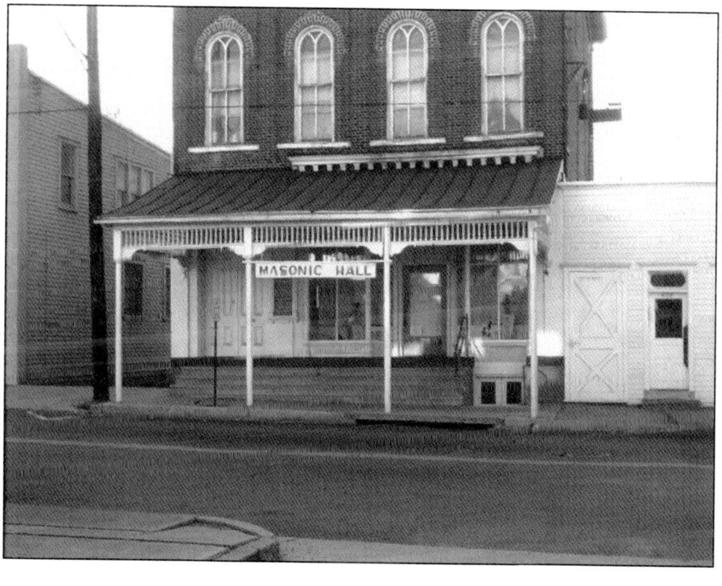

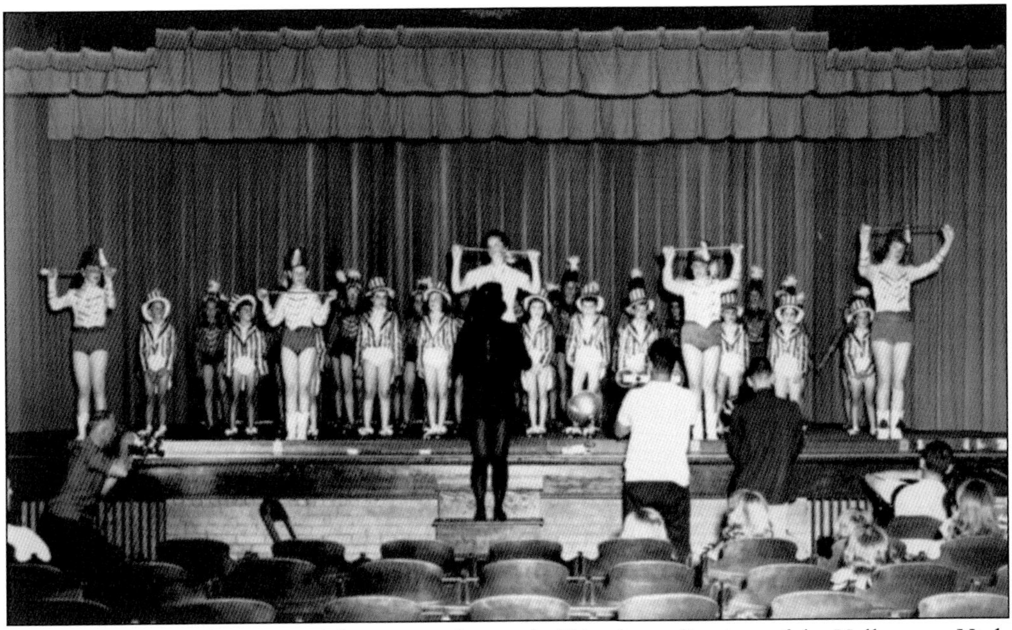

Only about two or three annual dance recitals were held in the auditorium of the Hellertown High School on Main Street. The American Legion served as a place to conduct the dress rehearsals. Although record players were the mainstay in the dance studio, the Frank Doddy Orchestra provided live music for the recitals. Frank Doddy lived in Wassergass at the time and was a local craftsman who made and fixed violins.

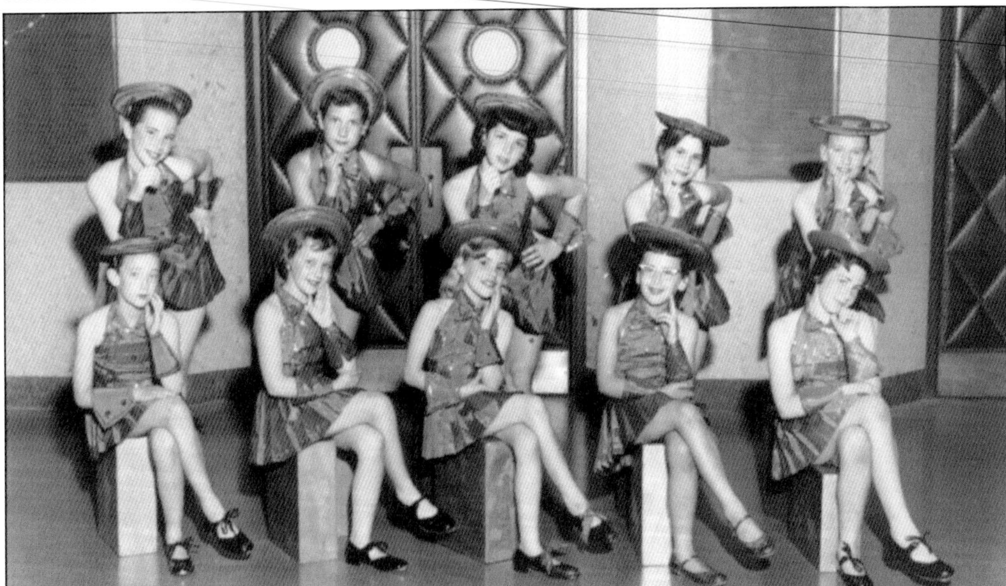

Group pictures of dance classes were a popular memento for parents to purchase. The portraits were nicely arranged by Mr. Spangenberg of the popular Society Portraits of Hellertown. Shown here are, from left to right, (first row) Anita Graham, Debbie Fehr, Joan Martin, Beth Doddy, and Joanne McCall; (second row) Cheryl Ruth, Barbara Koch, Judy Doddy, Bonnie Frey, and Annette Graham.

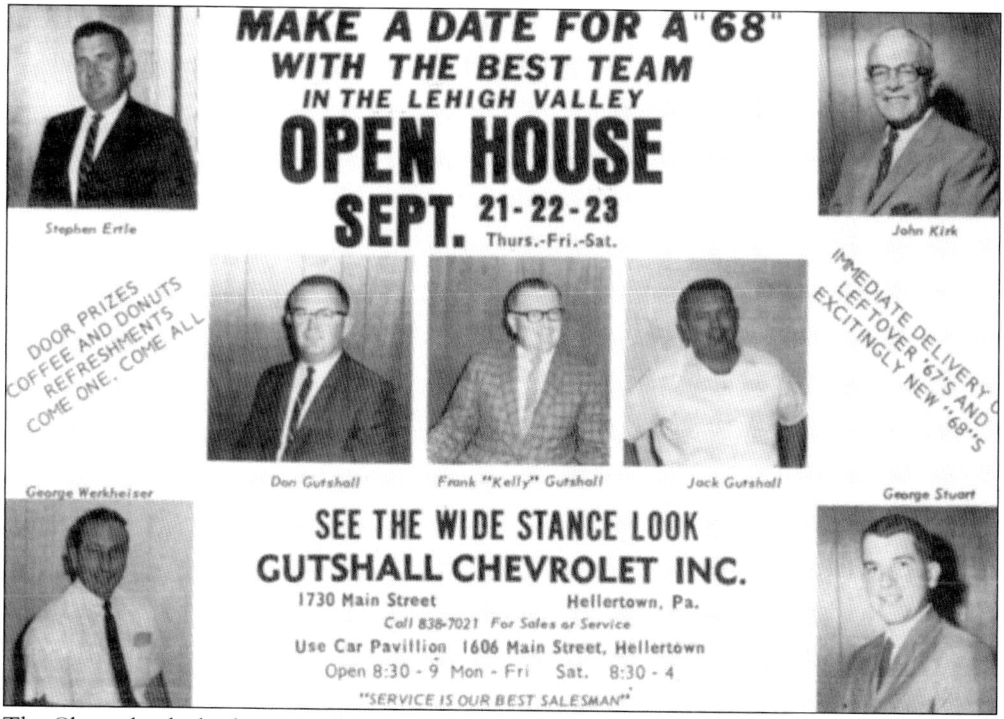

The Chevrolet dealership in Hellertown, at 1606 Main Street, went through a few name changes in its history. Initially called Bob's Place (Rickert Motor Company), it then became Spaeth's Chevrolet, then Gutshall's Chevrolet Inc. Clift Motors, a Chrysler dealership just over the town boundary at 1730 Main Street, was acquired by Gutshall's in the late 1960s, which then moved its showroom from its original location.

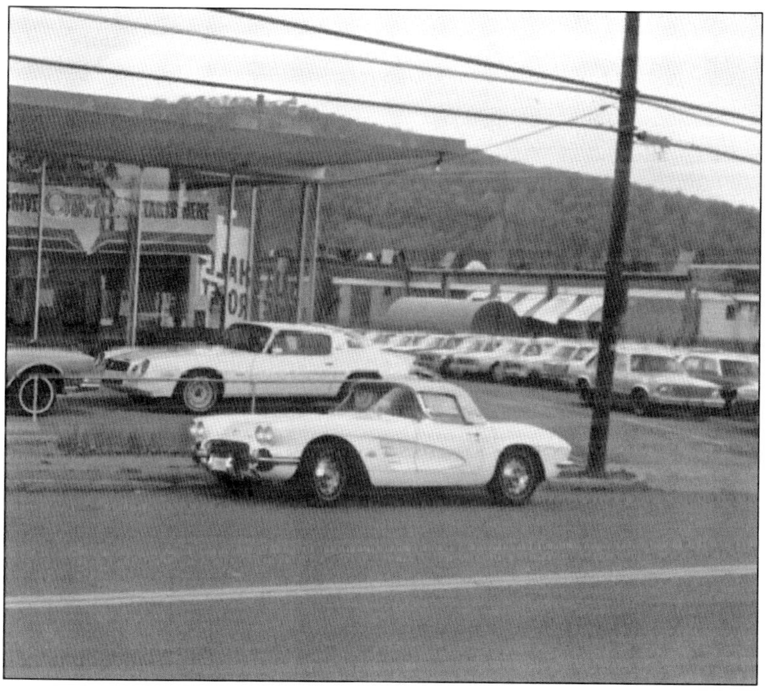

Located next to the Champion Spark Plug factory, built in 1918, this showroom was the final location of the Gutshall dealership. Previously, Clift Motors, a Plymouth dealership, had occupied the site.

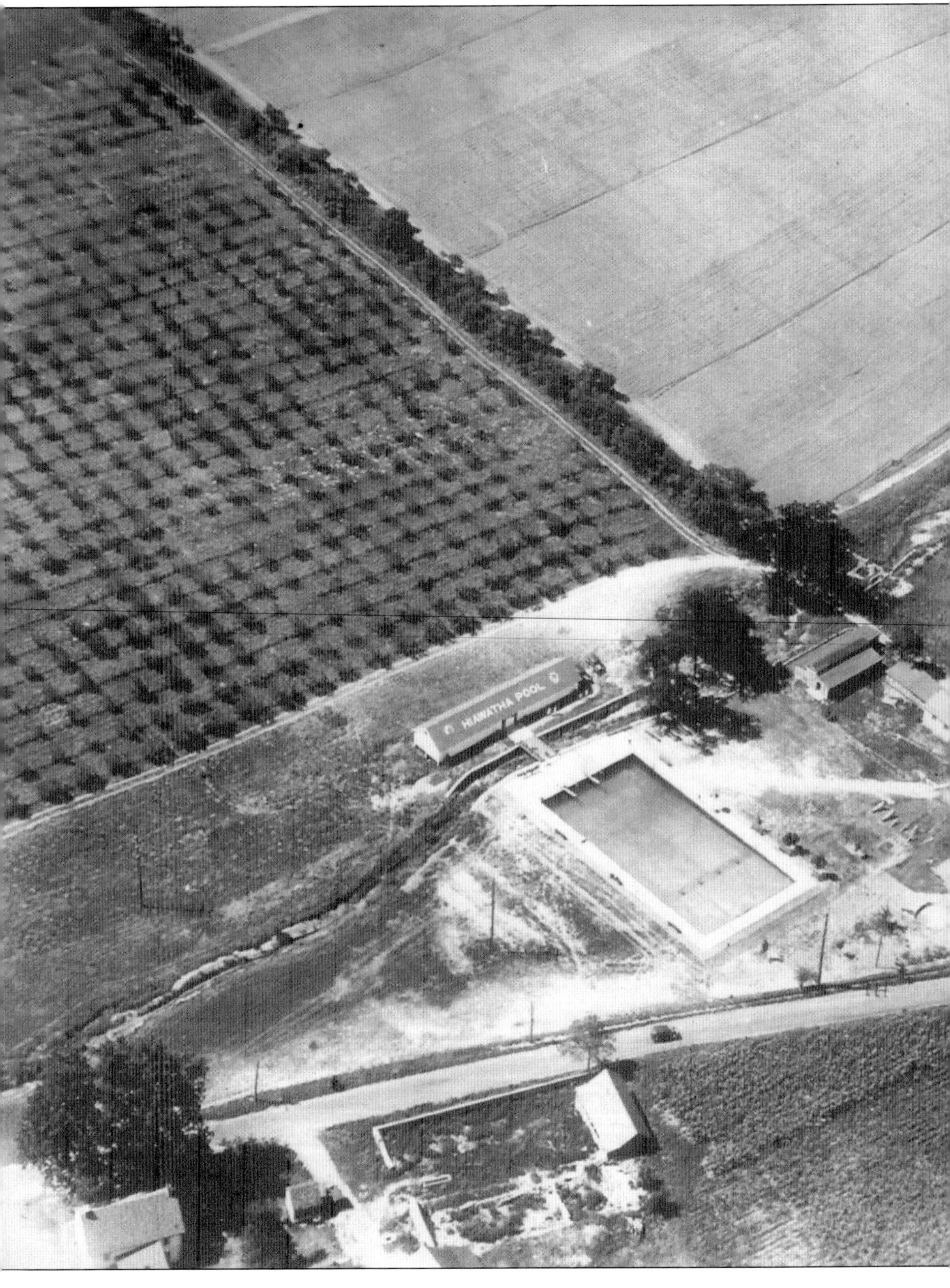
HIAWATHA POOL

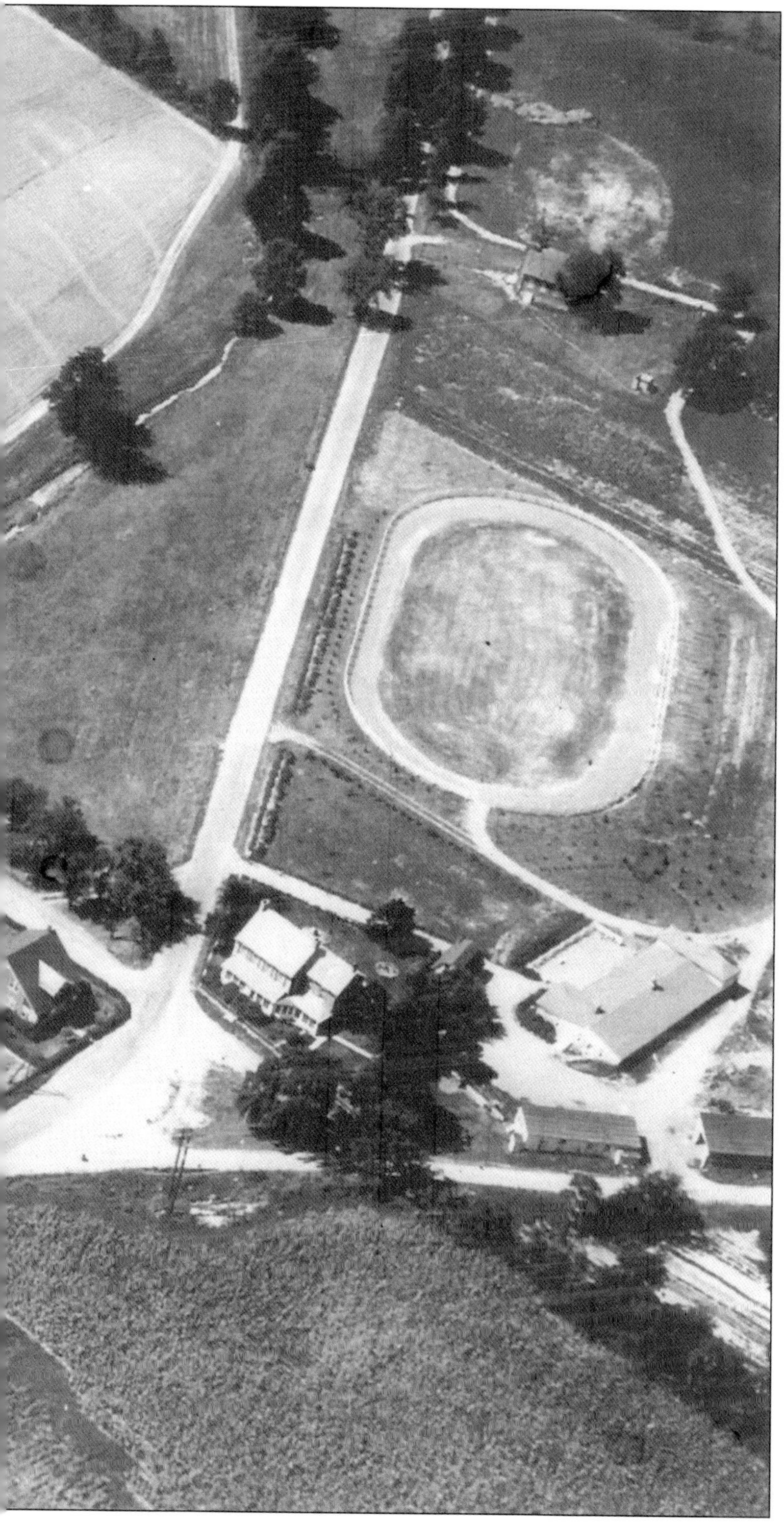

This aerial photograph shows two popular places for recreation, Hiawatha Pool and Patterson Stables. They were located near the intersection of Bingen and Friedensville Roads. Hiawatha was an Olympic-size cement pool in Lower Saucon Township. Frank and Jenny Kardos operated the pool next to their home on Bingen Road for about a decade. In 1947, they sold the property to Bob and Vivian Fitzsimons. Bob was a physical education teacher and swim coach for Easton Area School District. The Fitzsimons sold the property to Bethlehem Steel in 1960, due to maintenance costs and the polio scare. Bethlehem Steel demolished the pool in 1961. The Patterson Stables was owned by Edward C. and Marion M. (McIntyre) Marshall. (Courtesy of the Hellertown Historical Society.)

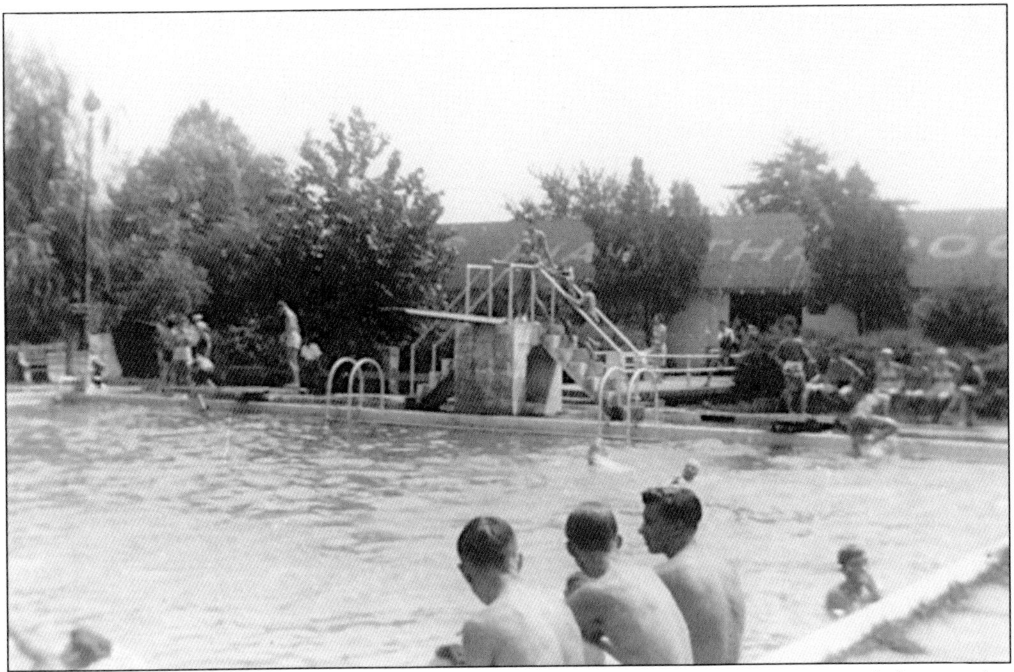

Hiawatha Pool is seen here at the time that Robert and Vivian Fitzsimons owned the popular pool near Black River Creek. Both Fitzsimons had careers as educators and must have enjoyed the sounds of children having fun. Their home was on the hillside above the pool. The pool had to be emptied and cleaned every three weeks and then refilled from an artesian well.

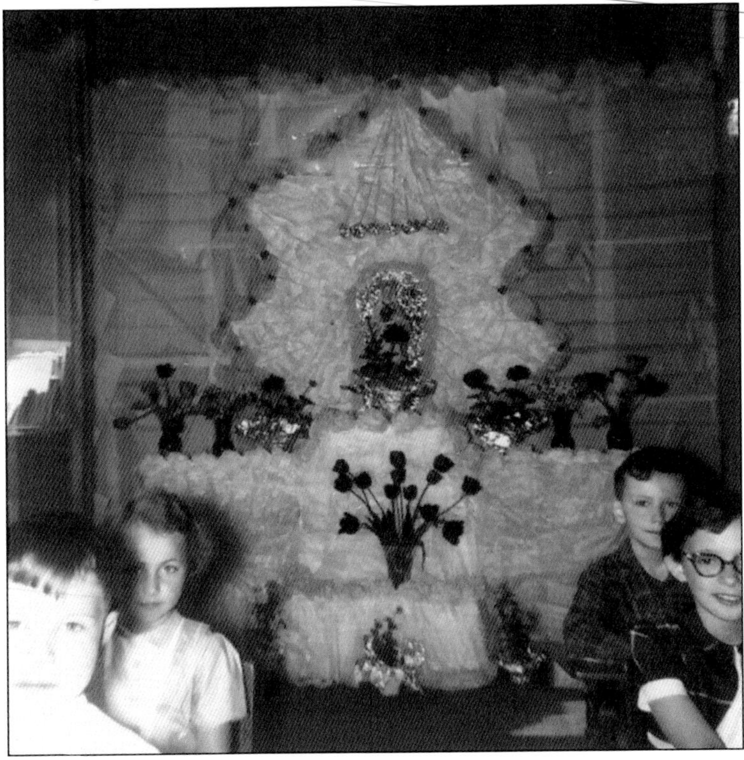

Jennie and John Chaffier opened the Casco Manufacturing Company in the 1940s, on Thomas Avenue. The company made sportswear and employed several Hellertown women as sewing-machine operators over its 41 years. The Chaffiers, being members of St. Theresa's Catholic Church, offered space in their factory as a temporary location for parochial school needs. Shown here in the 1950s are, from left to right, Francis Check, Elizabeth Duffy, Regis Sopko, and Laverne Resicks.

Five

Big Businesses

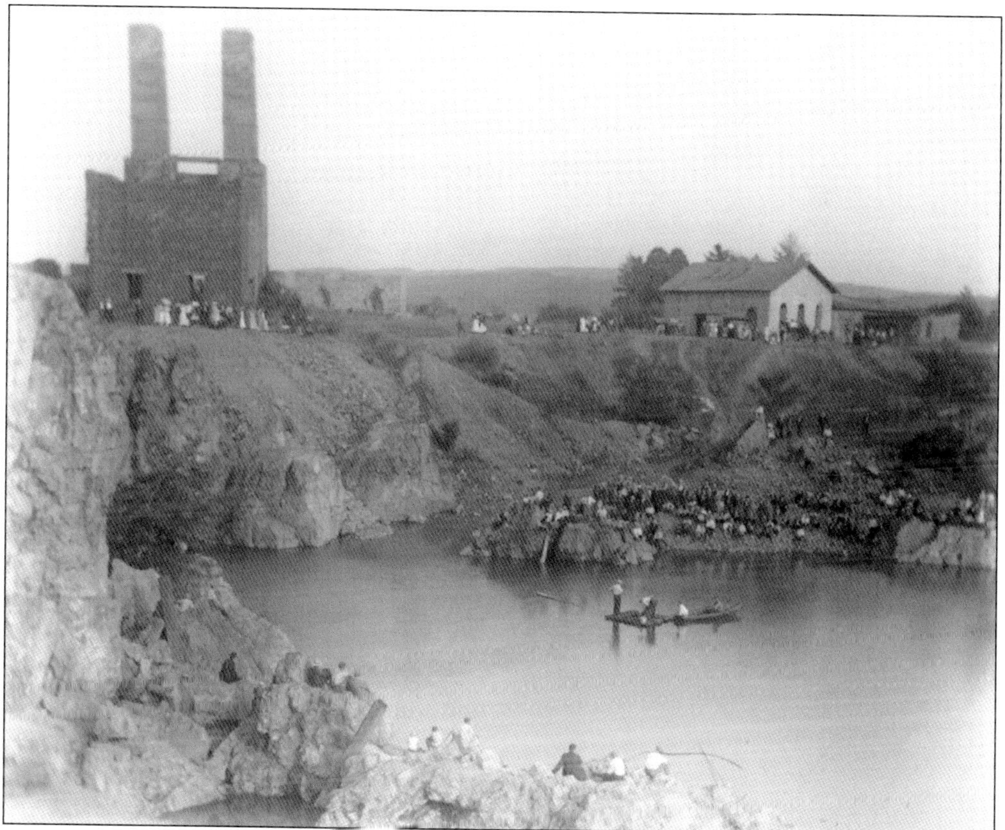

In the mid-1800s, Samuel Wetherill invented a process for making zinc oxide from calamine ore. He used zinc oxide as a substitute for lead in his paint manufacturing business. Wetherill leased the Ueberroth property in Friedensville and began the mining of the calamine ore deposits (pictured). He erected furnaces on the south side of the Lehigh River to process the ore. This photograph shows the search for a man who was swimming in the deep pit. Sadly, he had drowned.

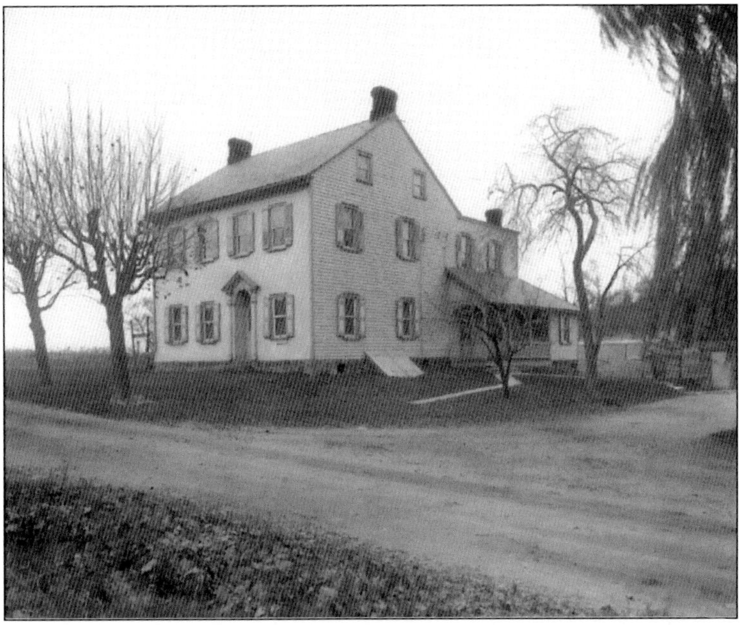

The Bethlehem Steel Farm was the idea of Charles Schwab, CEO of the corporation. The farmhouse was home to the Lloyd Koch family. Lloyd Kock, Dick Kantor's grandfather, managed the farm between 1910 and 1930. The dwelling was razed in 1941 at the outset of World War II; it had been built in 1812.

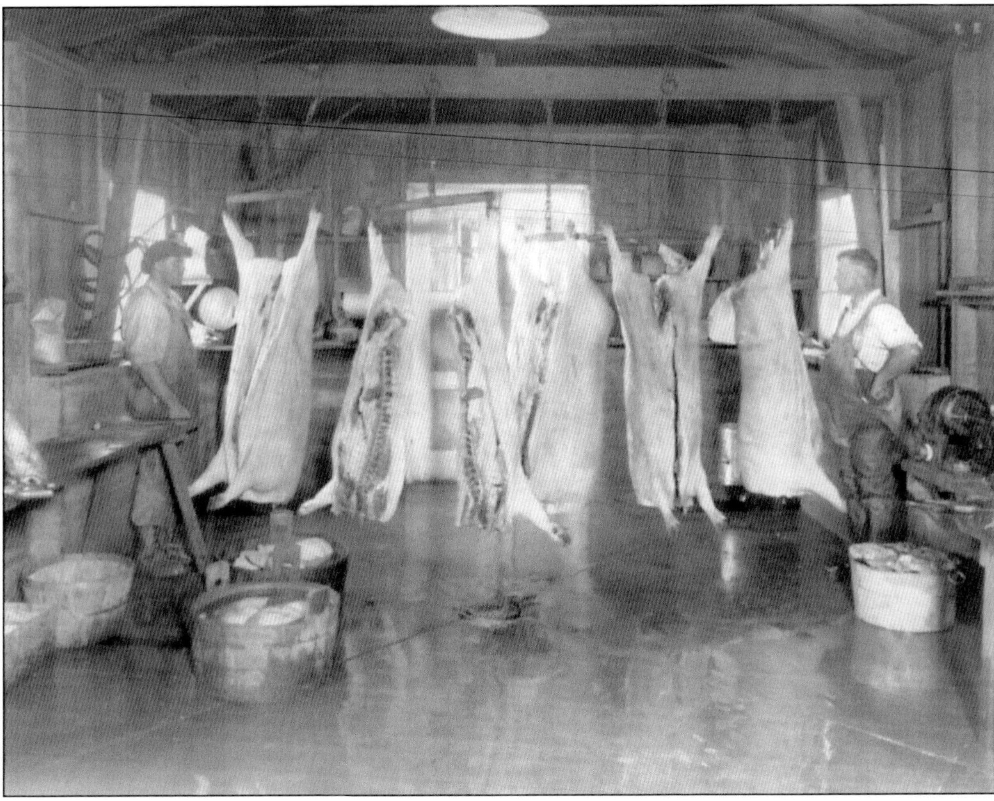

The farm raised poultry and pork, which provided foods on the menu at Bethlehem Steel's headquarters on Third Street, Bethlehem. The executive dining area and the regular workers' cafeteria served poultry, eggs, and pork from the farm. Butchering went on all year long. Seen here are Bill Sutton (left) and Lloyd Koch.

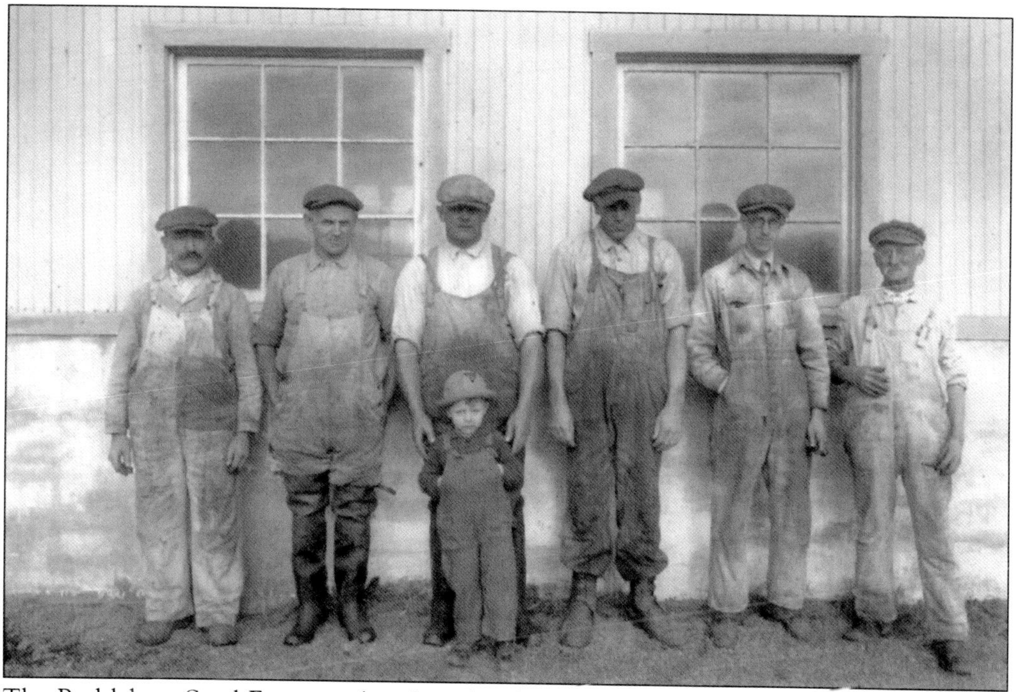

The Bethlehem Steel Farm employed six farmhands. Pictured from left to right are Albert Siegfried, Robert Koch, Lloyd Koch (with his son Leon), Bill Sutton, Raymond Siegfried, and Samuel Fehr.

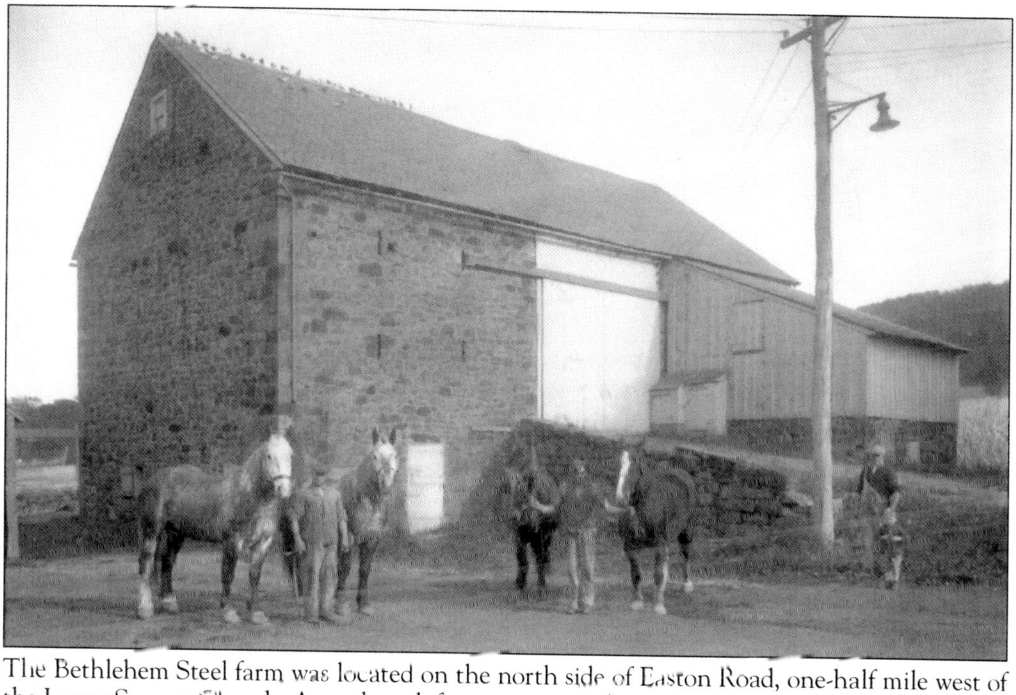

The Bethlehem Steel farm was located on the north side of Easton Road, one-half mile west of the Lower Saucon Church. A truck took farm-grown products to Bethlehem twice a week, year-round. Pictured from left to right are Rob Koch, Bill Sutton, and Lloyd Koch (with his son Leon). The horses were used for regular farm work, such as plowing the fields.

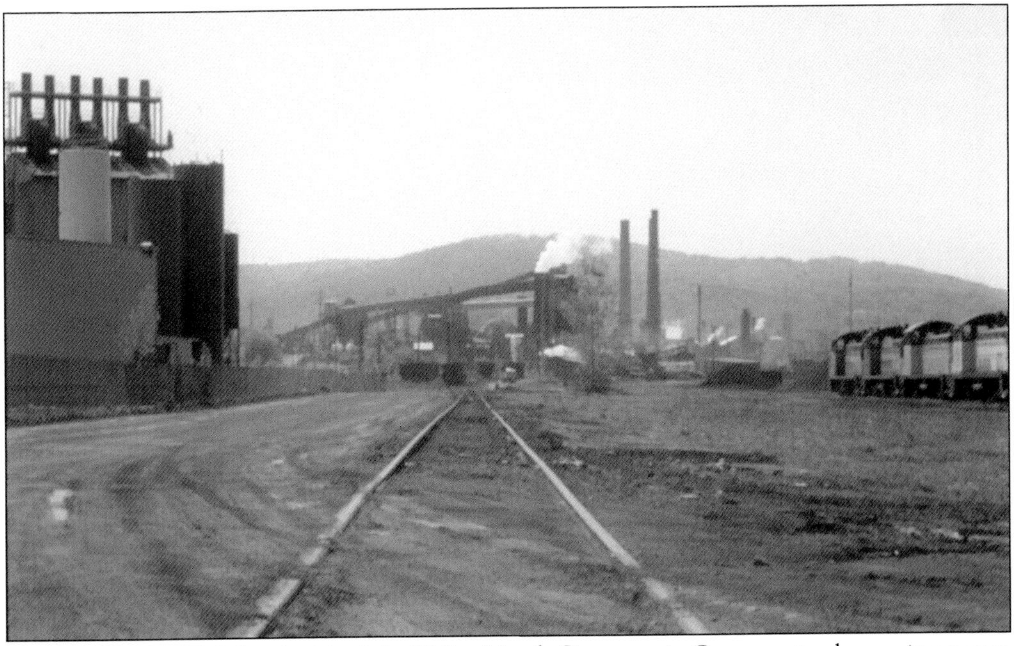

In 1908, Charles M. Schwab visited the Didier-March Company in Germany to observe its process of making coke. Schwab signed a contract with Didier-March to build a plant in Bethlehem to supply Bethlehem Steel with coke. However, when World War I broke out, Didier-March was forced to sell the plant to Bethlehem Steel for $8 million in 1917.

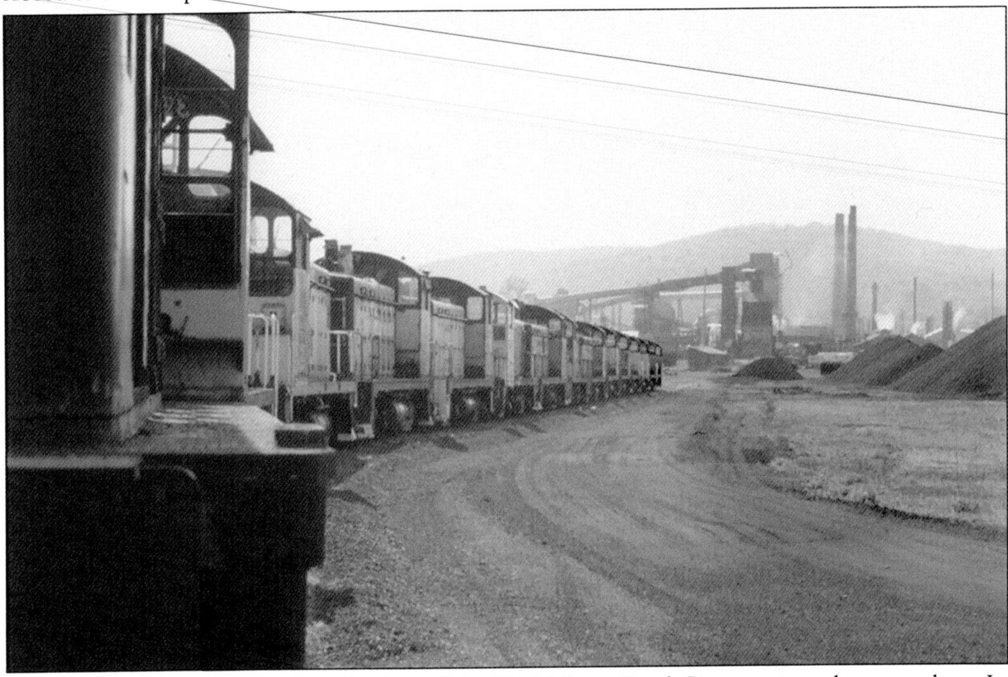

The Coke Ovens Division was the last of the Bethlehem Steel Corporation plants to close. In March 1998, 800 coke works employees were informed of the closure. The plant was known for its difficult working conditions. It was located on 160 acres between Hellertown and Bethlehem and employed 30,000 at the height of production.

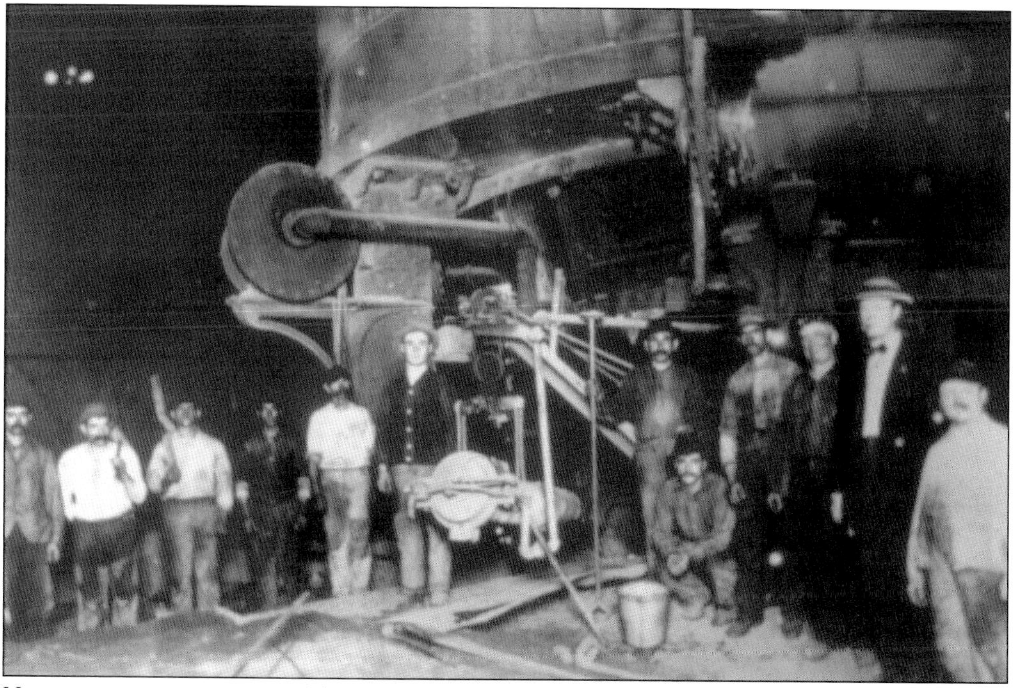

Here is a rare interior view of the Thomas Iron Company, in Lower Saucon. The firm purchased the foundry from the Saucon Iron Company in 1884. The stacks of the two furnaces measured 60 feet by 16 feet, and 50 feet by 16 feet. The furnaces annually produced 20,000 tons of fine-quality gray iron at the height of production. Thomas Iron designated the furnaces No. 10 and No. 11.

In 1955, three-year-old Joan (Jamiolkowski) Ruth helps water her father's garden, within view of the remains of the Thomas Iron Works. In 1921, the furnaces in the 73-acre tract were sold to the Reading Coal & Iron Company, which in turn sold them for scrap. The Jamiolkowski home, at the end of Thomas Avenue, previously served as a lab for the iron company.

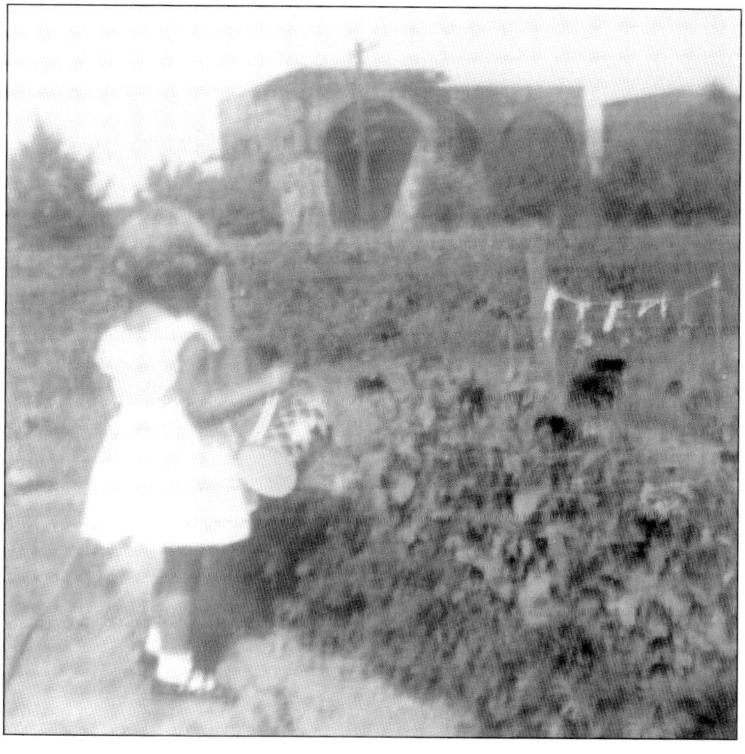

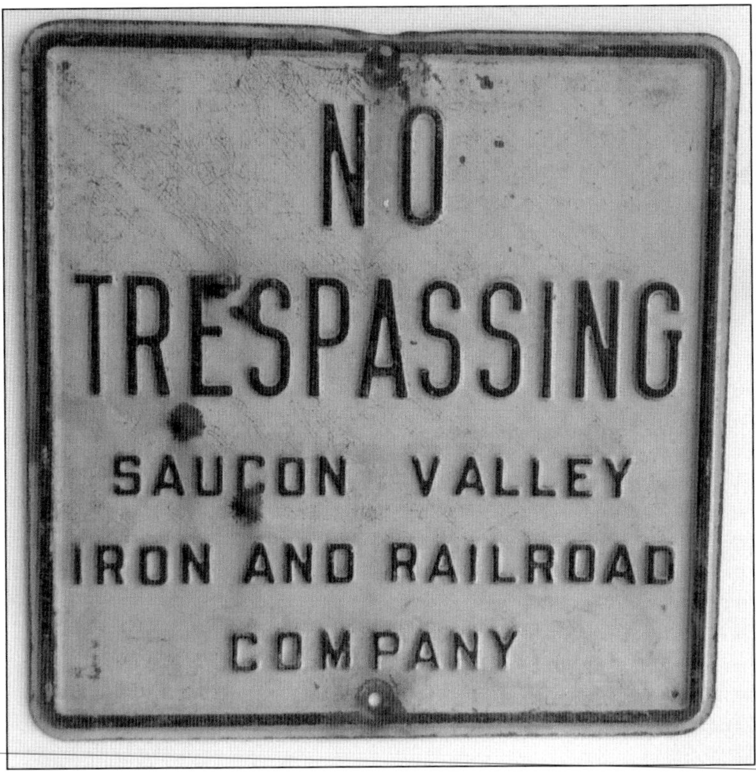

This is a "No Trespassing" sign from the Saucon Valley Iron and Railroad Company. The Saucon Iron Company was chartered and erected in Lower Saucon in 1866. The company owned the Saucon Valley Iron and Railroad Company, whose rails connected to the North Penn Railroad near Bingen. The Thomas Iron Company purchased the works in 1884.

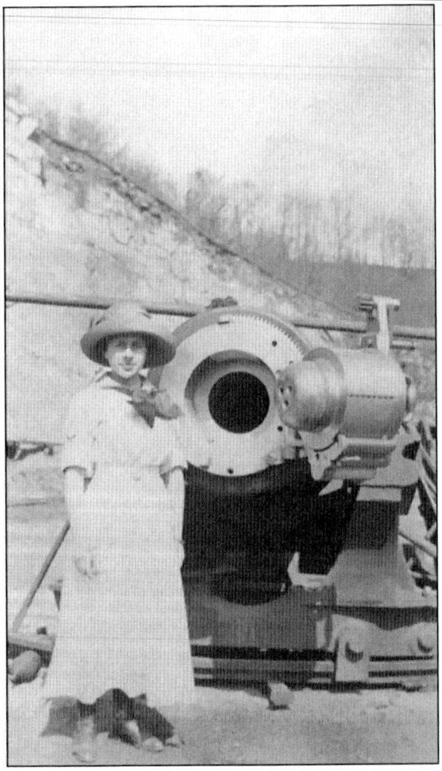

Frances E. Knoll poses beside an artillery gun at the Redington Proving Grounds. In 1887, the Bethlehem Steel Company leased property in Redington to create a proving ground. It was the only privately owned proving ground in the country at the time. The property gave Bethlehem Steel a tremendous advantage, allowing it to produce munitions to completion. Knoll was a resident of Butztown. (Courtesy of David Jacoby.)

Six

Town and Country

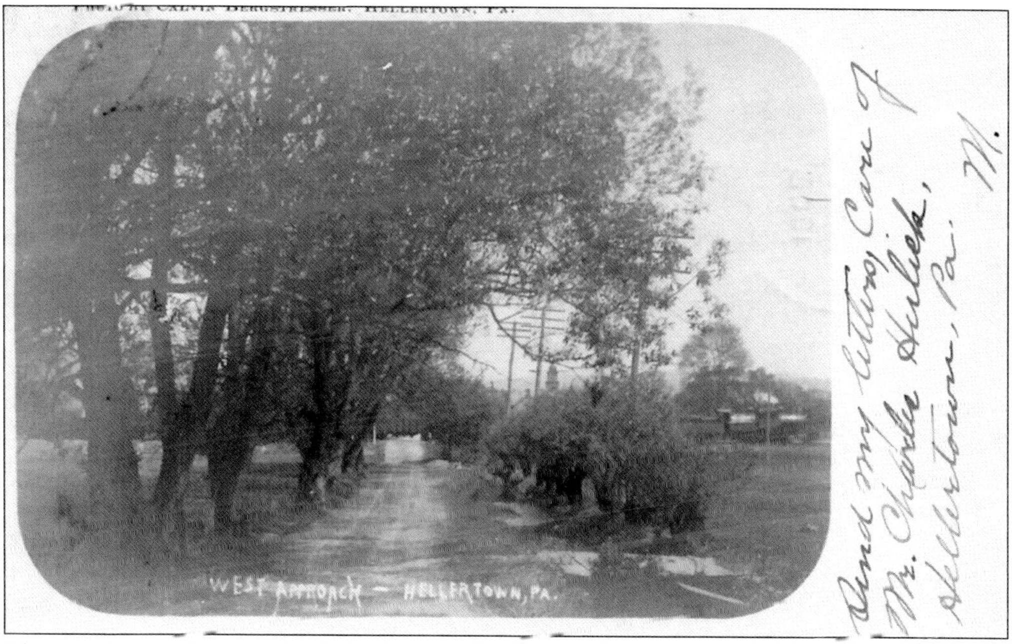

This east-facing photograph of the Saucon Creek was taken in the early 1900s from the Water Street Bridge in Hellertown. The tracks of the Pennsylvania & Reading Railway Company, laid down in the 1860s, are visible. In the distance is the steeple of St. Paul's Evangelical Church, which later became the Methodist church, located on Main Street.

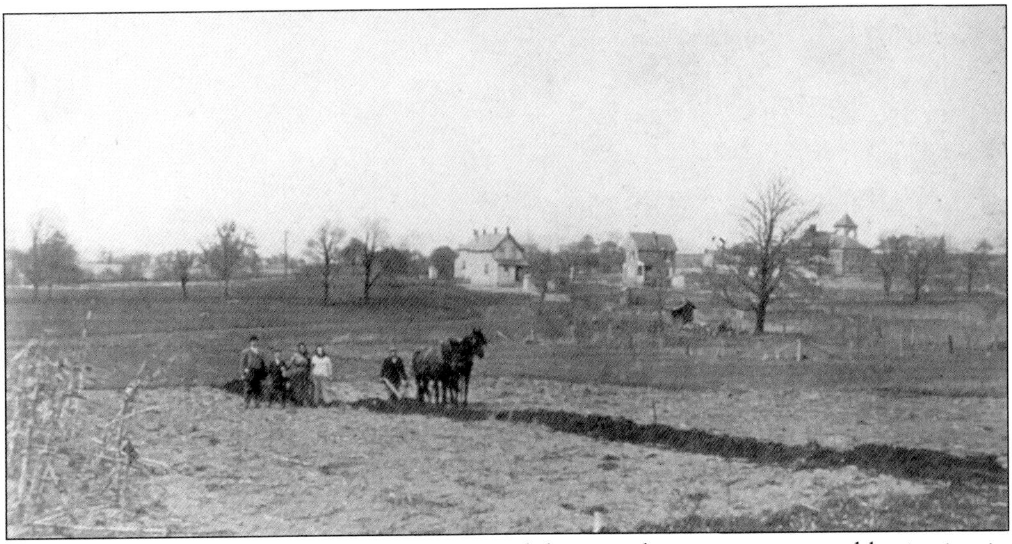

The Wagner farm became Wagner Terrace, a subdivision that was constructed beginning in 1909. Wagner Terrace was laid out in lots bordered by Route 412, Cherry Lane, and Zimpfer Lane. The typical home in the development is a brick, three-bedroom, Cape Cod structure. Most of the homes were built in the 1940s and 1950s for Bethlehem Steel Corporation employees. The steepled building on the right is the Lower Saucon High School, later known as Zawick Manufacturing Company.

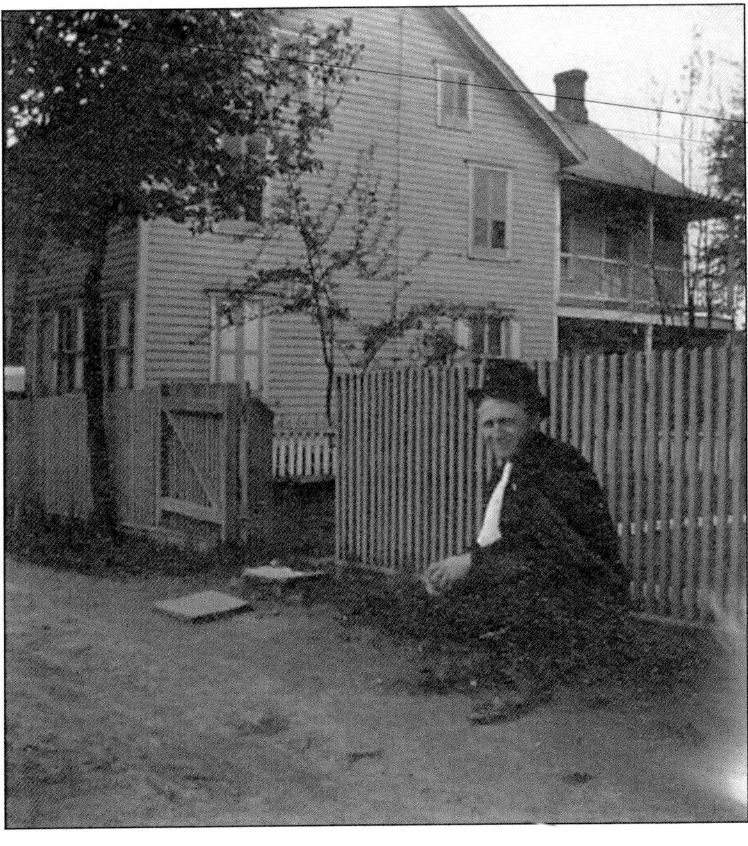

The home shown here stands immediately to the right of the new CVS on Main Street. It appears that the home retains its entire original configuration, including the intact rear section.

The Lutz-Franklin Schoolhouse is seen here in the early 1950s. During the years that the building was used as a school (1880–1958), there was no running water, and the students used two outhouses in the rear of the property. Electricity was installed in 1952. Alumni of the school say they received an excellent education there.

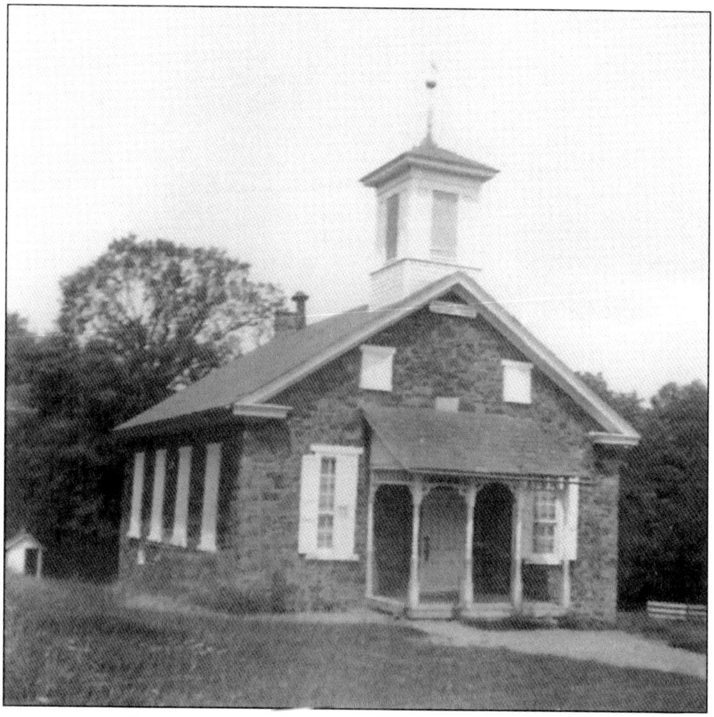

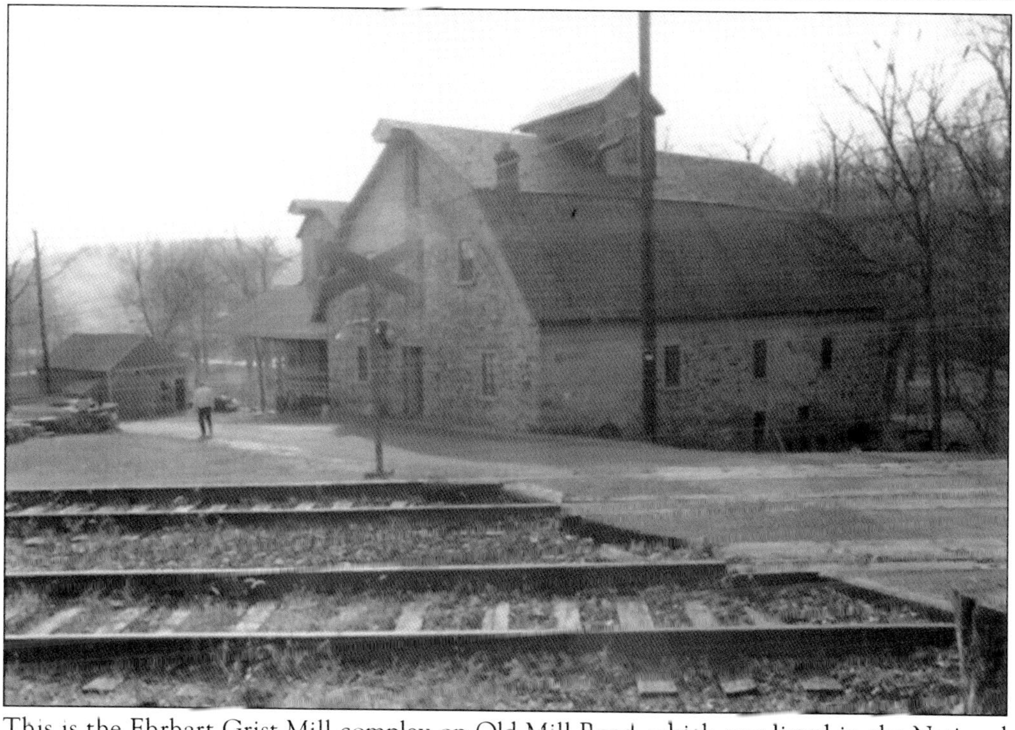

This is the Ehrhart Grist Mill complex on Old Mill Road, which was listed in the National Register of Historic Places in 1987. In the mid-1800s, the mill was operated as a gristmill and feed store. An arsonist set fire to the mill in 1995 and destroyed the building. This site is readily visible from the Saucon Rail Trail.

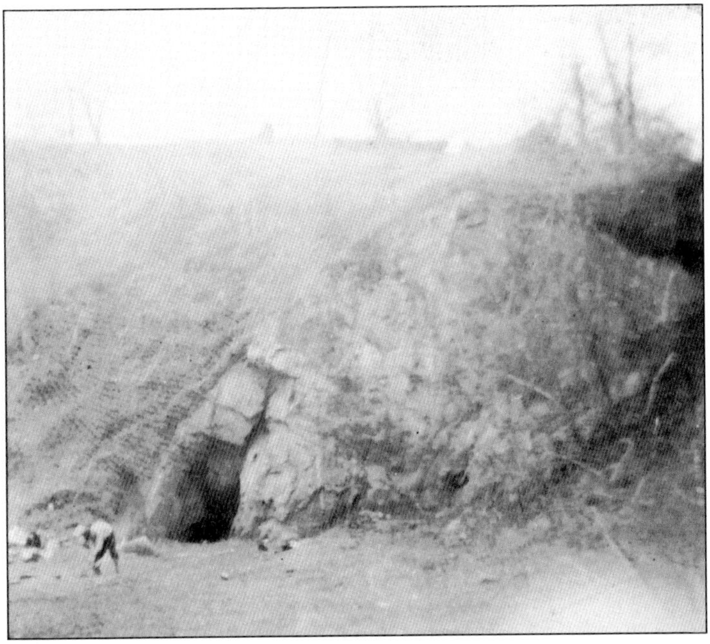

In 1883, during a dig in a limestone quarry in Hellertown, the Lost Cave (also known as Rentzeimer's Cave) was discovered. The cave has five chambers, and a crystal-clear stream flows through them. In 1930, Erwin C. and Maria Gilman started the Lost River Caverns as a tourist attraction. Over time, despite challenging economies, it survives as a valuable tourist attraction. The Gilmans built a large structure in front of the entrance. (Courtesy of Lost River Caverns.)

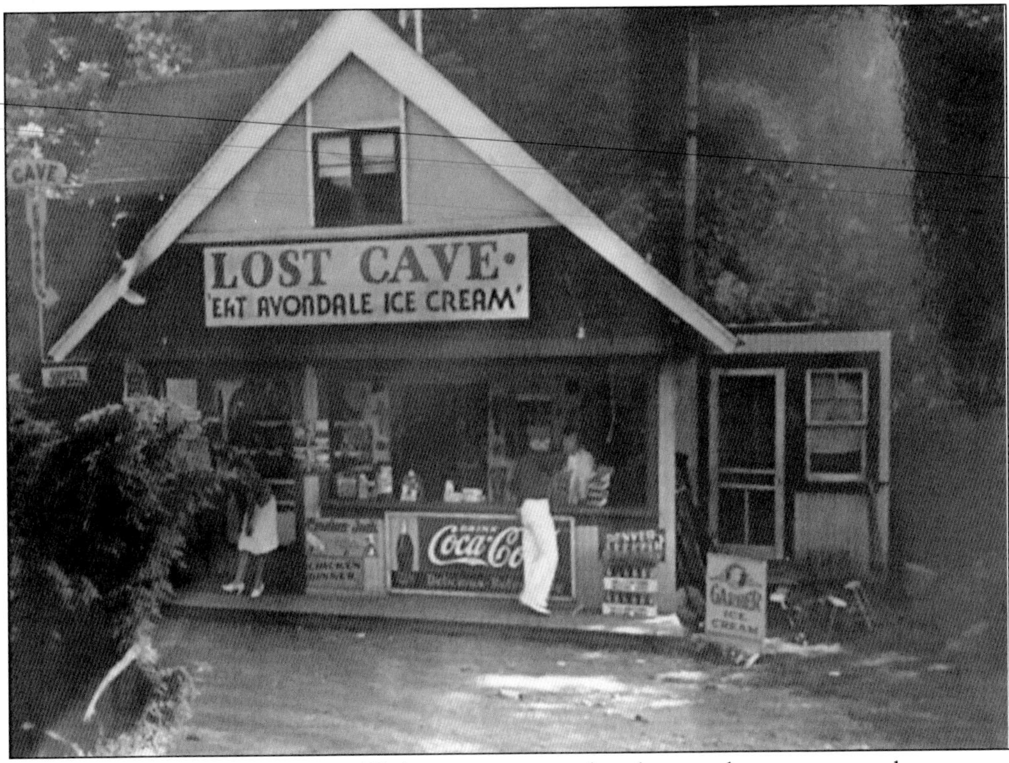

Although the cave is a constant 52 degrees year-round and great place to escape the summer heat, a scoop of ice cream at the Avondale Ice Cream parlor was very popular in the late 1930s. Harry Normington of Lanark, Pennsylvania, established a chain of Avondale ice-cream parlors in 1934. He was forced to close his business in 1941, a casualty of the Great Depression. (Courtesy of Lost River Caverns.)

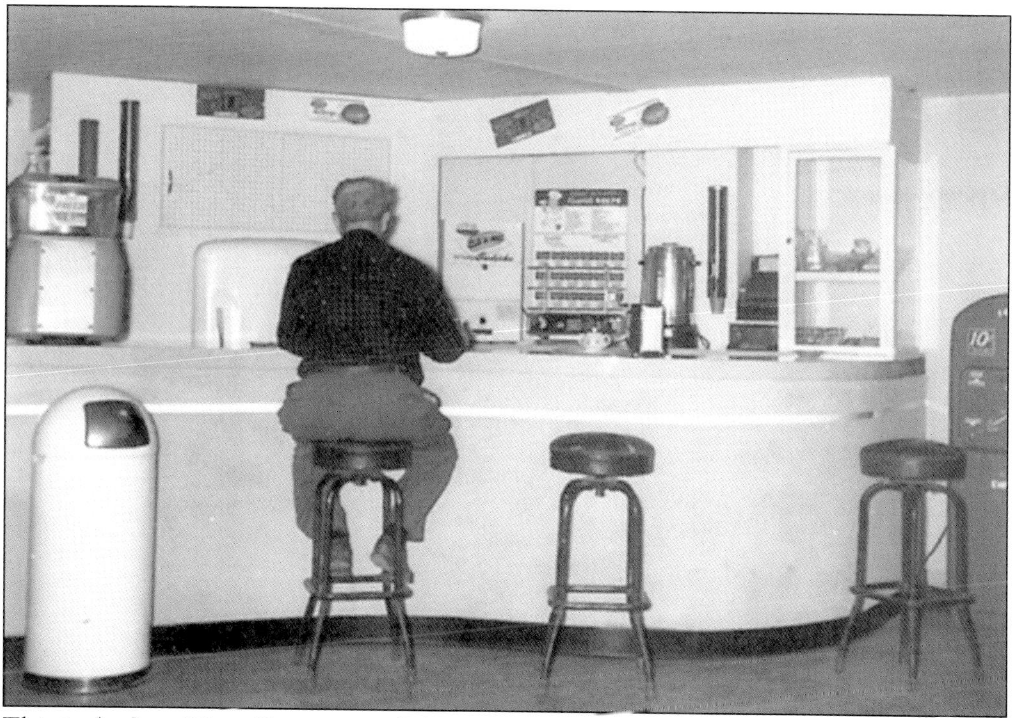

This is the Lost River Caverns snack bar. It closed, as tourists prefer to picnic in the grove next to the caverns, enjoying packed lunches in the covered pavilions with a view of nearby Silver Creek. (Courtesy of Lost River Caverns.)

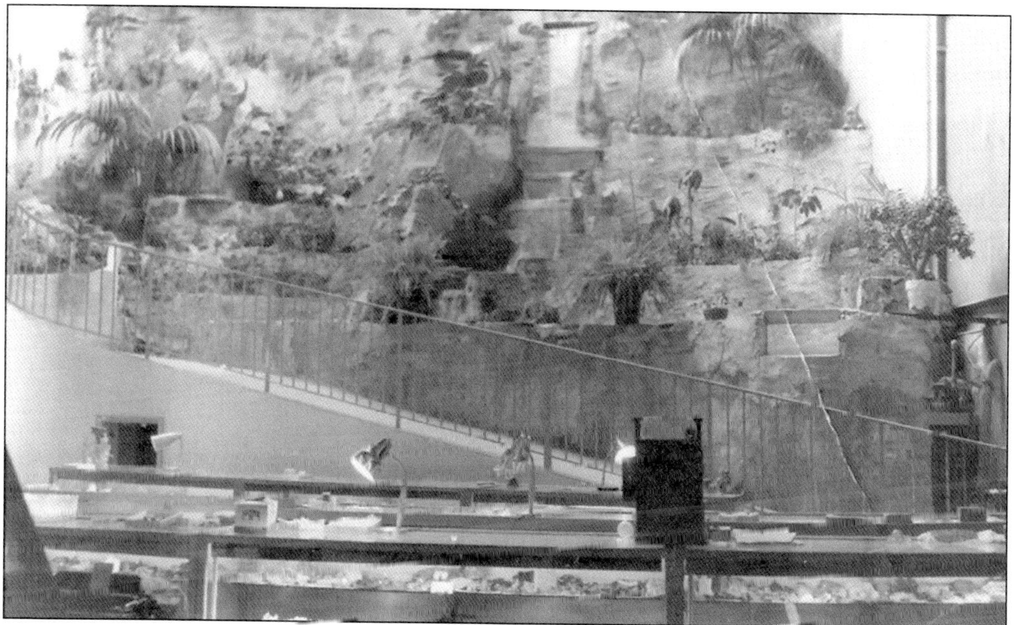

In 1930, the Gilmans offered a few samples of local rocks to be sold as souvenirs. Over the years, there was an increased demand for rocks, minerals, lapidary equipment, tools, metalsmith items, and, eventually, fine jewelry. The gift shop has been expanded to sell these items. (Courtesy of Lost River Caverns.)

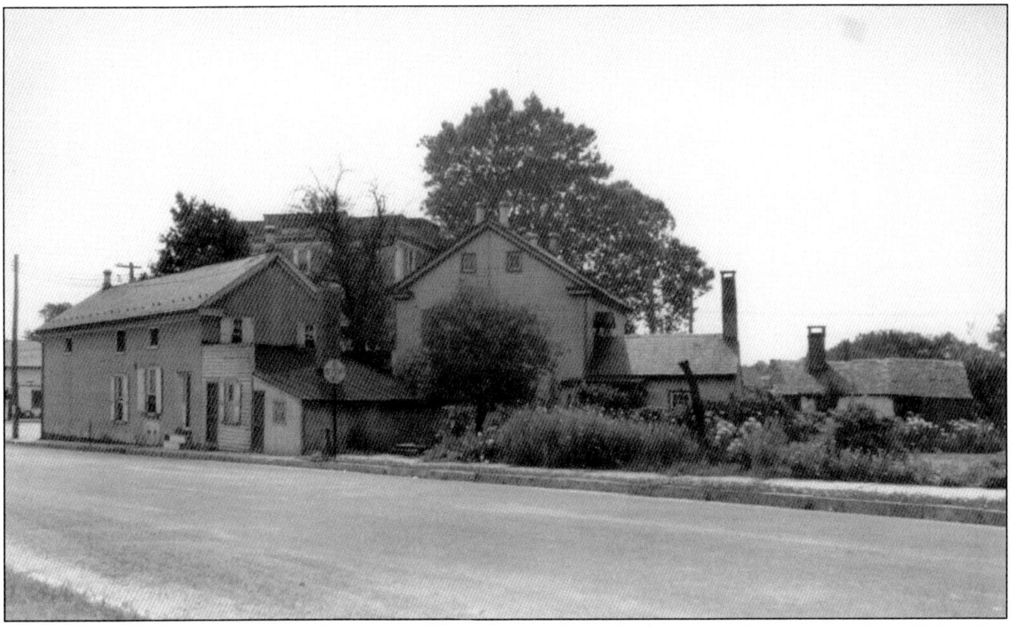

Ed Weisel operated the Weisel Harness Shop from 1895 until 1940, when it was demolished to make way for Detwiller Plaza. He was a business partner with Ted Hagey, who tanned leather across Main Street. Ed Weisel's knowledge of Pennsylvania German came in handy, as he was called upon to communicate with German-speaking guests at the Park Hotel. (Courtesy of the Hellertown Historical Society.)

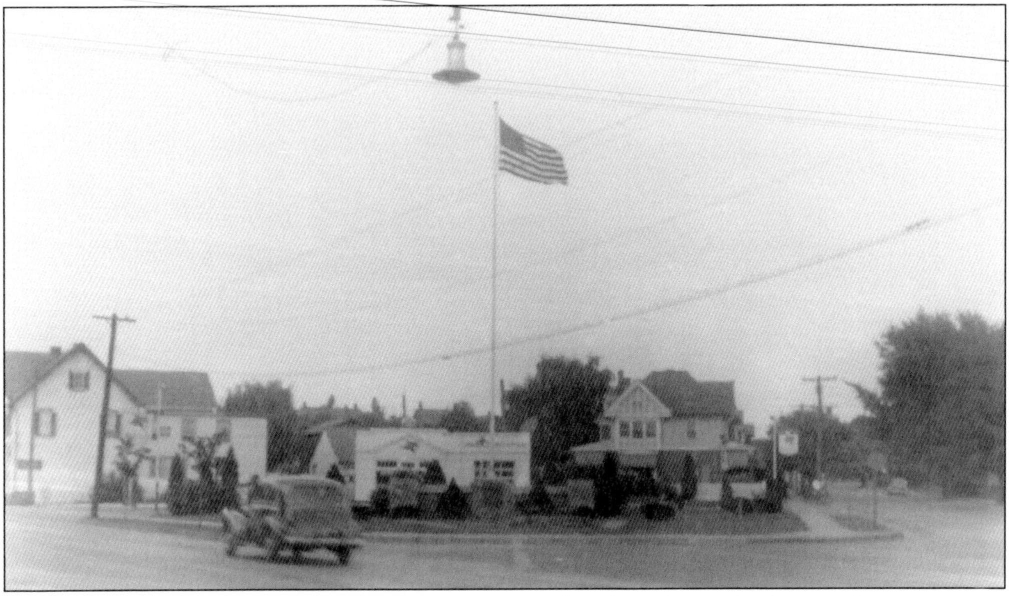

This intersection at Easton Road and Main Street has long been the heart of commerce in Hellertown. The Weisel Harness Shop and the old post office stood at the intersection until the buildings were demolished in 1940 to create the Detwiller Plaza (pictured). Stone from the old buildings was used to build the fountain, pool, and base of the flagpole on the plaza. The lights in the fountain came from the 1964 New York World's Fair. (Courtesy of Hellertown Borough Water Authority.)

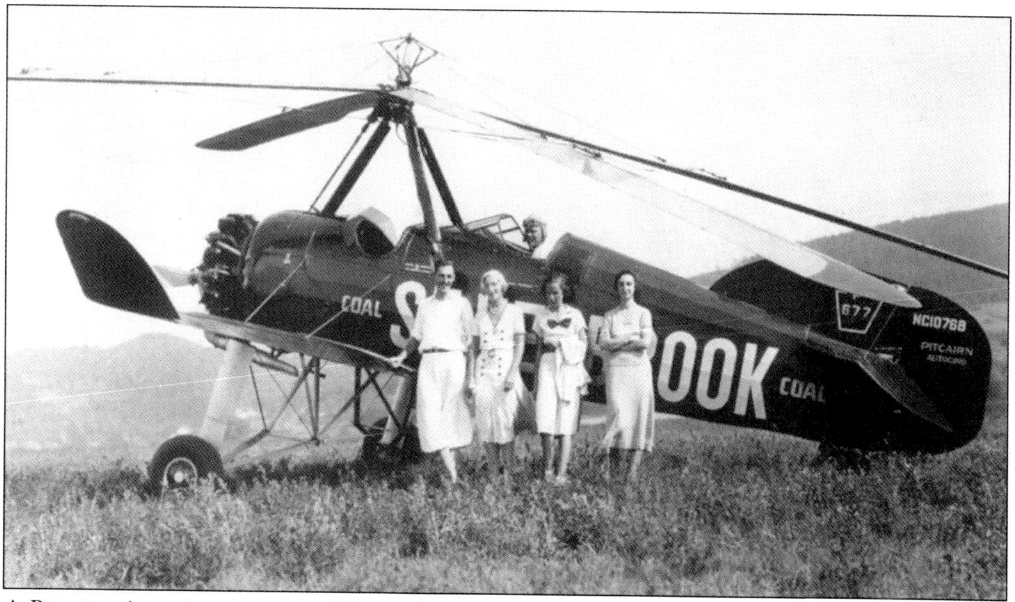

A Pitcairn Autogiro is seen in 1931 at the Bethlehem Municipal Airport. The autogiro was first flown in 1923 at Cuatro Vientos Airfield in Madrid. A motor was not used to spin the giroplane's rotor blades. Instead, air currents moved the blades, causing the aircraft to lift into the sky slowly and smoothly. By the mid-1930s, the giro had faded away, replaced by helicopters. (Courtesy of David Leidig.)

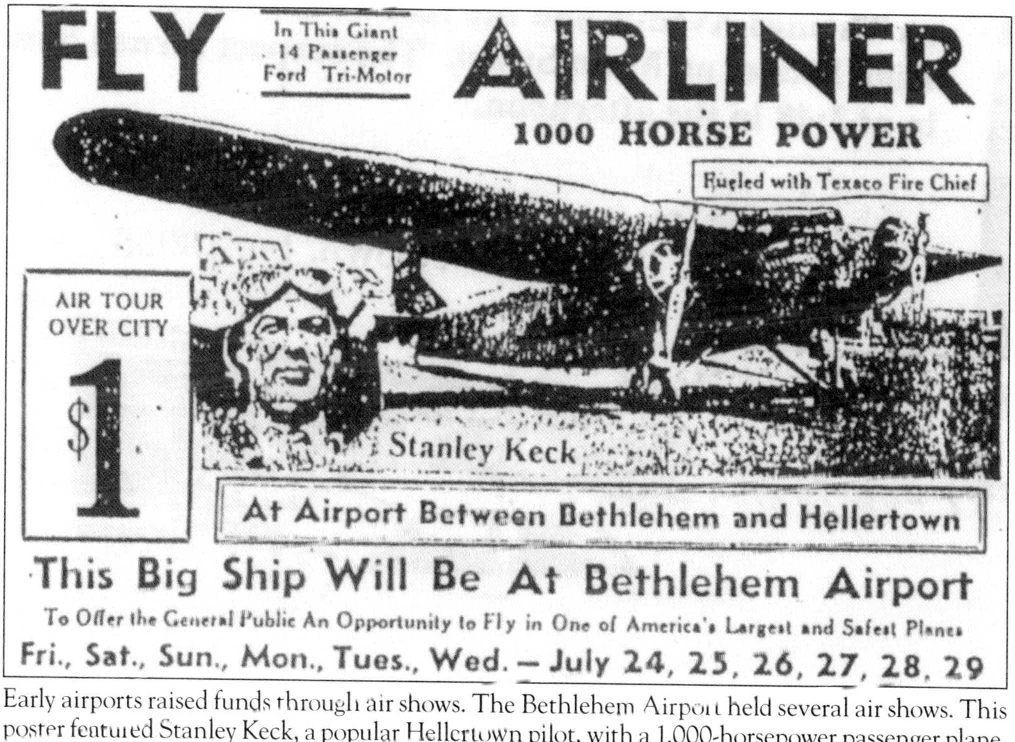

Early airports raised funds through air shows. The Bethlehem Airport held several air shows. This poster featured Stanley Keck, a popular Hellertown pilot, with a 1,000-horsepower passenger plane. Keck learned to fly at age 20. He went on to become known for being a master at aerobatics, aerial photography, and organizing air shows. (Courtesy of the Hellertown Historical Society.)

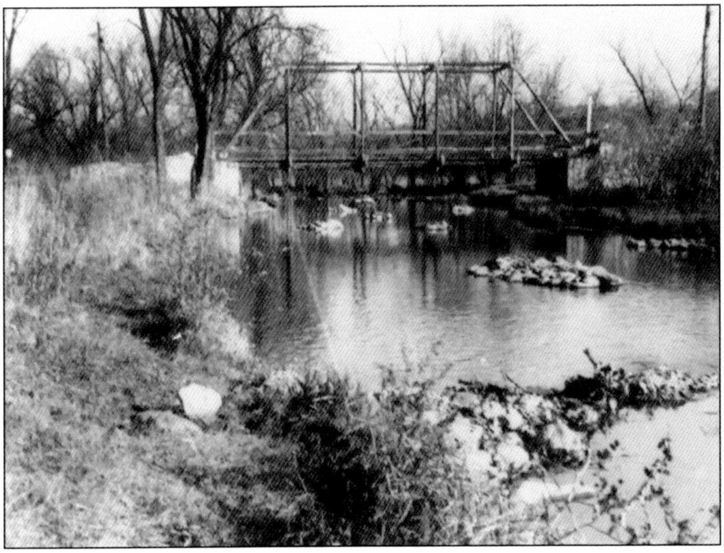

Here is a view of the Walnut Street Bridge spanning the Saucon Creek. It is the only high-truss span bridge, built by Charles N. Beckel, known to exist. Built in 1860, the all-metal bridge was considered the state of the art. A bridge at that location was needed for local farmers to reach the Wagner gristmill. Over the years, the bridge has also been called Wagner's Bridge and the Pony Bridge.

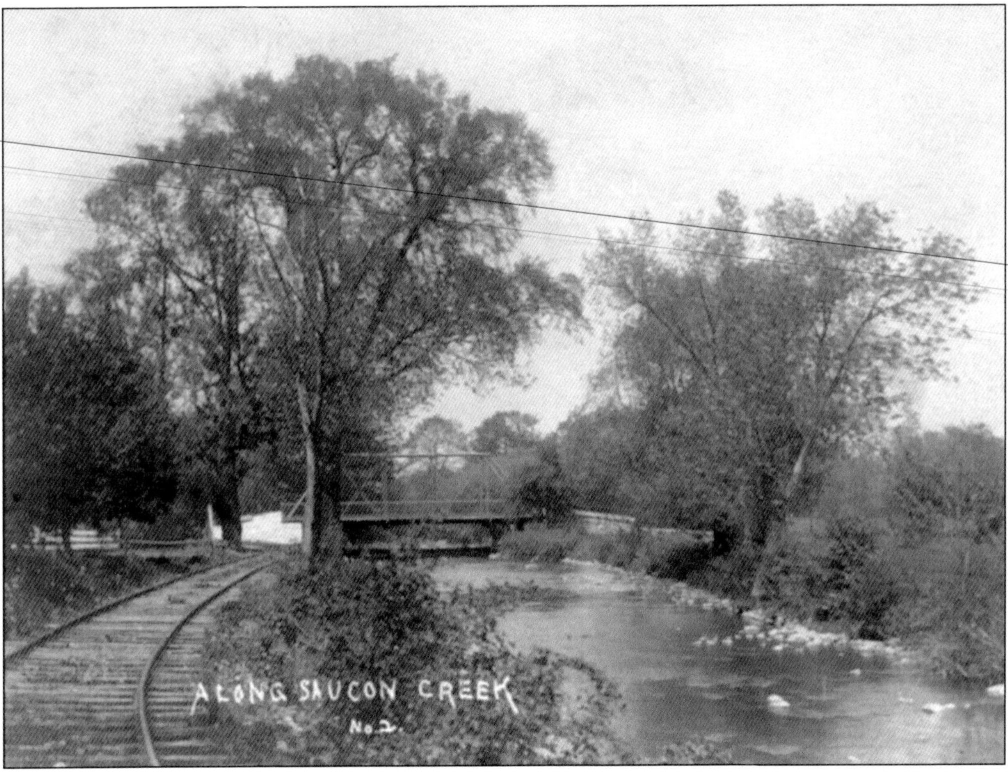

This image of the Saucon Creek was captured by Prof. Bergstresser, a Hellertown teacher and photographer. The Walnut Street Bridge is in the distance. Charles and Lawrence Beckel built this historically important bridge in 1860. The bridge is seen here in its original location, on Walnut Street in Hellertown. One of the oldest all-metal bridges in the United States, it was saved from destruction by the Hellertown Historical Society. The railroad tracks belong to the Thomas Iron Company. (Courtesy of the Hellertown Historical Society.)

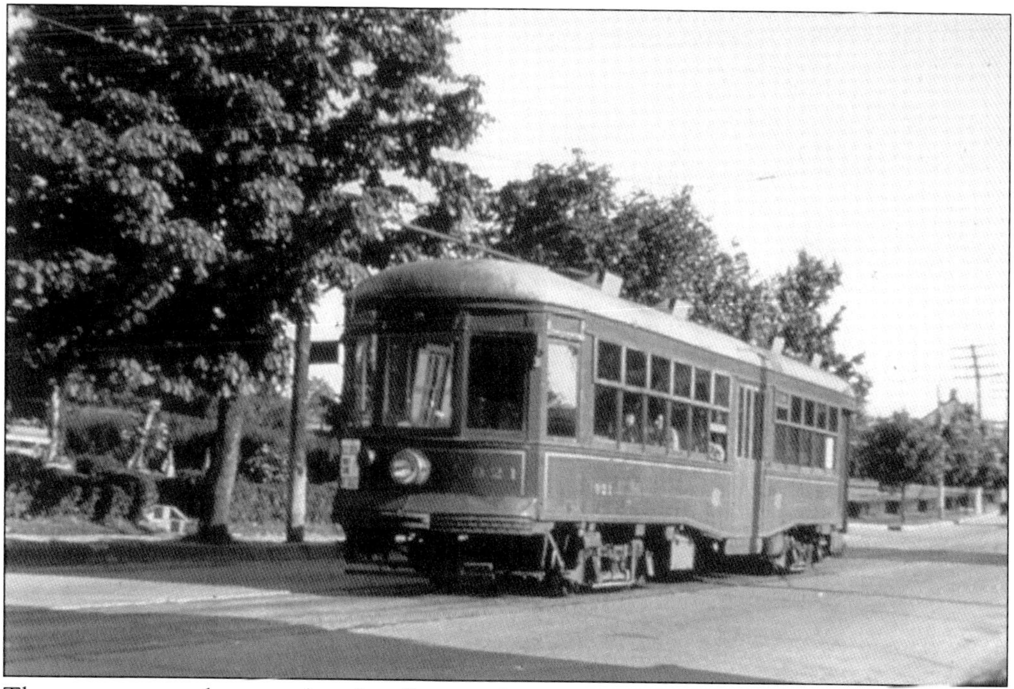

There are many photographs of trolleys at this termination point at Walnut Street. This rare view shows a trolley with its doors located in the center. (Courtesy of the Hellertown Historical Society.)

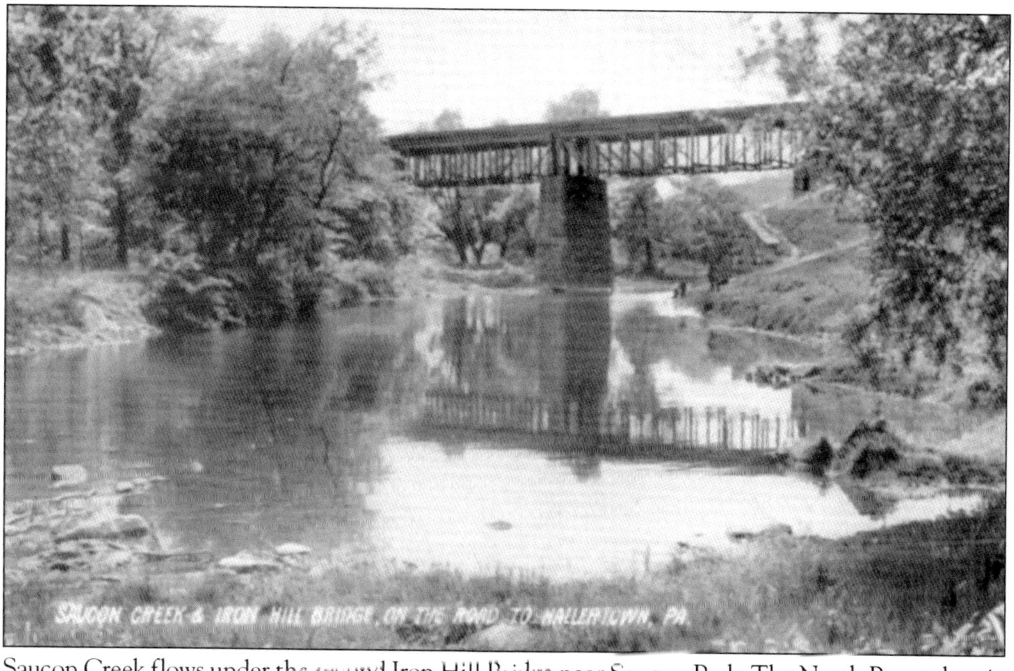

Saucon Creek flows under the second Iron Hill Bridge near Saucon Park. The North Pennsylvania Railroad built the bridge, which was located a few miles north of Hellertown. This bridge, the railroad company, and the village of Iron Hill no longer exist. Note the misspelling of the name "Hallertown," which indicates that the photographer was not from the area.

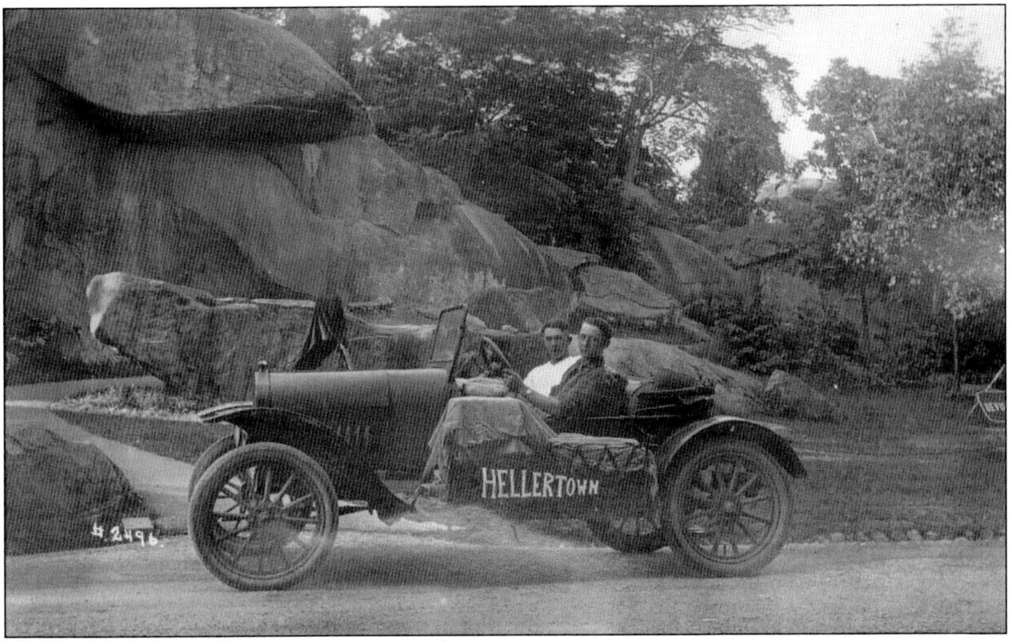

Here, locals Kenneth Ruch Kunsman and Lester Fluck sightsee at Gettysburg's famous Devil's Den. Lester Fluck was a bread delivery man in the borough. He is recorded making his rounds in a 1938 Charles Hartman 8 mm home movie. A digital recording of this movie is available at Lower Saucon Township Historical Society.

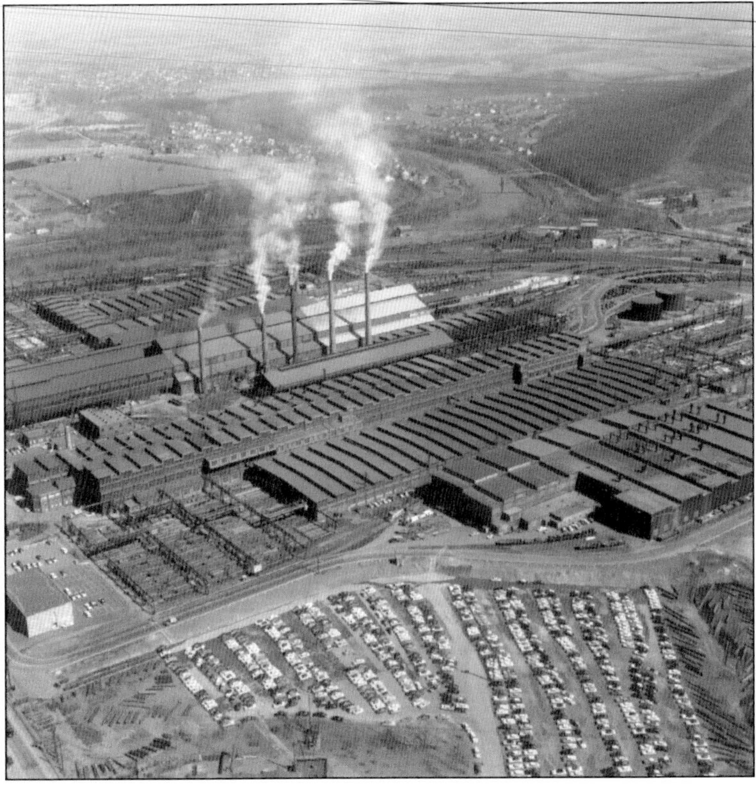

This aerial photograph captures two communities. Steel City is to the right of the river, in upper portion of the photograph. Freemansburg is on the left side of the river at the top of the image. (Courtesy of David Jacoby.)

In 1921, the first mayor of Bethlehem, Archibald Johnston, arranged for Bethlehem Steel Corporation to donate 100 acres to the city for the first public park. The Saucon Creek runs through the park and supplied water for the first pool (pictured). Saucon Park's stonework was completed as a Works Progress Administration job in the 1930s.

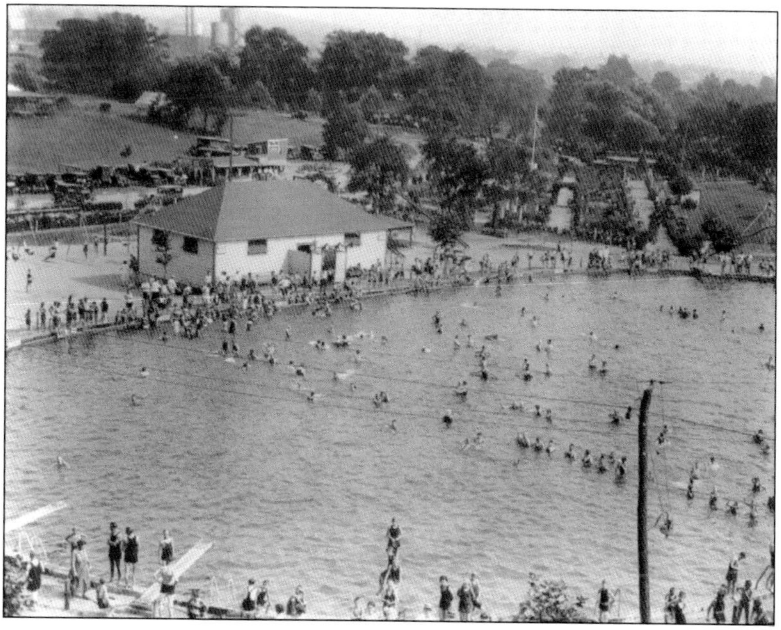

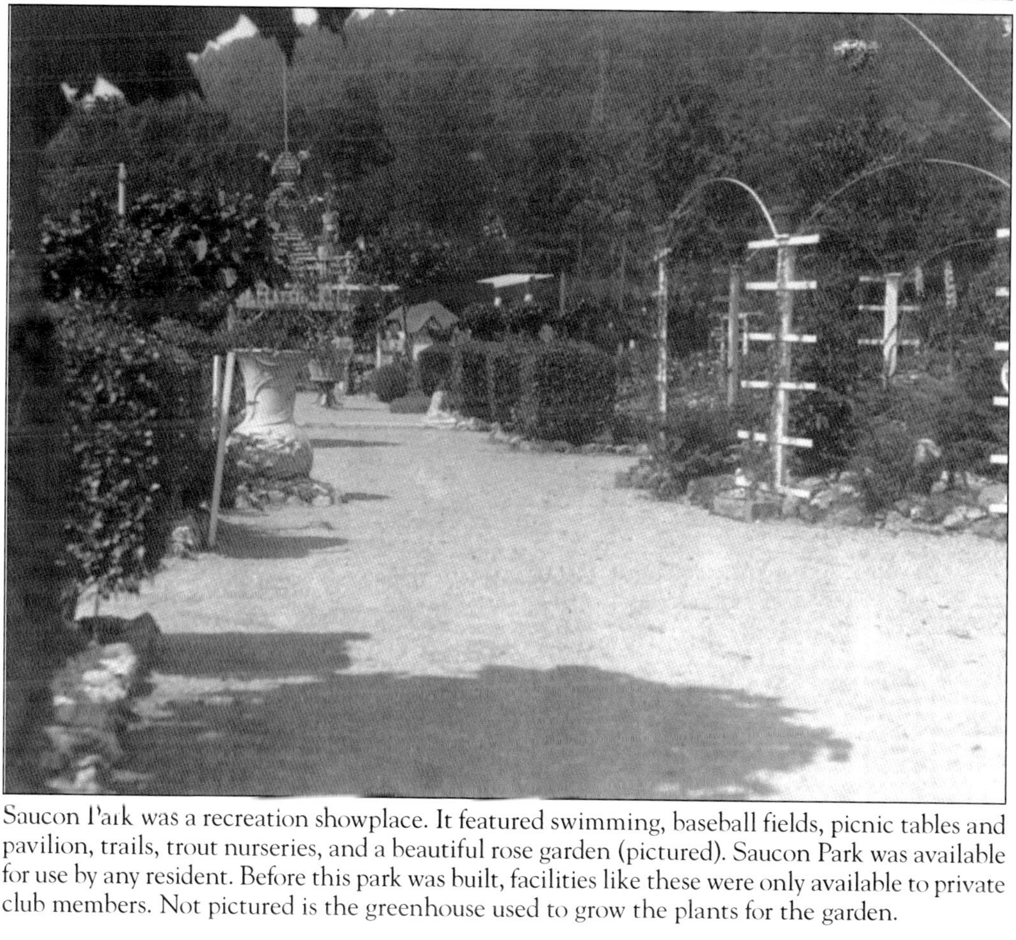

Saucon Park was a recreation showplace. It featured swimming, baseball fields, picnic tables and pavilion, trails, trout nurseries, and a beautiful rose garden (pictured). Saucon Park was available for use by any resident. Before this park was built, facilities like these were only available to private club members. Not pictured is the greenhouse used to grow the plants for the garden.

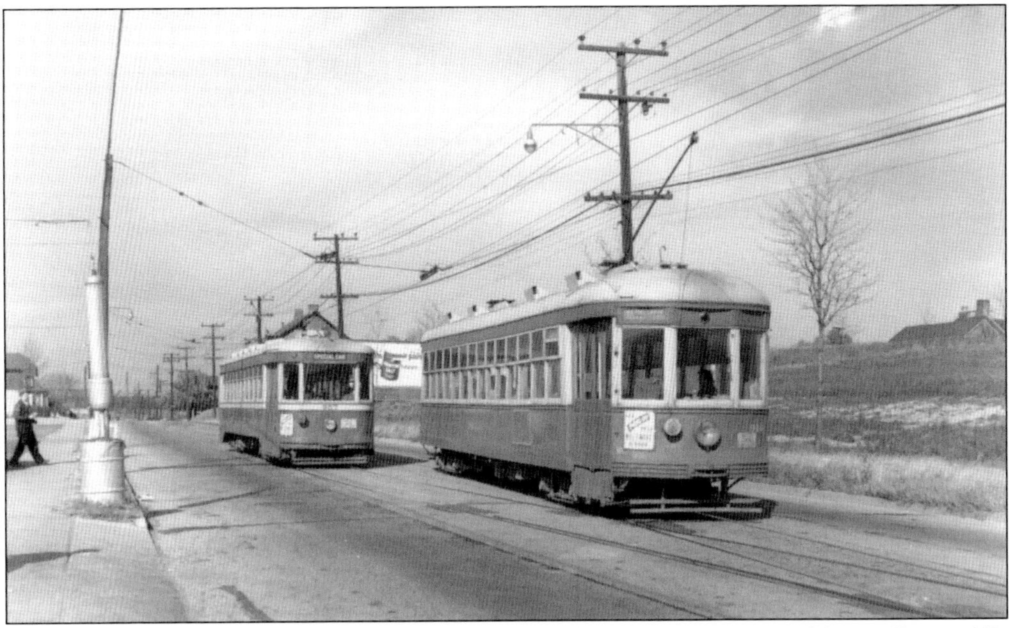

These trolley cars would create havoc with today's traffic exiting Interstate 78 onto Route 412, the area depicted here. Since the route to Hellertown was primarily a single track, opposing trolley traffic could be passed at this siding. The route in Hellertown ended at Walnut Street. The advertisements on both trolleys for Philco's 1953 Multiwave Radio dates this photograph to near the end of trolley service to Hellertown. Service ended on October 26, 1952.

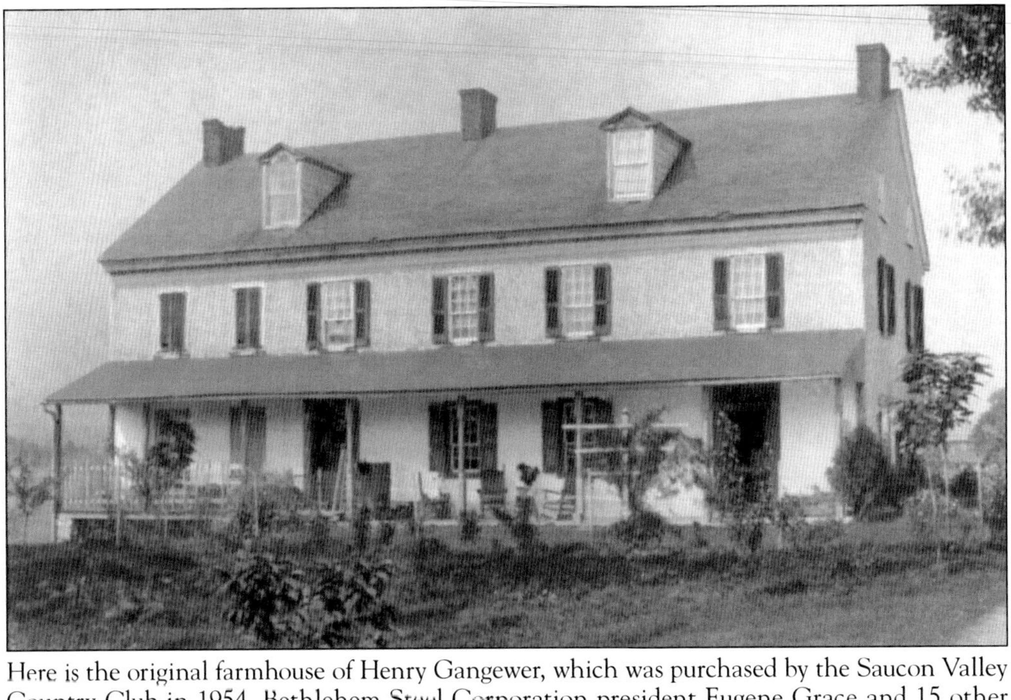

Here is the original farmhouse of Henry Gangewer, which was purchased by the Saucon Valley Country Club in 1954. Bethlehem Steel Corporation president Eugene Grace and 15 other businessmen organized the club in 1920. The country club turned the 559-acre farm into the 18-hole Weyhill course. The farmhouse structure is incorporated into the Weyhill guesthouse.

Here are some of the double Dutch doors on the Wagner farm barn. The Moravian-like wrought-metal hinges on the doors are very rare. There are seven double Dutch doors along the front of the barn. The current owner, Gerald Holum, has kept this beautiful barn in tip-top shape.

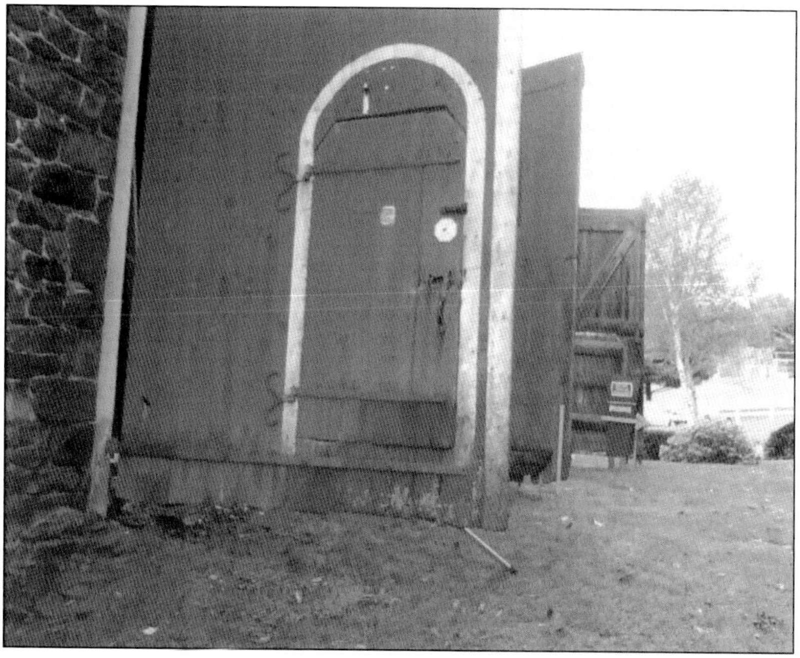

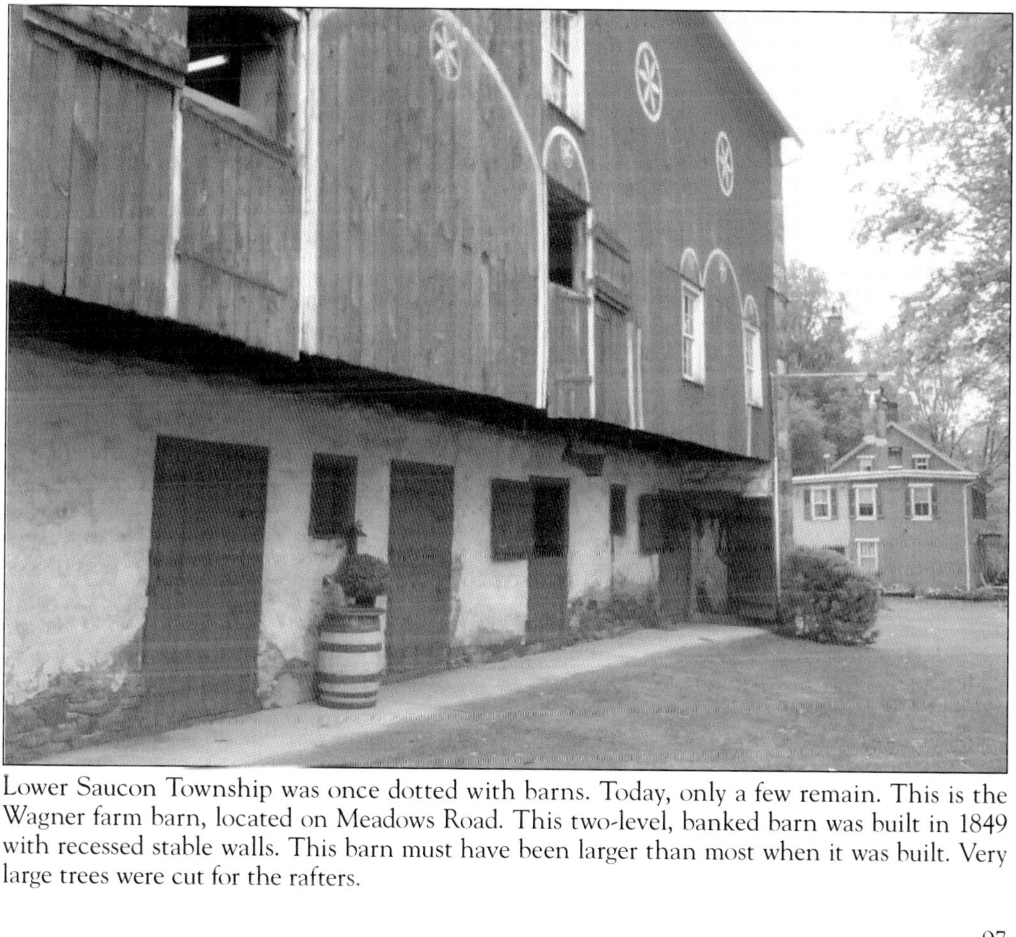

Lower Saucon Township was once dotted with barns. Today, only a few remain. This is the Wagner farm barn, located on Meadows Road. This two-level, banked barn was built in 1849 with recessed stable walls. This barn must have been larger than most when it was built. Very large trees were cut for the rafters.

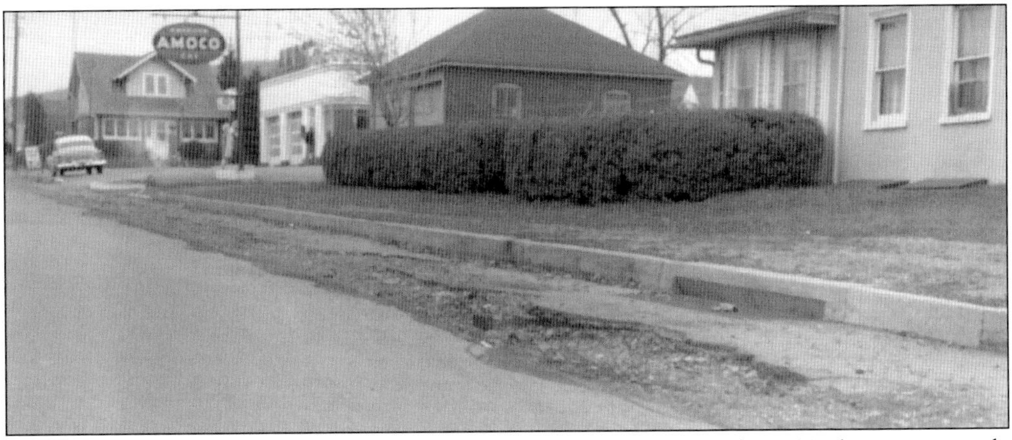

Leaded gas was about the only fuel one could buy at a gas station since the 1920s, but many people needed "white gas" for applications in which the lead additive was not used due to its fouling properties. This gas station on Cherry Lane satisfied this need, as AMOCO (Standard Oil) Corporation continued to produce lead-free gasoline. No ethanol here! (Courtesy of Hellertown Borough Water Authority.)

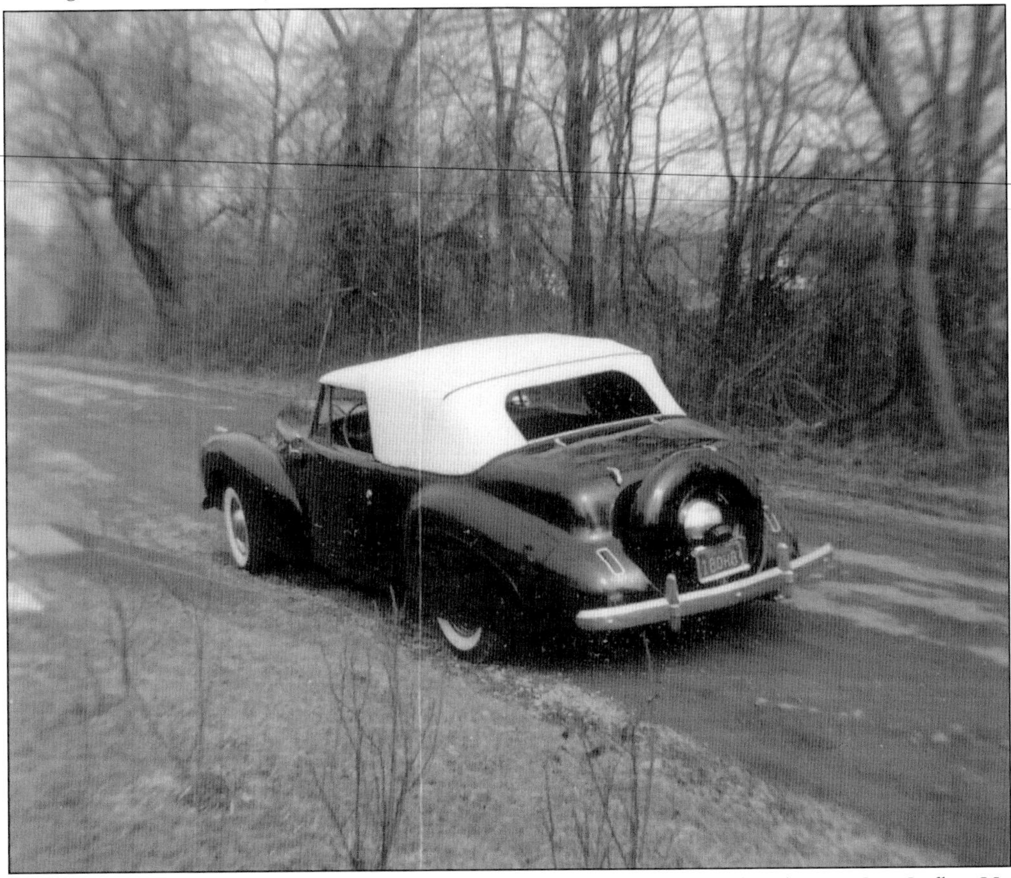

This prewar Lincoln Continental Cabriolet convertible belonged to local artist Joe Sofka. He sold it to William "Skeeter" Ruth. Ruth sold it, unrestored, in the early 1970s. Fewer than 400 of these cars were produced. (Courtesy of Joe Sofka.)

Road rallies on rural roads attracted large crowds, as shown in this 1960s photograph. This particular event took place outside of Springtown, on Drifting Drive. (Courtesy of Pete Conner.)

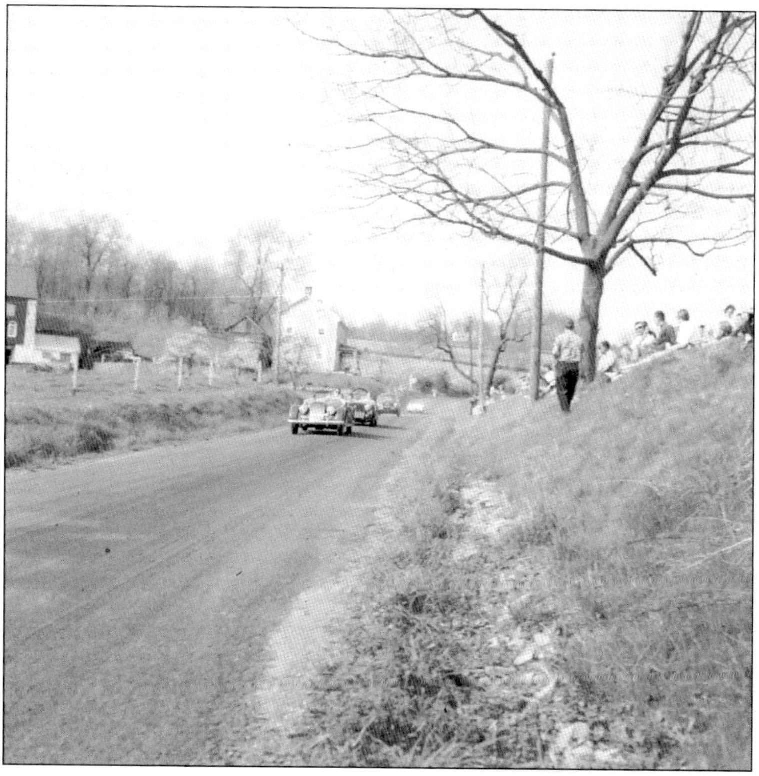

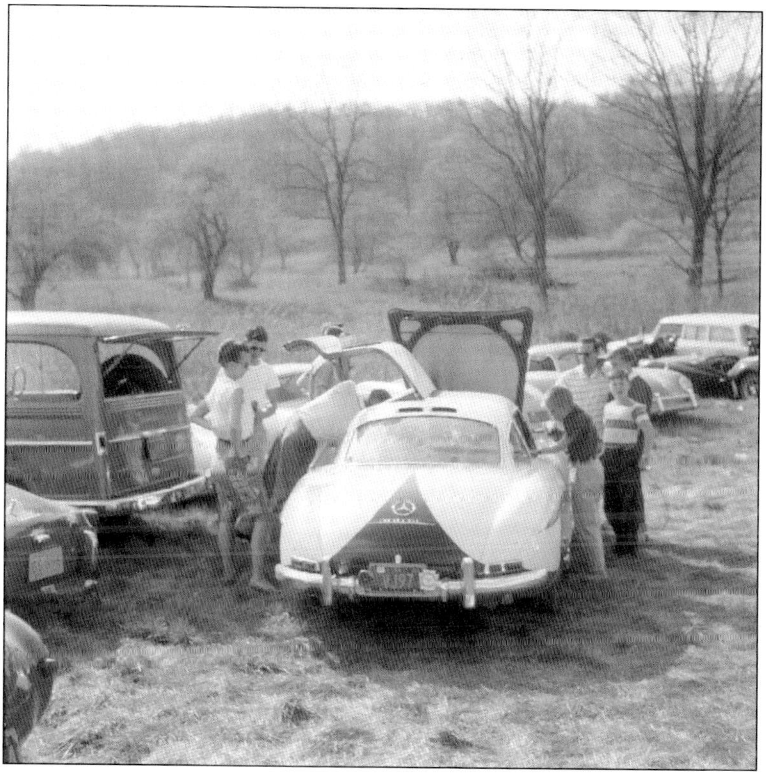

It seems almost unbelievable that cars like this 1954 Mercedes-Benz 300SL "gullwing" were running around the back roads of the countryside. These cars now command high prices when fully restored. (Courtesy of Pete Conner.)

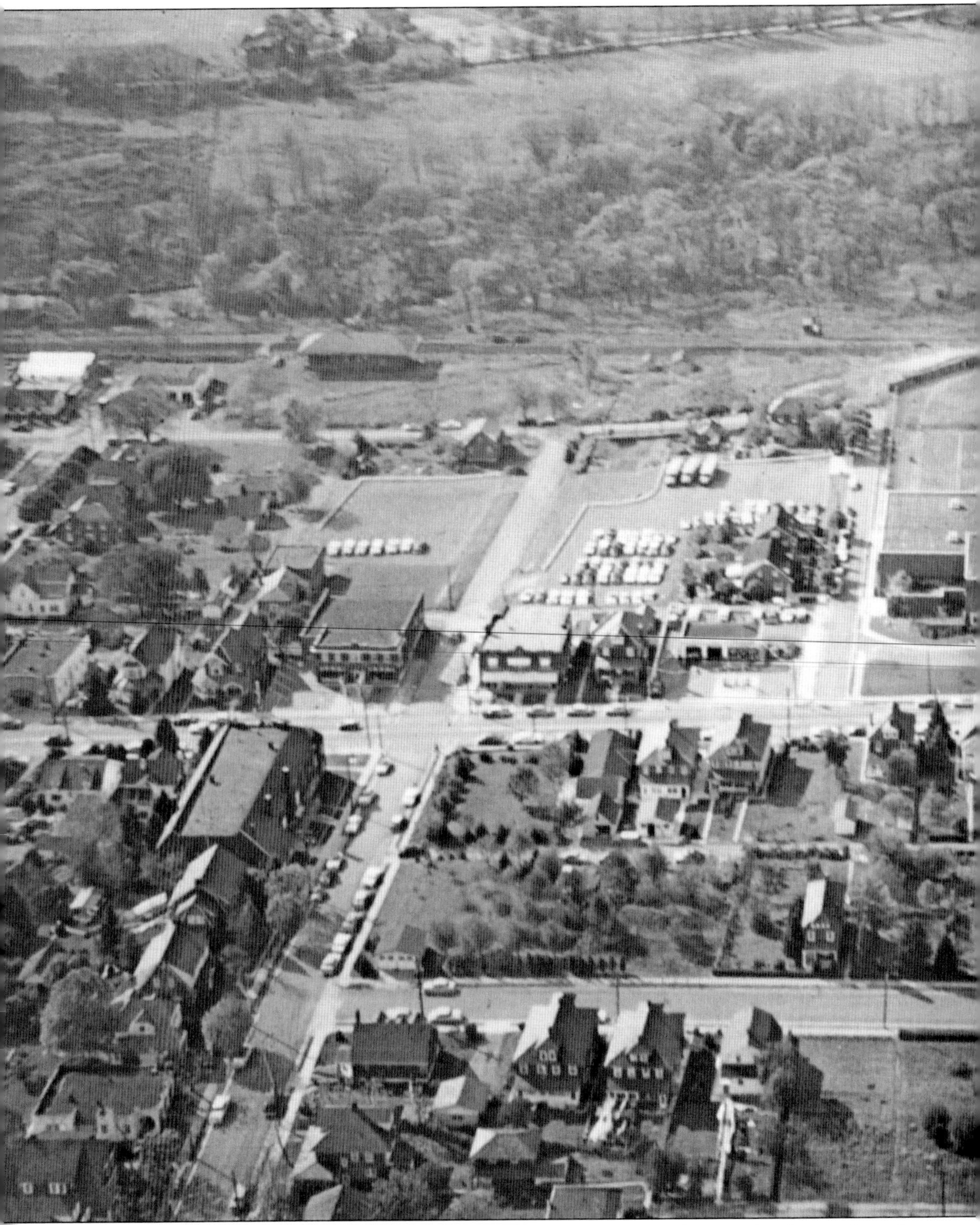

Taken in the early 1960s, this photograph reveals many interesting changes that have taken place in these neighborhoods. The remains of the Thomas Iron Works are not yet lost to nature, and the Hellertown train station is still standing. The main structure is the recently enlarged Hellertown

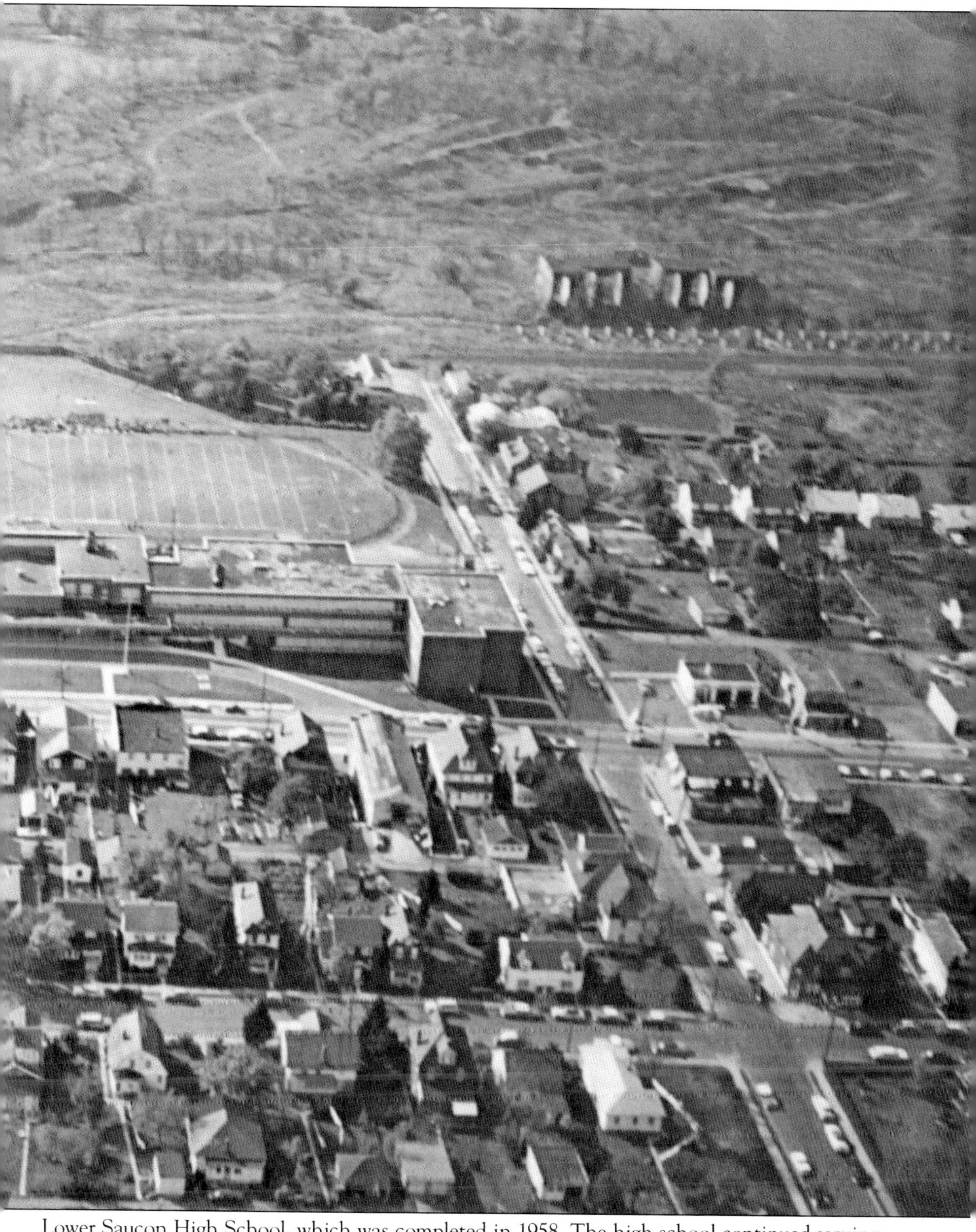

Lower Saucon High School, which was completed in 1958. The high school continued serving as an educational facility until about 2003, when it became a facility for senior citizens, many of whose taxes ironically went to build this structure for the education of their children.

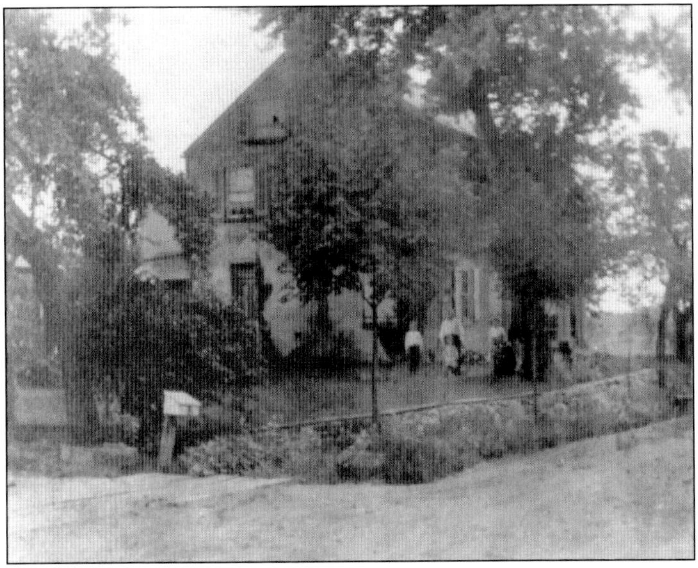

Five generations of the Pflueger family have lived in this dwelling. It is located across the street from the Lower Saucon Township Municipal Complex on Old Philadelphia Pike. John Friedrich Pflueger (1801–1866) farmed the land and was a shoemaker and cigar maker. This home was a stop on the Underground Railroad. Today, descendants Herman and Sue Hackman reside here. (Courtesy of Herman Hackman.)

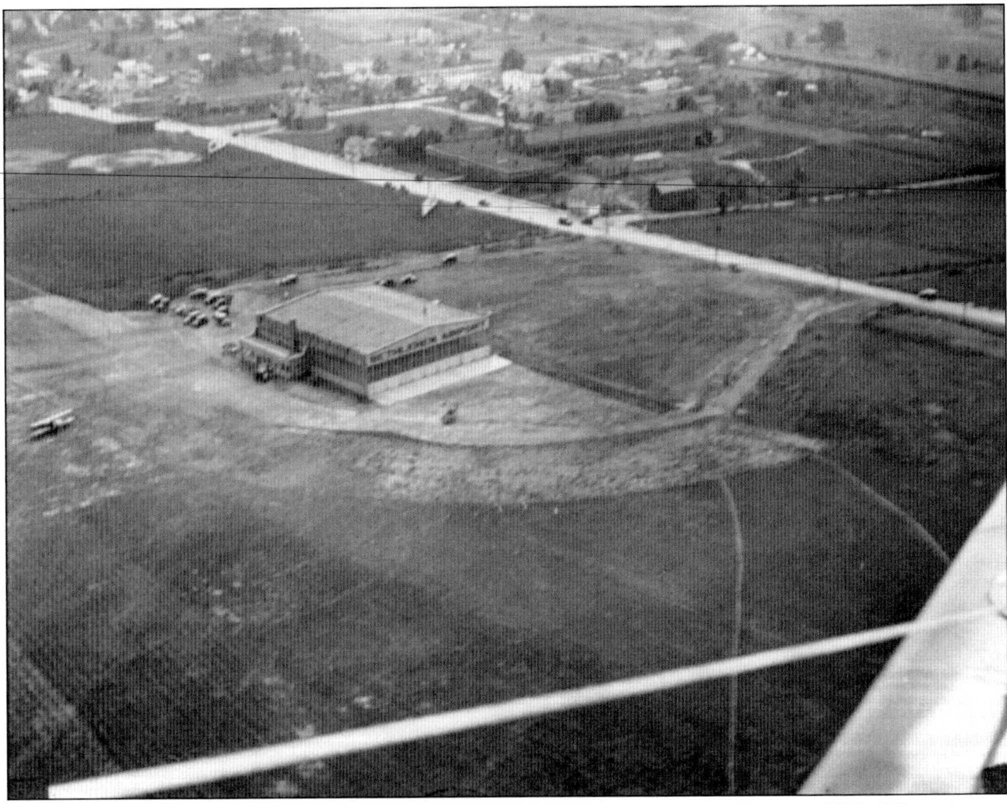

This aerial photograph of the Bethlehem Municipal Airport was taken in 1931. The airport was located across Route 412 from present-day Wendy's, or Vassi's Drive-In. Bethlehem Steel Realty sold land where the current Hellertown interchange to Route 78 exits today, to the city of Bethlehem for use as an airport in 1928. This was the first airport in the Lehigh Valley. The airport ceased operating in July 1934. The city council was in a cash crunch due to the Great Depression. (Courtesy of David Leidig.)

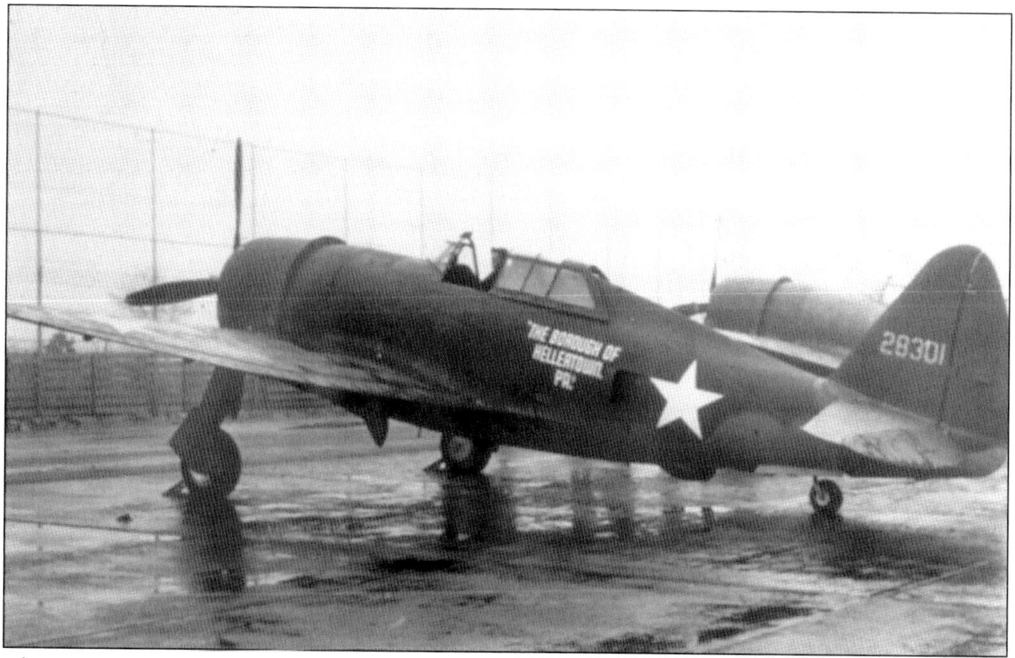

This World War II monoplane aircraft trainer has "The Borough of Hellertown, PA" painted on its side. These trainers were essential to fighting the war, as they offered the first flying experience for Navy pilots. The residents of Hellertown raised over $500 in war bonds to restore this plane as a trainer. (Courtesy of the Hellertown Historical Society.)

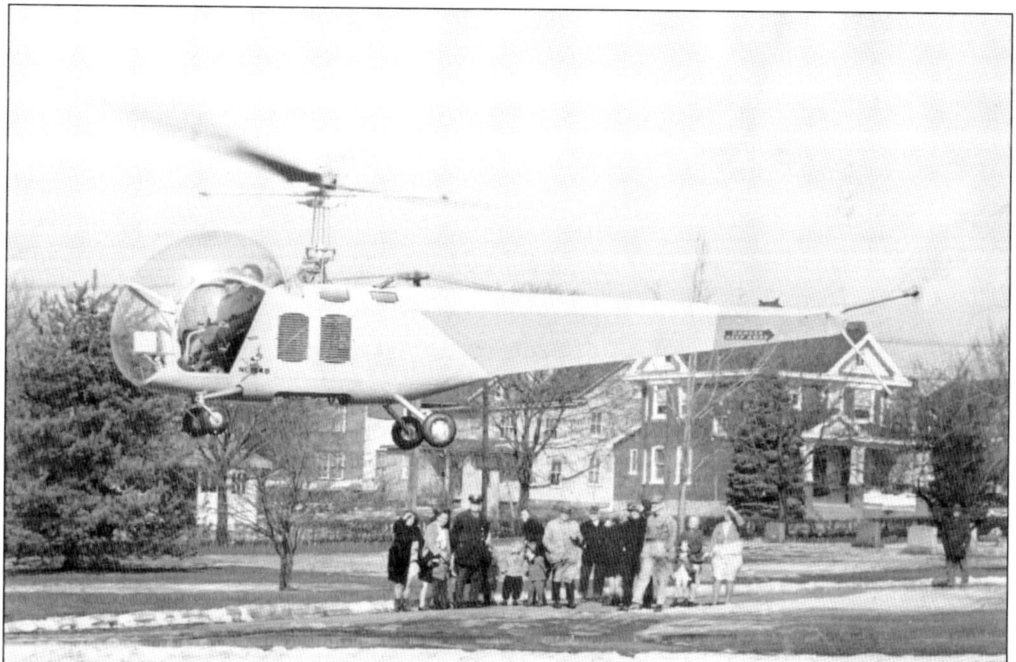

A Boeing helicopter lifts off in 1948, with Hedwig Fischel sitting next to the pilot. Neighbors have gathered to watch the helicopter on a cold day in February. The house at right still stands today, on the corner of Walnut and New Streets. (Courtesy of John Fischel.)

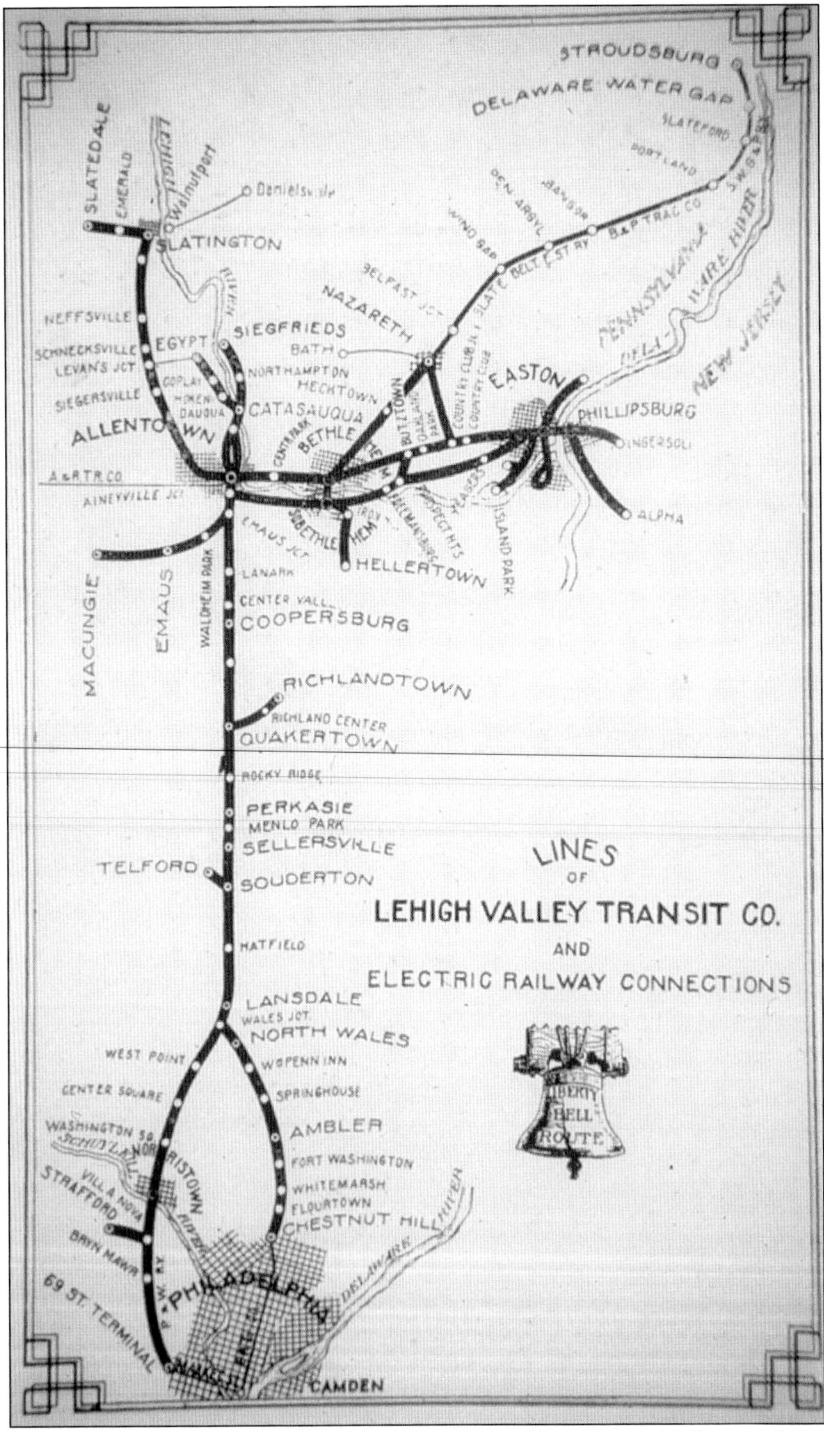

The trolley was the primary mode of transportation used by Saucon Valley residents to go to work at the Bethlehem Steel Corporation in the first half of the 20th century. This map shows the extensive coverage of local routes in and around the Lehigh Valley while also showing the Liberty Bell route directly linking Allentown to Philadelphia. (Courtesy of Douglas E. Peters.)

This was the plan for building lots for the Wydnor development, created in 1915. The village of Wydnor is three miles south of Bethlehem in Lower Saucon Township, near the intersection of Old Philadelphia Pike and Black River Road. The development was slow in attracting buyers, as it was considered too far from Bethlehem Steel Corporation.

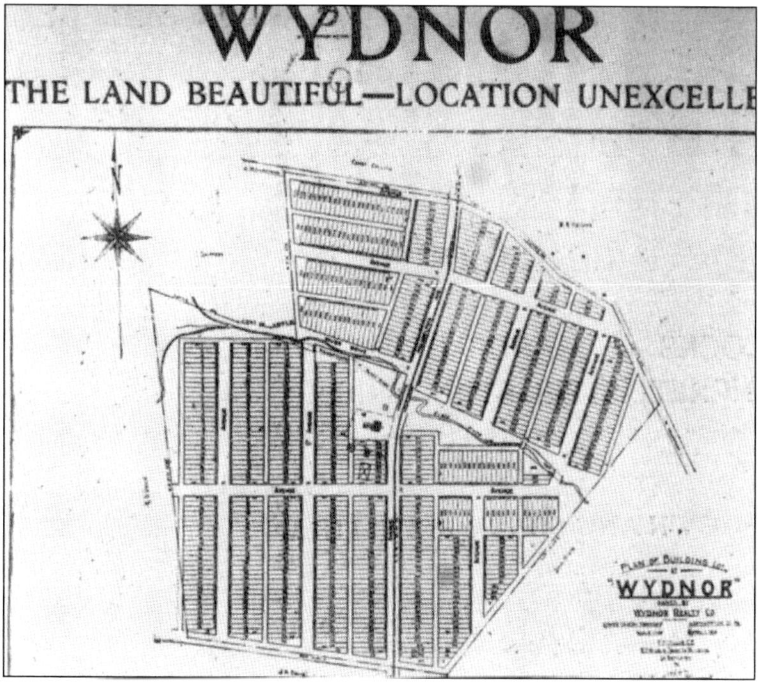

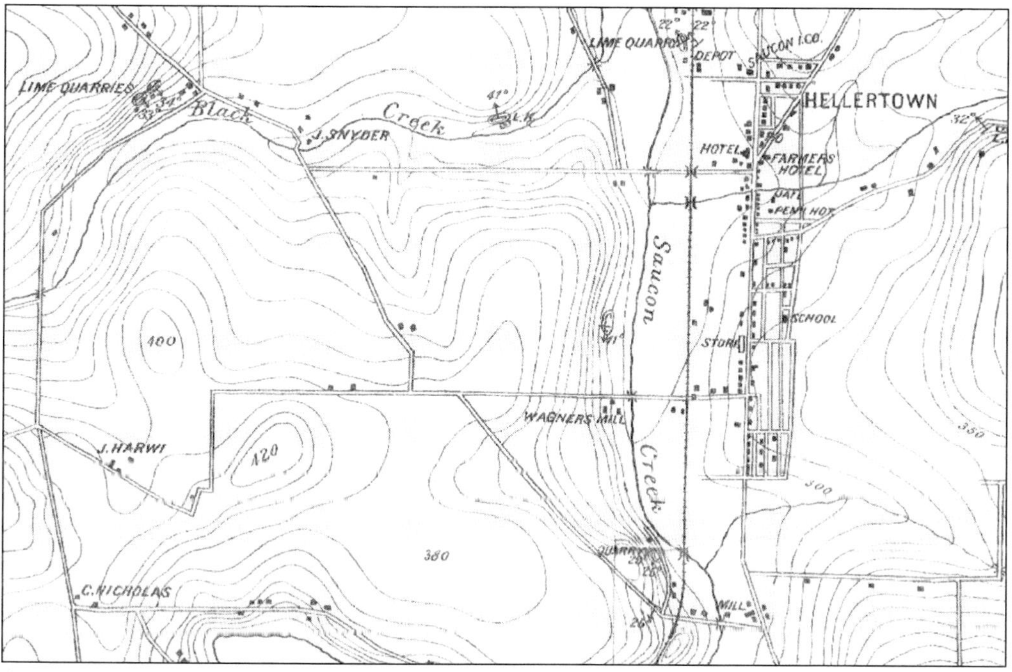

Commuters try to imagine a convenient shortcut that would reduce travel time between two frequently traveled locations. Here is an example of a road that satisfied that condition. It was eventually closed because of the intrusion it introduced to the inhabitants living along the route. In the center of the map is the road that ran past the Wagner Grist Mill. It carried traffic clear over to Bingen Road before it was closed. (Courtesy of Fran Robb.)

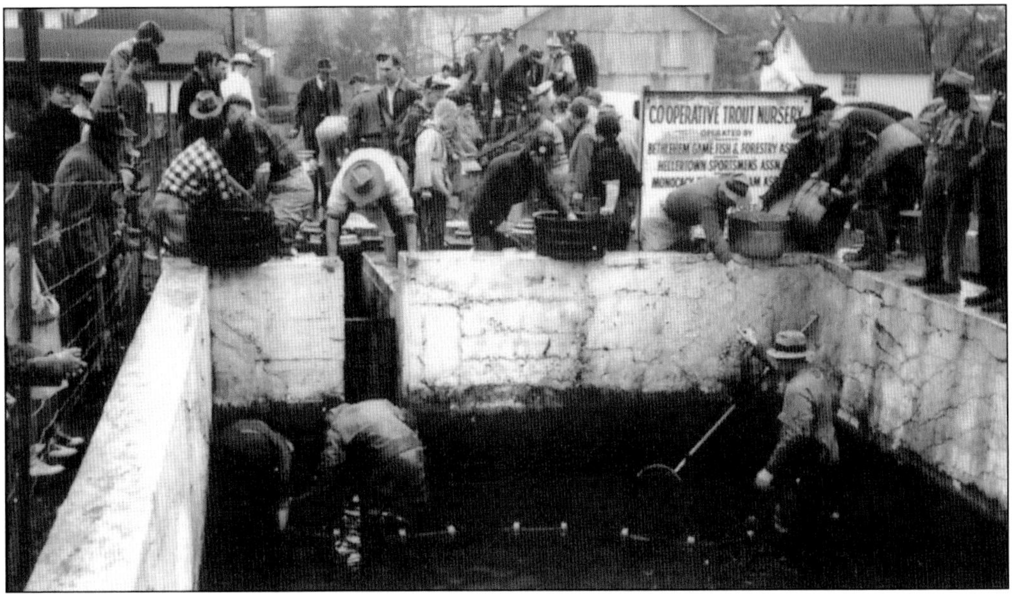

The Park Hotel was once known for its numerous fishponds and hatcheries. Shown here are the remains of one of the trout hatcheries, long after the hotel was demolished. The hatcheries were a tourist attraction. Often, the large trout jumped high above the water, causing the spectators to exclaim with delight. In February 1973, the hotel was demolished to make way for a parking lot for a tire business. (Courtesy of the Hellertown Historical Society.)

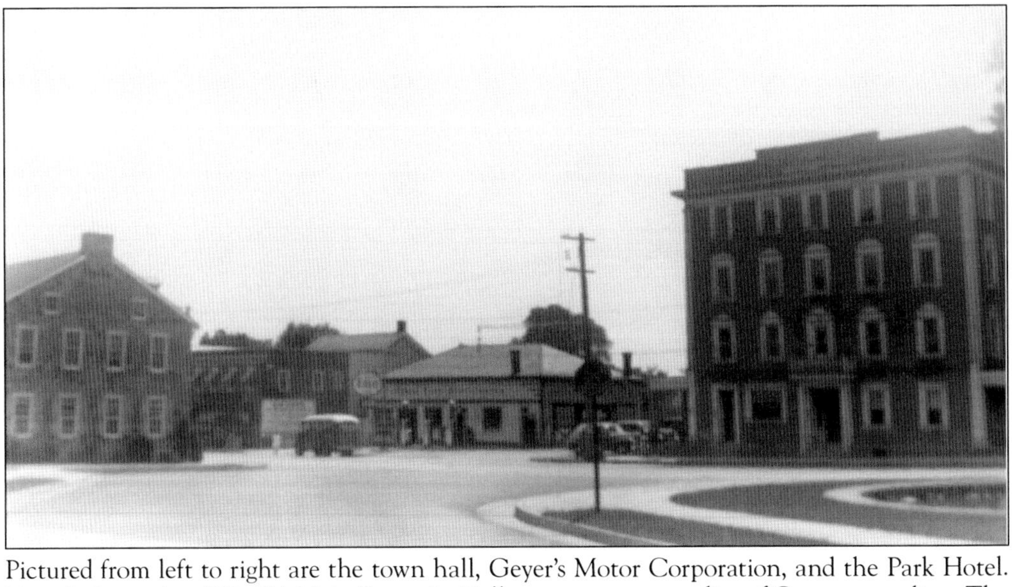

Pictured from left to right are the town hall, Geyer's Motor Corporation, and the Park Hotel. Geyer's, located at 706–714 Main Street in Hellertown, was a supplier of Conoco gasoline. The station's slogan was "Gas With Geyer's." Walter and Jack Geyer began the family business in 1921, converting a horse stable into a garage. (Courtesy of Hellertown Borough Water Authority.)

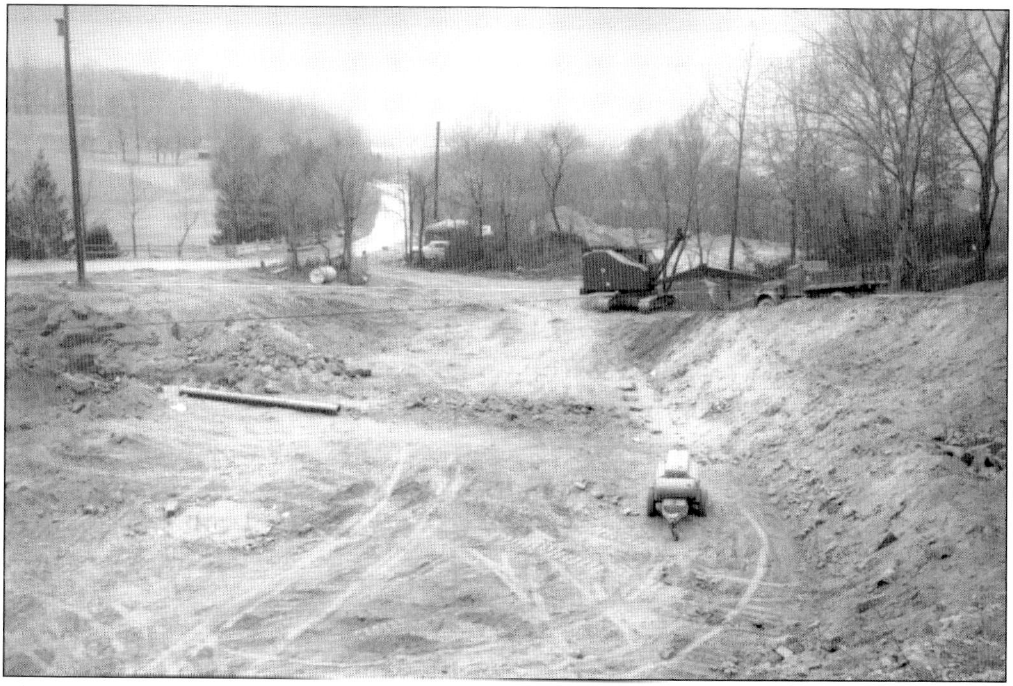

This area of a former sand company became a place to explore for children in the 1950s. Located just off Apple Street, many shooters used the sand bank as a safe place to fire their long guns for target practice. Children would then collect the spent .22 and shotgun cartridges to use as toys.

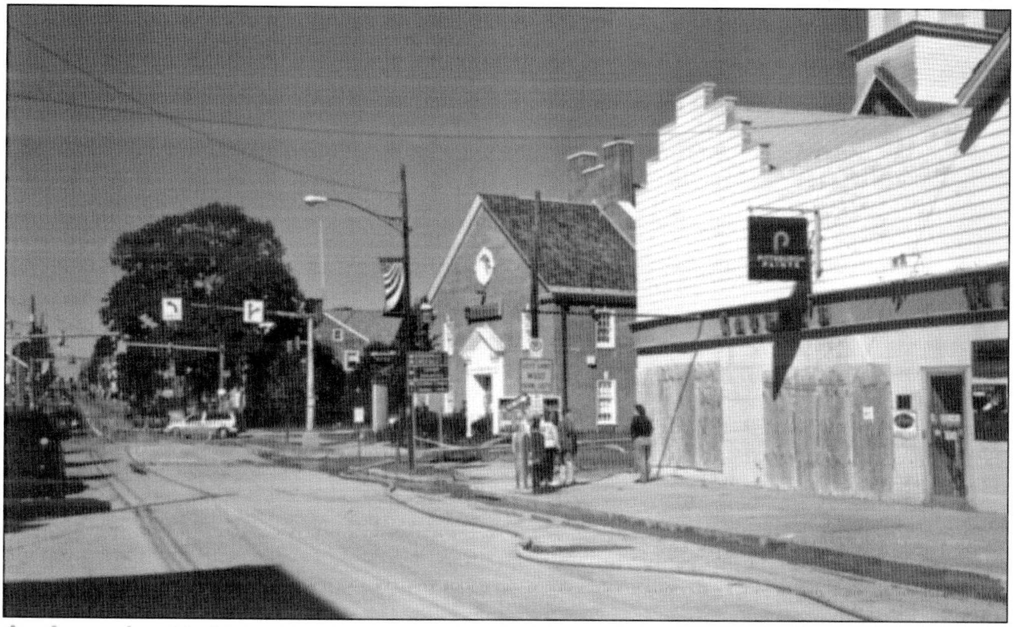

On September 18, 2004, Hurricane Ivan flooded Carson's Hardware Store with three feet of water. The flood damaged the structure of the store and most of the inventory. This photograph, taken the following day, shows Carson's (right) with boarded-up windows. Main Street was still covered in mud. Carson's, a staple of Main Street Hellertown for 25 years, was forced to close in 2005. (Courtesy of Hellertown Borough Water Authority.)

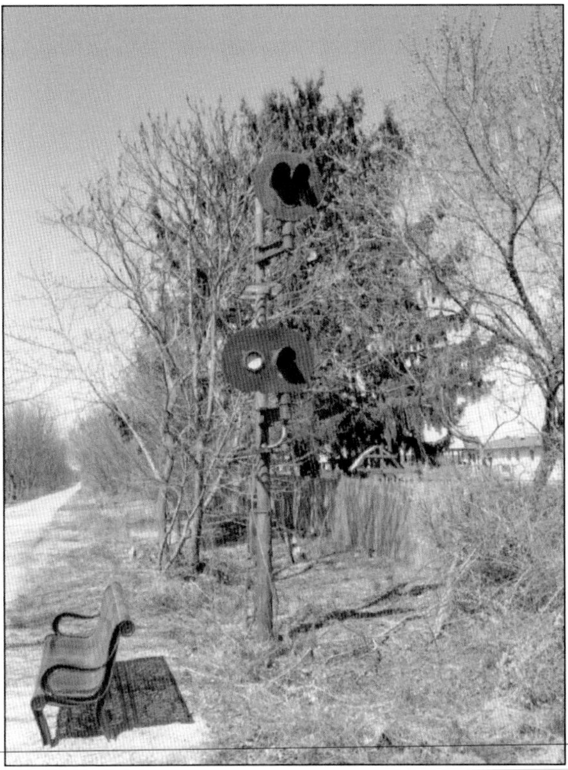

After being converted to a rail trail in 2011, a number of artifacts of the old North Penn Railroad remained. This is one of the railroad signals along the path. Hellertown Borough plans to refurbish and restore a similar railroad signal located farther along the Saucon Rail Trail.

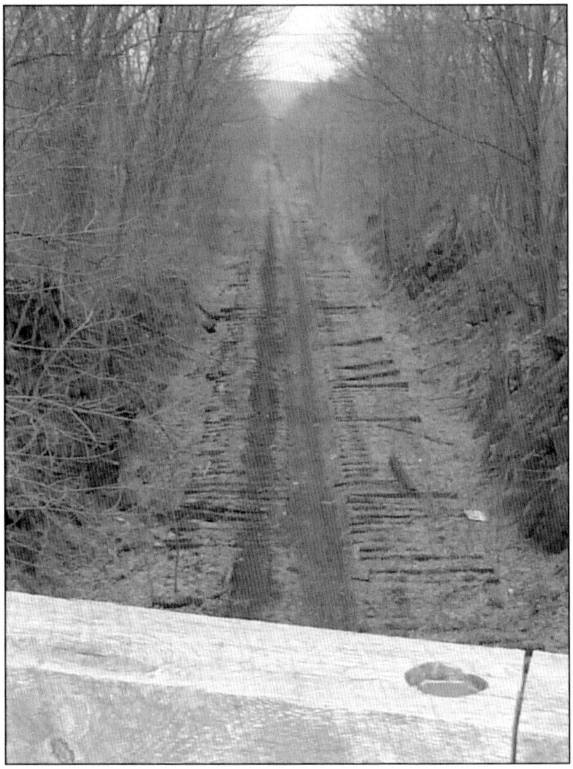

Since commuter rail service terminated on July 1, 1981, this stretch of the former North Pennsylvania Railroad line in Hellertown lay dormant. This 2005 view from the now-closed High Street wooden bridge shows the path to be relatively unobstructed from natural encroachment. But, within a few years, nature would reclaim most of it.

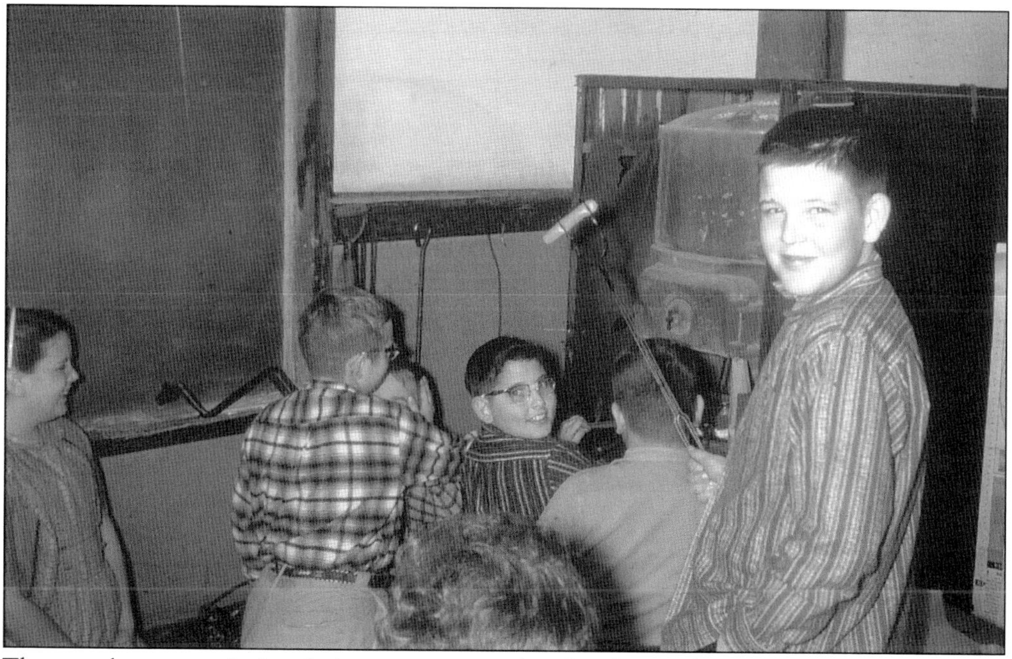

These students are enjoying their time warming their lunches in the corner stove in Seidersville School in 1956. No doubt, this same scene could be witnessed in many of the schoolhouses across the township. (Courtesy of John Fischel.)

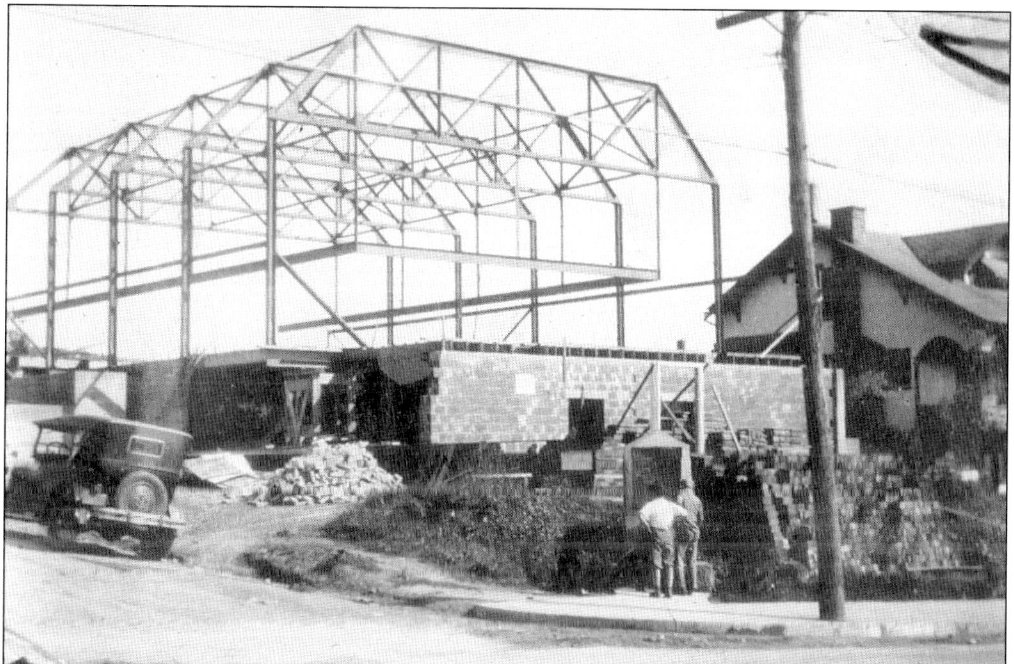

The Edward H. Ackerman Post 397 American Legion building was constructed on this site, at Main and Chestnut Streets, beginning in 1924. It opened in 1927 and served as a place for various community functions. Despite a five-year closure due to financial hardships, this post reopened in 2013 and is once again a respite for patriots and veterans.

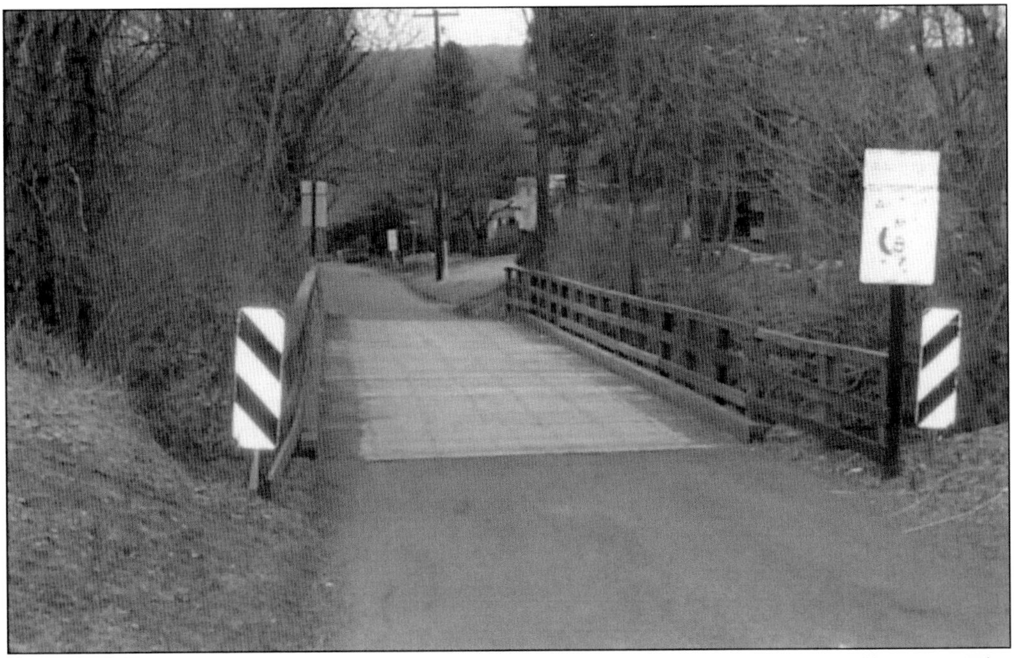

The High Street Bridge is a one-lane timber bridge built in 1910 in western Hellertown. The span crosses the abandoned Norfolk Southern Railroad track, where Seidersville Road and High Street meet. The bridge was closed in 2011 and is due to be demolished and replaced by the city of Bethlehem.

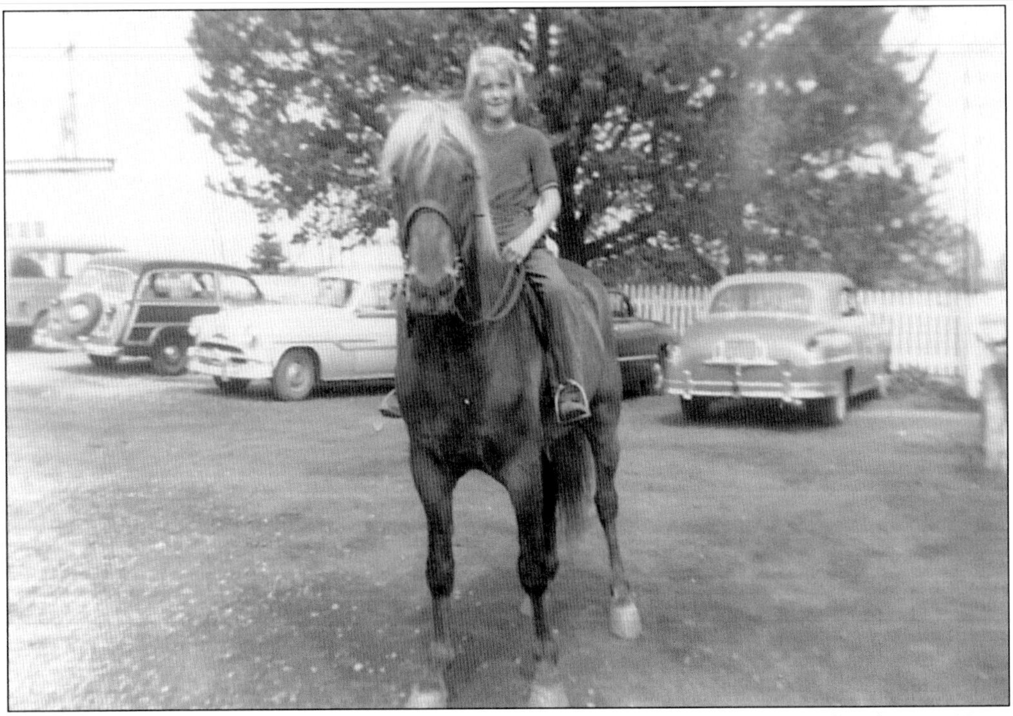

Patterson Stables was a great place for young and old alike to spend some time riding horses. Here, Carianne Webster rides "Peanuts" in 1953. (Courtesy of Joanne Jones.)

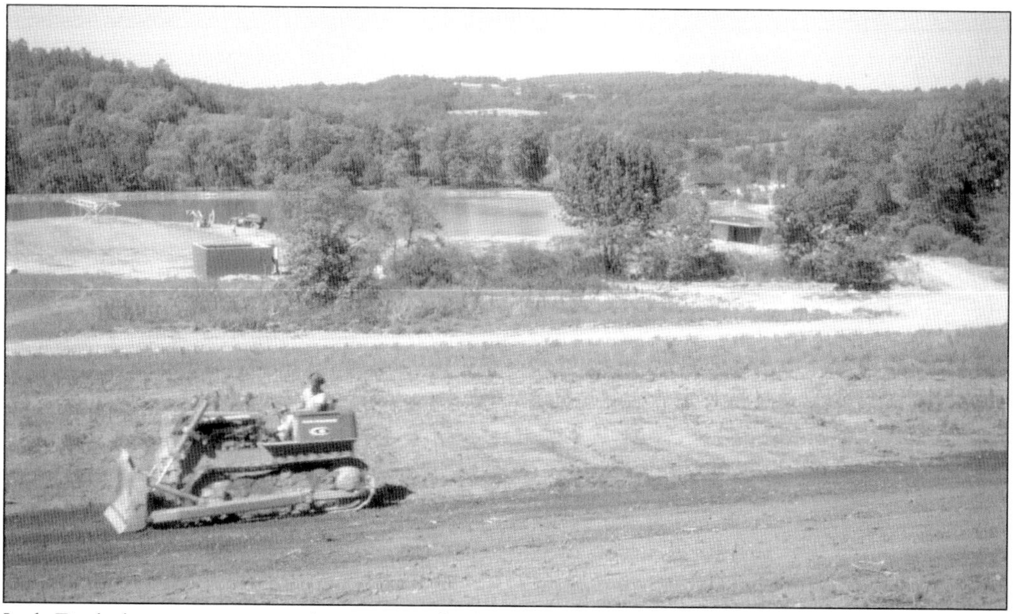

Jack Fischel, an engineer and excavator, built Marlin Lake out of swampland near Wassergass in the early 1960s. Fischel combined portions of the names of daughters Margaret and Linda to produce the name Marlin Lake. This photograph was taken in 1963, when the finishing touches were being completed on the lake property. (Courtesy of John Fischel.)

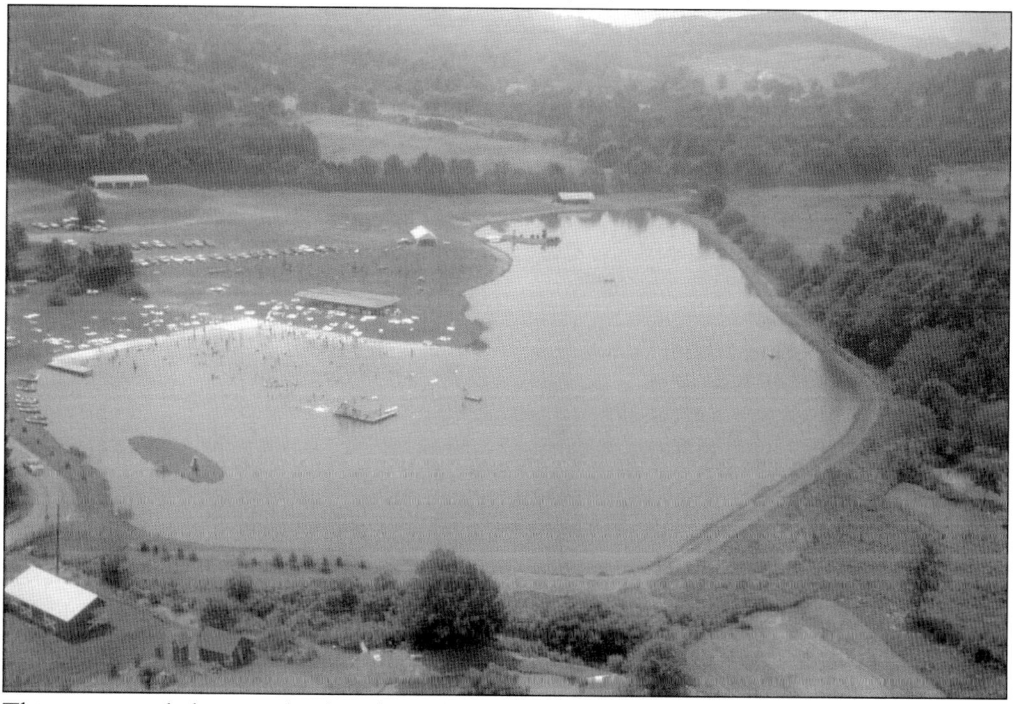

This is an aerial photograph of Marlin Lake, a man-made swimming, fishing, and boating basin along Lower Saucon Road. The lake covers eight acres and is about 10 feet at its deepest point. The deep areas permit boating. Visible here are three pavilions and a picnic grove surrounding the lake. (Courtesy of John Fischel.)

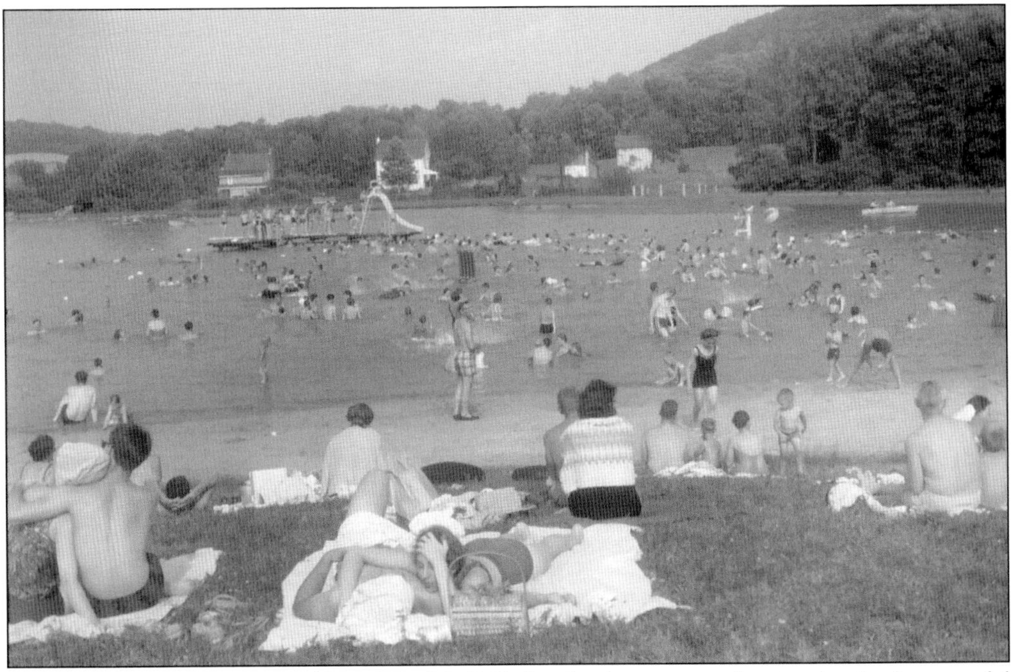

Since its opening on Memorial Day, May 30, 1963, families have enjoyed swimming in the peaceful setting of Marlin Lake. There is a raft in the middle of the lake for diving, and a snack bar for lunch. For anglers, the lake held catch bass, bluegill, perch, and catfish. (Courtesy of John Fischel.)

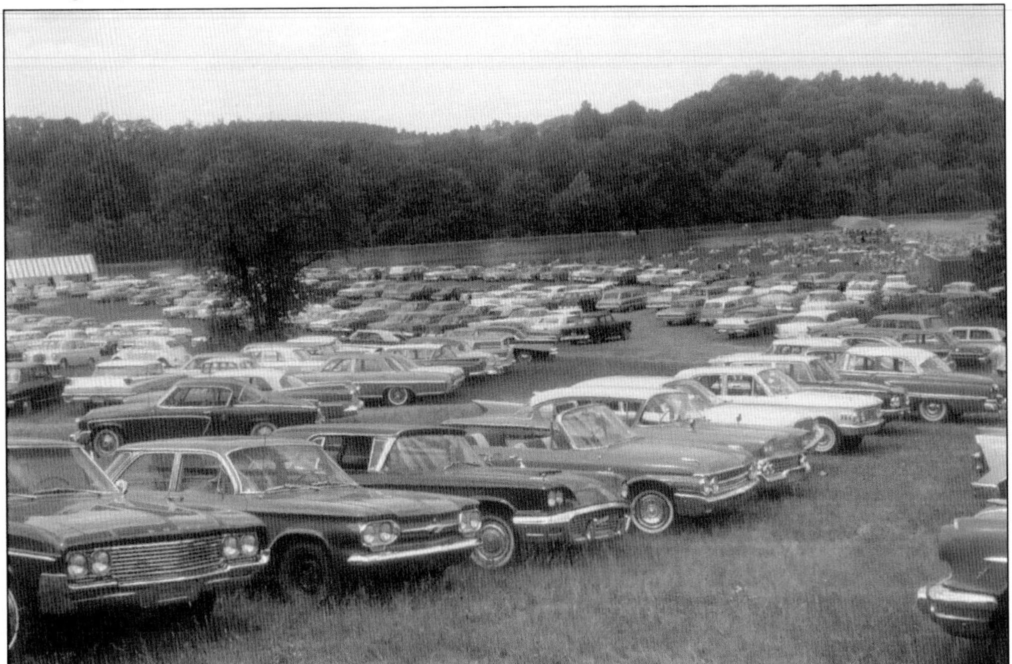

Marlin Lake drew as many as 2,000 visitors a day on a hot Saturday or Sunday. The parking lot is seen here in 1966, with no open parking space in sight. Before air-conditioning was common, the lake was the place to beat the heat. (Courtesy of John Fischel.)

Seven

Gone But Not Forgotten

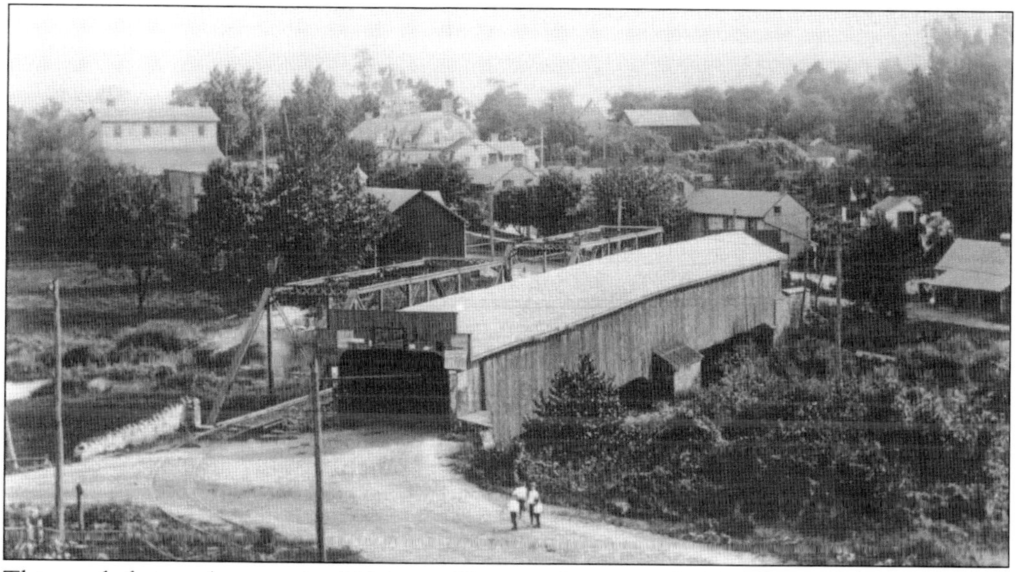

This south-facing photograph of Shimersville was taken around 1900, showing the old covered bridge that spanned Saucon Creek. Next to it is a steel bridge that carried trolleys between South Bethlehem, Iron Hill, Shimersville, Freemansburg, and Butztown. This community no longer exists. (Courtesy of David Jacoby.)

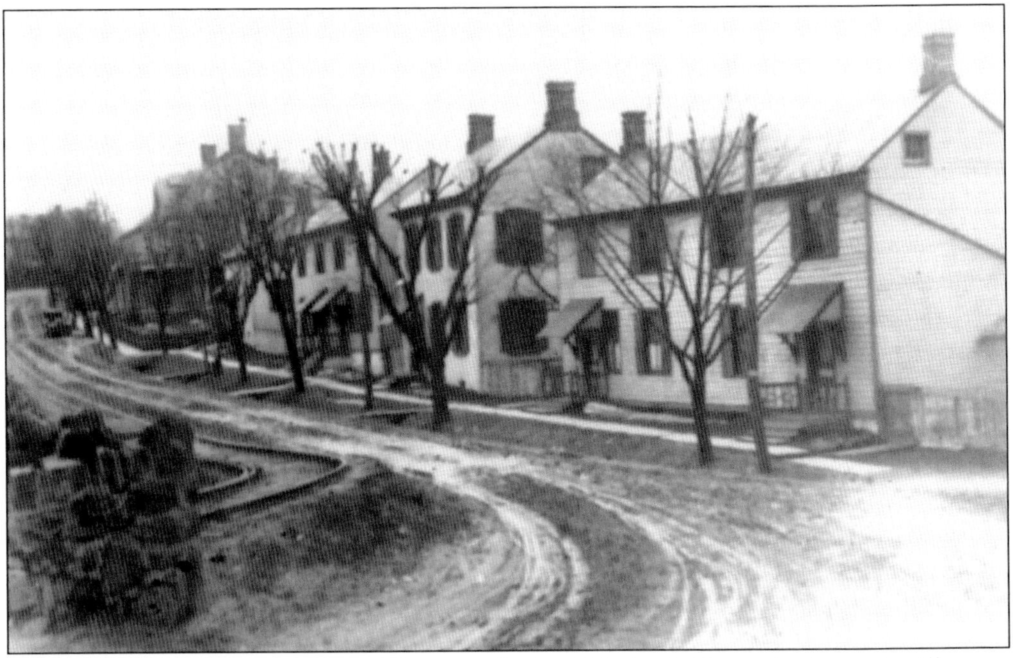

These houses stood in the center of Shimersville. In 1812, Jacob Shimer built an oil mill; soon, a village grew around these structures. For five generations, the Shimer family added various industries. As a result, workers were encouraged to build homes and live in the village.

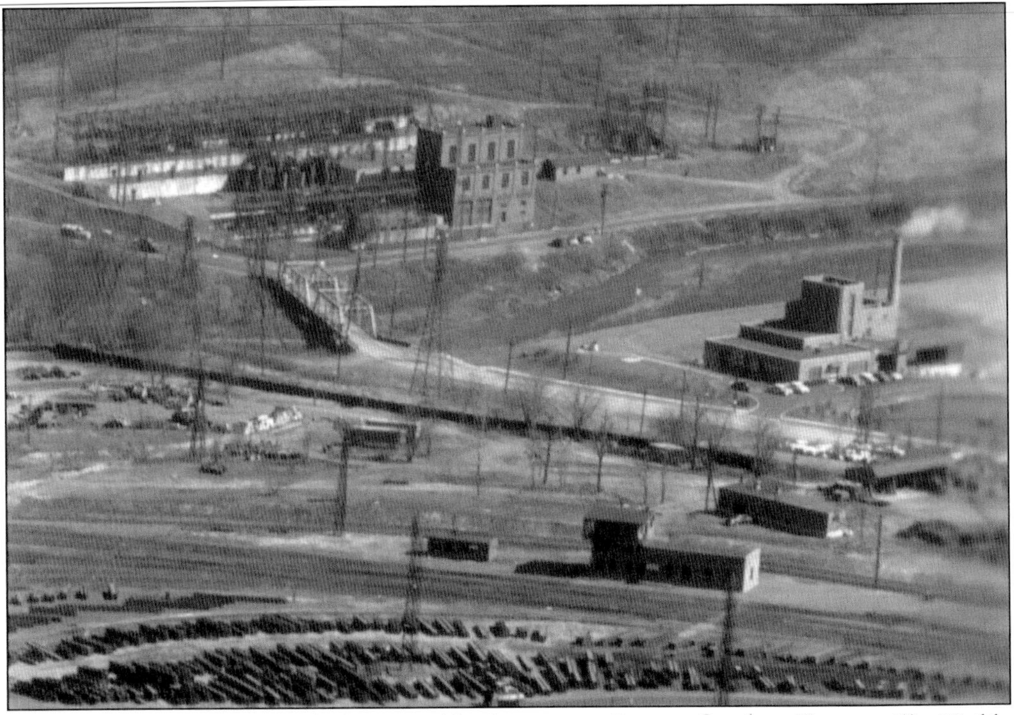

This is a rare photograph of the last metal bridge to cross Saucon Creek at Shimersville. Visible here is the Freemansburg substation, which bordered on Applebutter Road. This whole section of roadway was replaced in 1968.

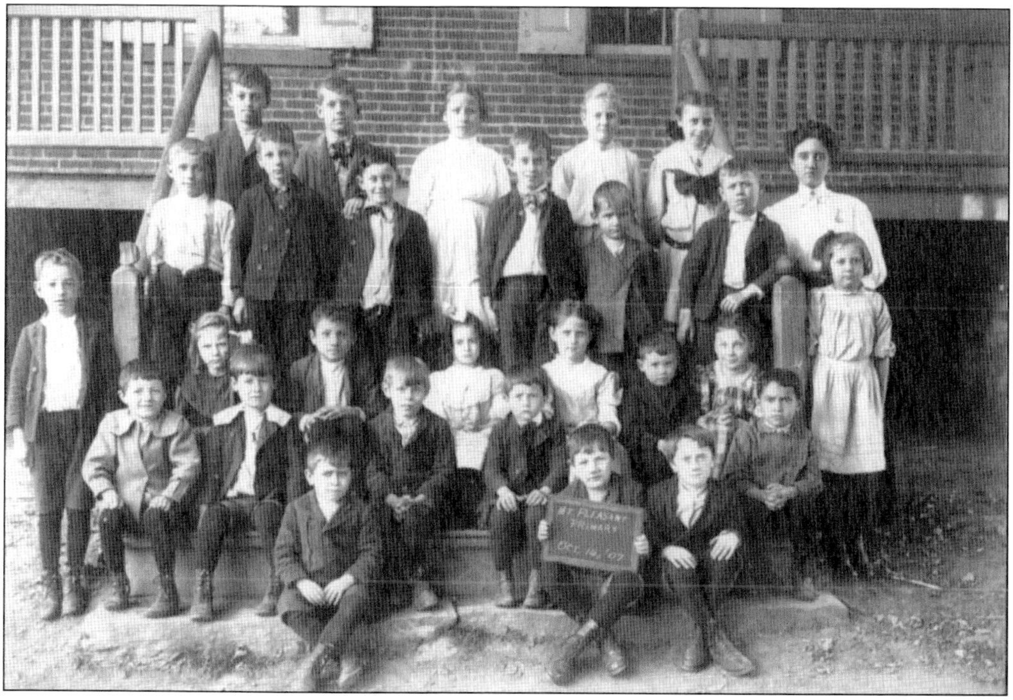

Here is a 1907 class photograph for Mount Pleasant School Primary in Shimersville. The teacher, Miss Kemerer (third row, far right), instructed 28 students in grades one through five. She received a salary of $42 a month for her work.

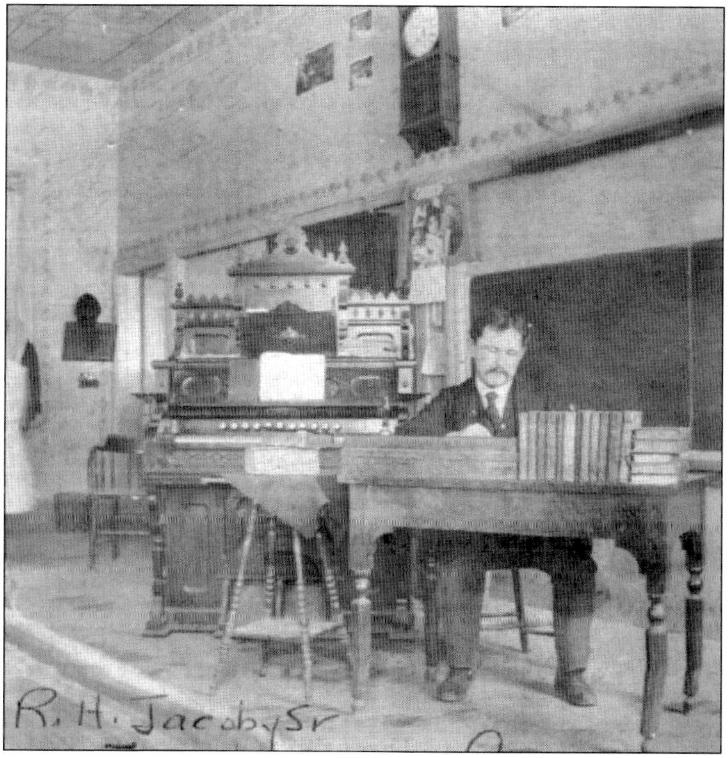

This rare interior photograph is part of the Jacoby family archives and dates to the early 1900s, when their ancestors were located in Shimersville. The only school in Shimersville at the time was the Mount Pleasant School. This school was described in the 1908 book *The History and Genealogy of the Shimer Family in America* as providing excellent academic instruction. (Courtesy of David Jacoby.)

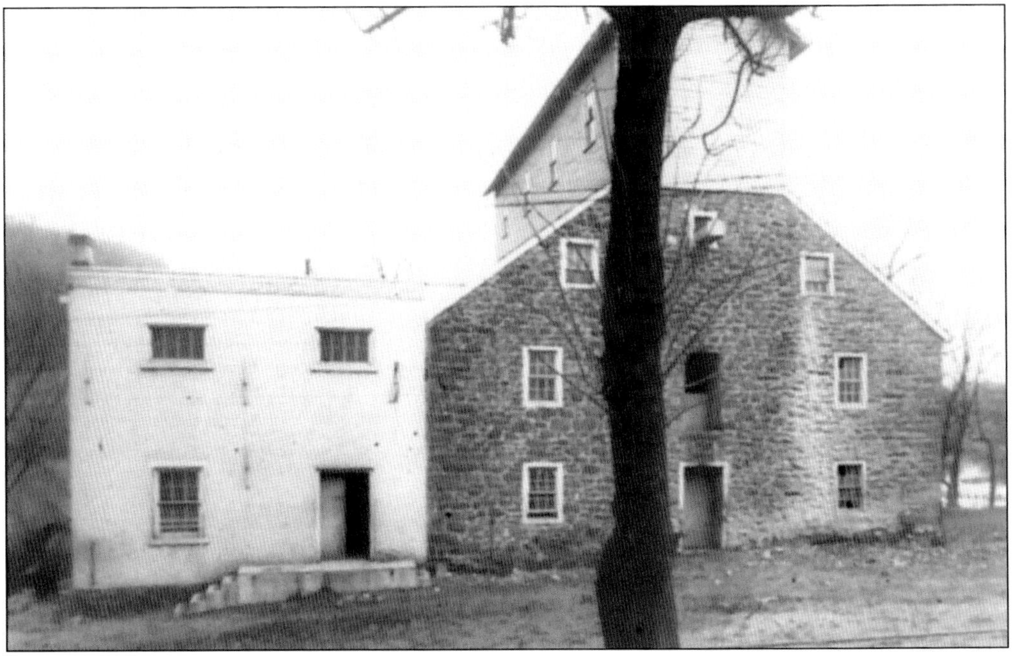

The Shimersville gristmill was last owned by John Knecht. Nathaniel Irish purchased 500 acres along Saucon Creek in 1735 and built the area's first gristmill along the creek in Shimersville sometime before 1740. There were so few mills at the time that the Moravians of Bethlehem had a road built especially to reach Irish's property.

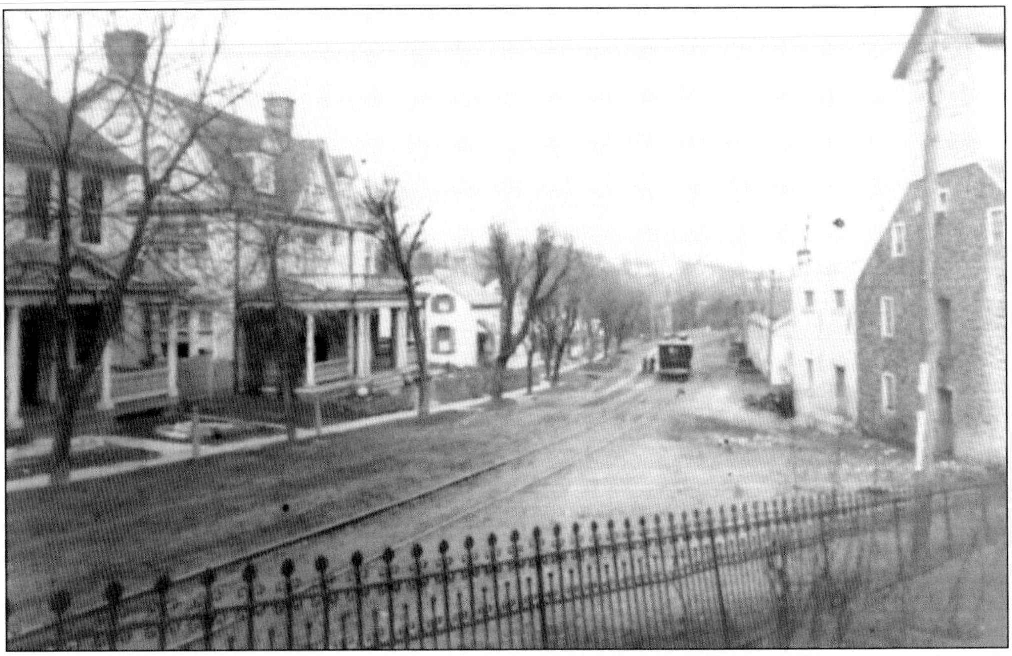

Shown in this north-facing photograph of the main street in Shimersville is a trolley running through the village. The Lehigh Valley Transit Company offered trolley service between Shimersville, Freemansburg, Northampton Heights, and South Bethlehem. A branch of the North Pennsylvania Railroad passed through the village.

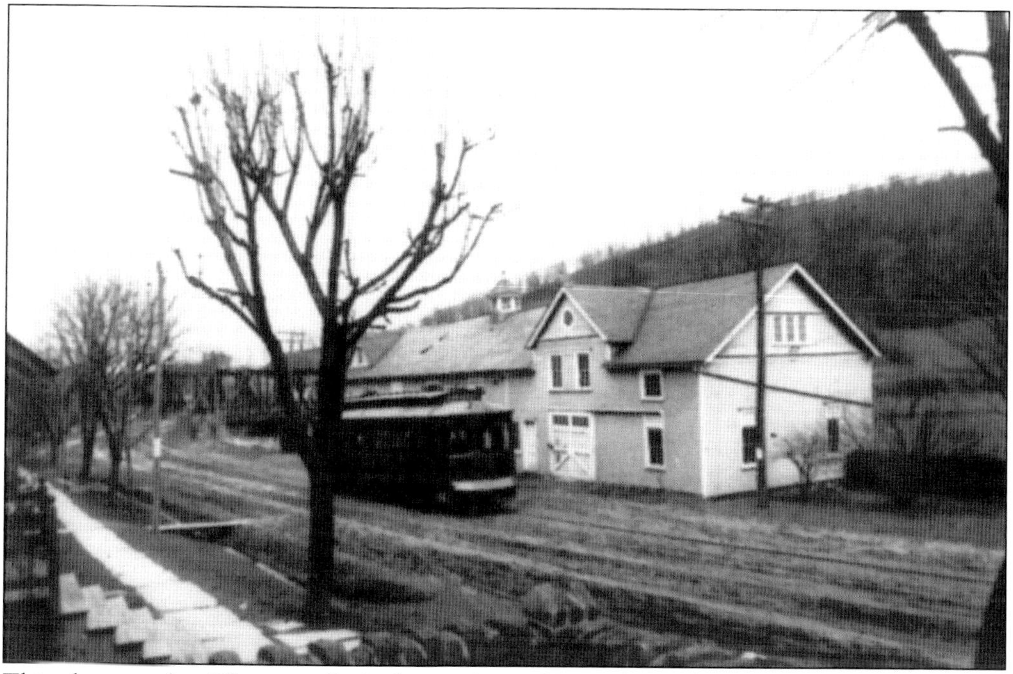

This photograph of Shimersville looks northeast. Howard Knecht sold the village to Charles Schwab, president of Bethlehem Steel Corporation, in 1915 for $500,000. Schwab then expanded the nearby company property toward the southeast. Bethlehem Steel used a portion of this property for a dumping ground for cinders. It was the oldest of the Lower Saucon Township villages.

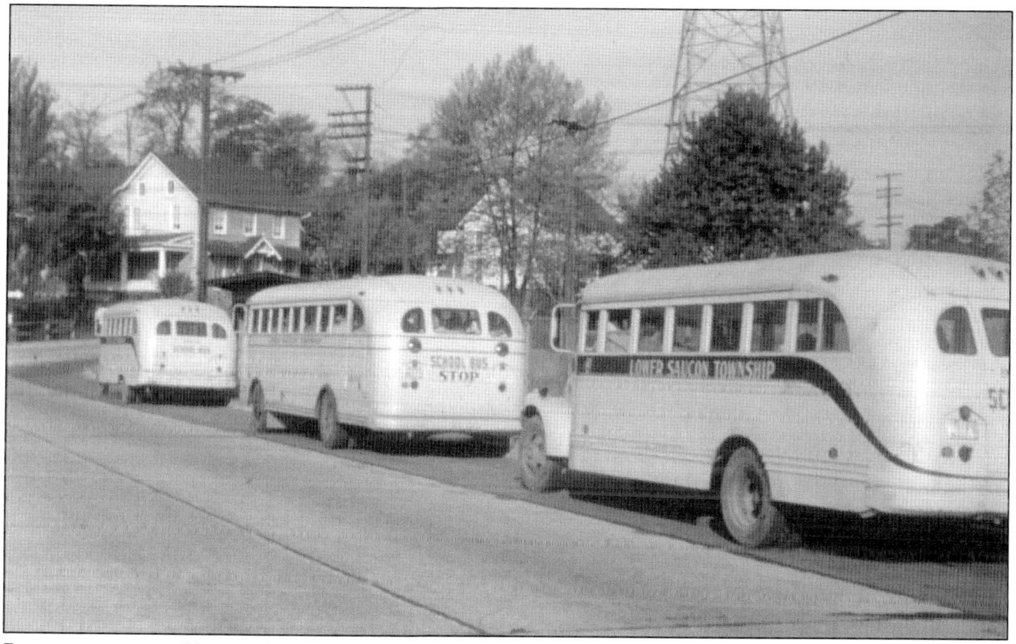

Buses congregated here, where Shimersville Road meets Hellertown Road, to reshuffle their student passengers. Buses coming from the Steel City and Lower Saucon areas carried students of different school districts and used this location to have students reach their respective schools.

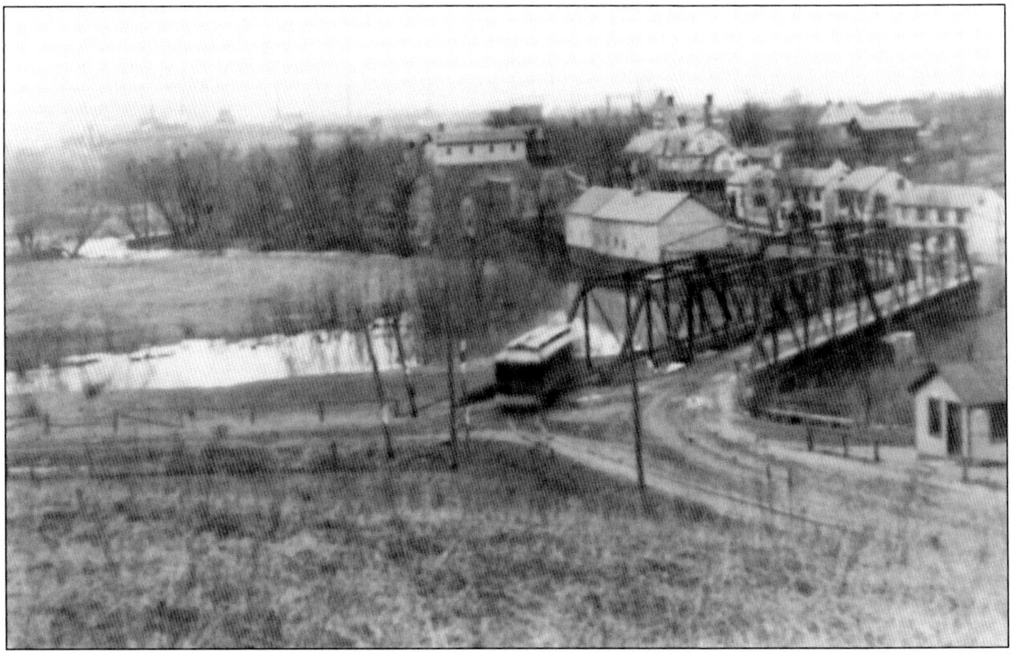

This photograph of the main street in Shimersville looks south. The village was located on the south side of the Lehigh River, near the mouth of Saucon Creek. In 1855, Shimersville had fifteen houses, one hotel, one store, one gristmill, one woolen manufacturer, and an iron foundry. Here, a trolley travels near the two-span iron bridge.

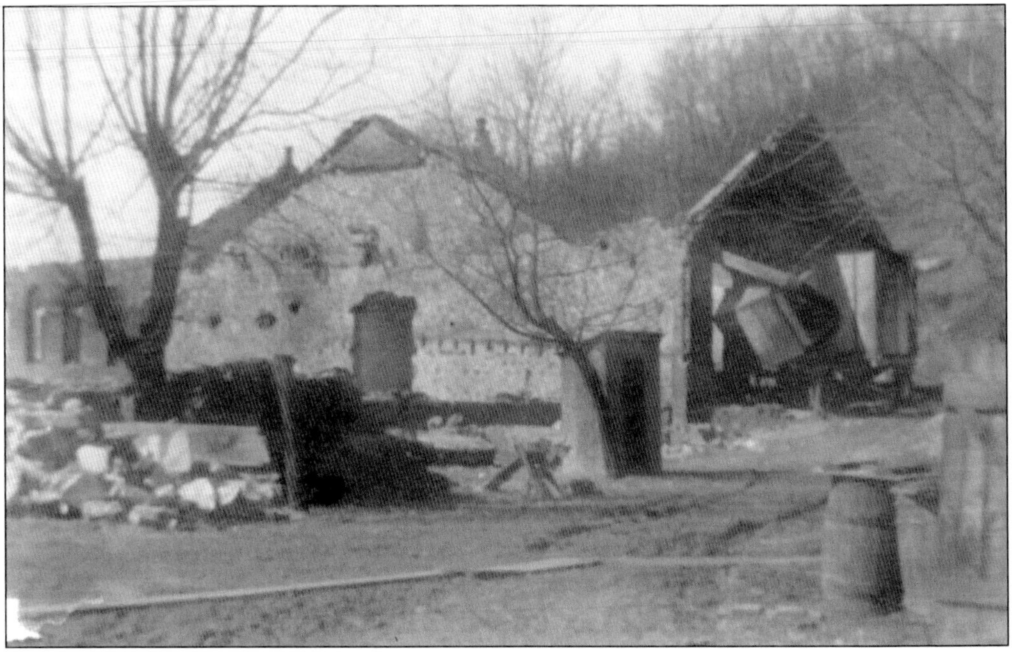

The William Shimer & Sons foundry was a complex of buildings on Applebutter Road, about 200 yards from the Freemansburg substation. William's father, John Shimer, started the complex in 1824. In 1875, the firm began the operation of a foundry and a machine shop. Toys were one of the products manufactured here. (Courtesy of Diane Weber Wampole.)

This is the Knecht home in Shimersville. It was built by John Knecht and then improved upon by his son Howard Knecht in the 1880s. Howard installed running water in the home in 1893, one of the first homes in Saucon Valley to have this luxury. Howard married Laurenti Walter in this home in 1882.

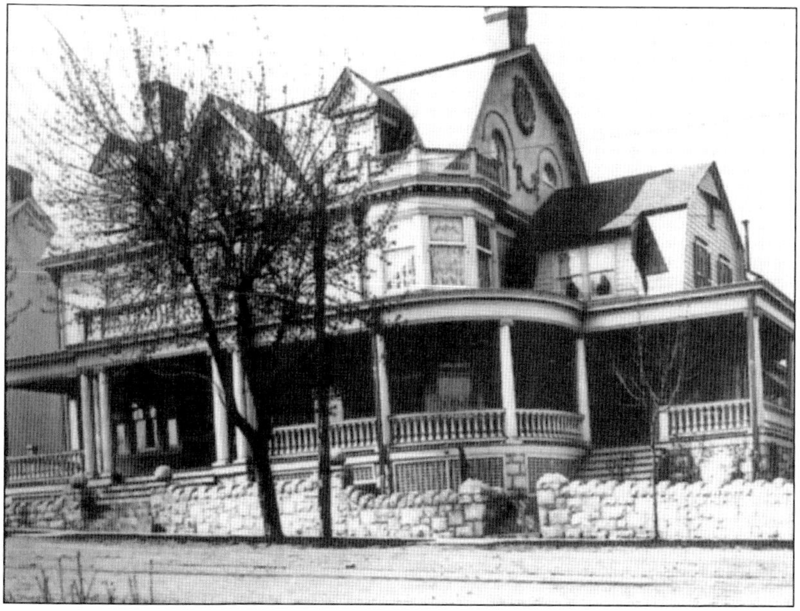

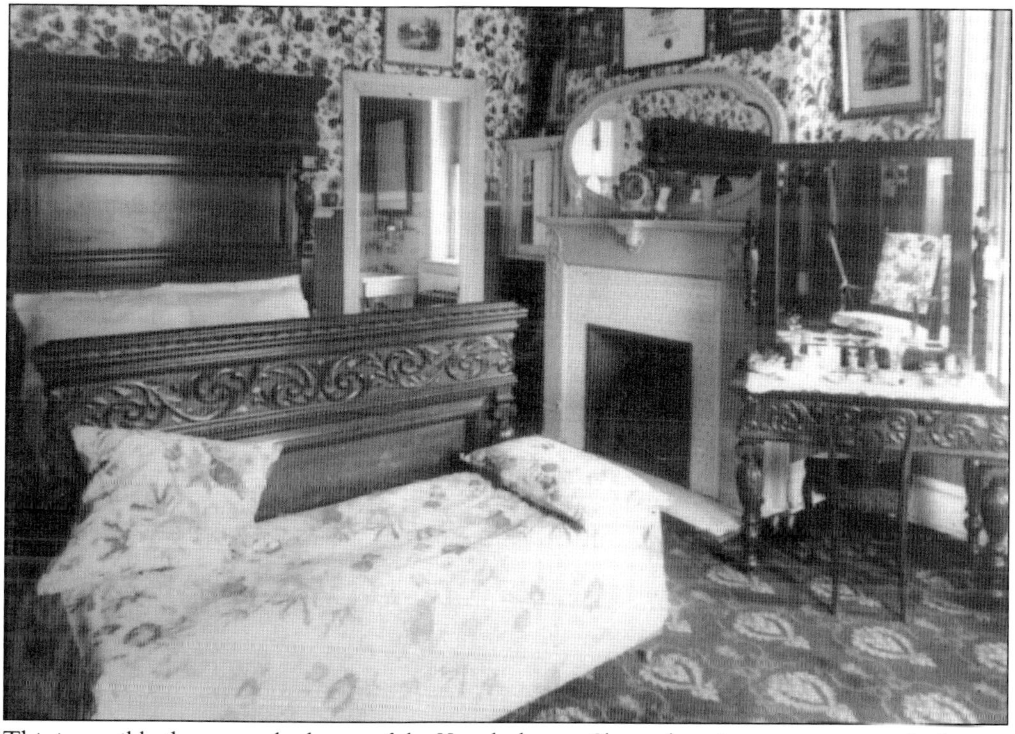

This is possibly the master bedroom of the Knecht house. Shown here is an entrance to a bathroom from the room. The household furnishings are of the late Victorian period, called Eastlake style. The multitude of busy patterns on the wallpaper, carpet, and upholstery was typical of this style. The fine, carved wooden furniture complemented the rush of patterns.

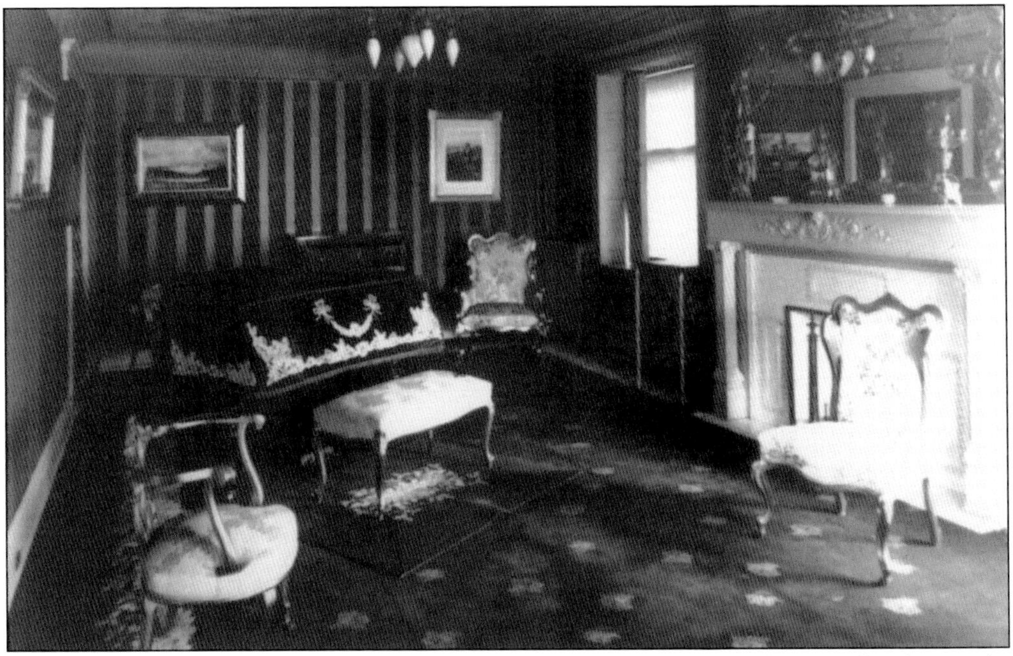

This is an interior view of the music room of the most luxurious home in Shimersville, the Knecht house. The painted ceiling and wall-to-wall carpeting made this a cozy place to entertain guests. Local newspaper accounts of the early 1900s reported the many visits by friends to Howard and Laurenti Knecht's home.

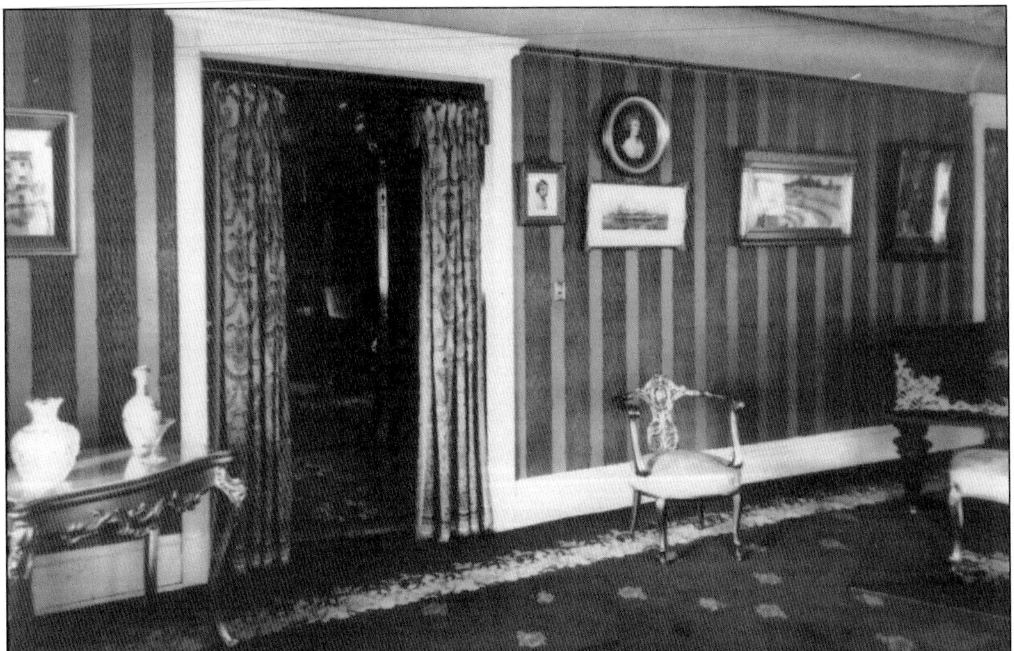

The music room is seen here from another angle. The striped wallpaper and curtained doorway give the appearance of entering a lush, extravagant space. The decorative square grand piano on the right was an expensive and rare musical instrument.

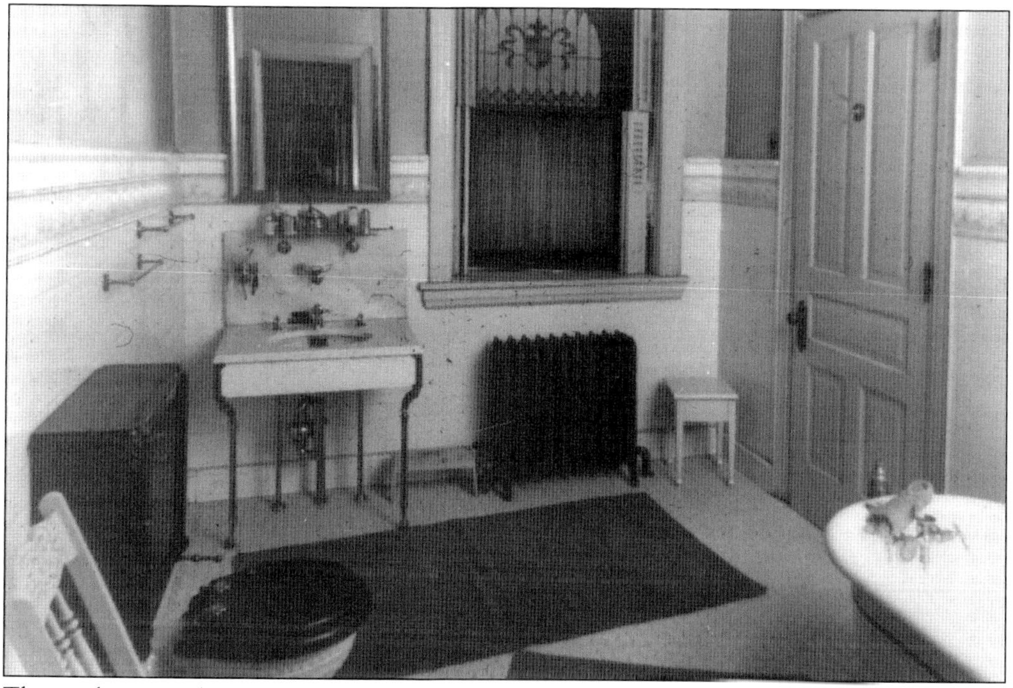

This is a luxurious bathroom that only a wealthy owner could afford in the early 1900s. A marble sink is next to a steam-heated radiator. The stained-glass window allowed light in but protected privacy. The white hexagon-shaped tiny tiles gave the bathroom a sanitary look.

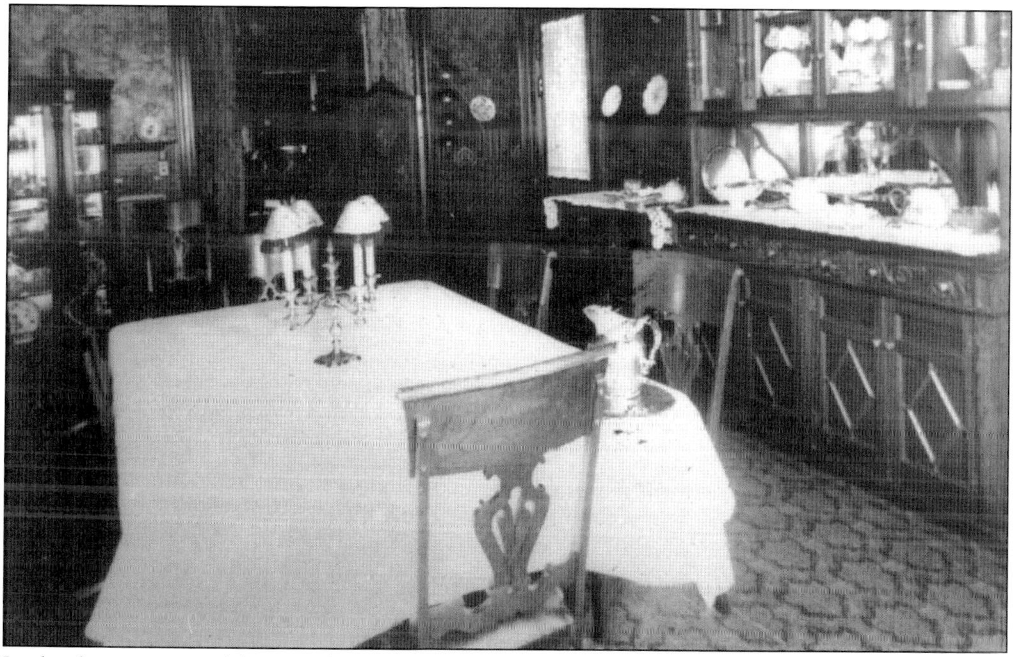

In the dining room of the Knecht home, the fine woodwork and rich patterns were carried out, as in the rest of the home. Most likely, the kitchen was in the basement, as the meals were prepared by servants away from the family and guests. This room had an intimate feel. The hutch was packed with china and anything else needed to serve guests.

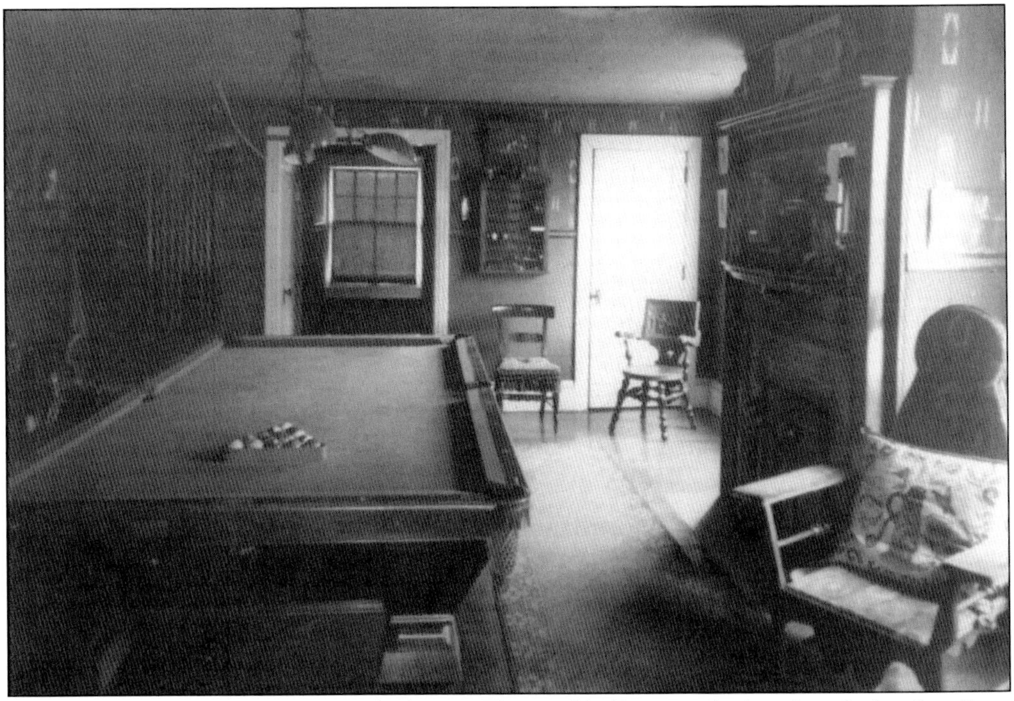

This is the game room of the Knecht house. The pool balls are racked and ready for play. Even the game room has an ornate fireplace mantle. The modern chandelier shines directly on the pool table. Many of the houses in Saucon Valley at the time of this photograph, in the early 1900s, did not yet have electricity.

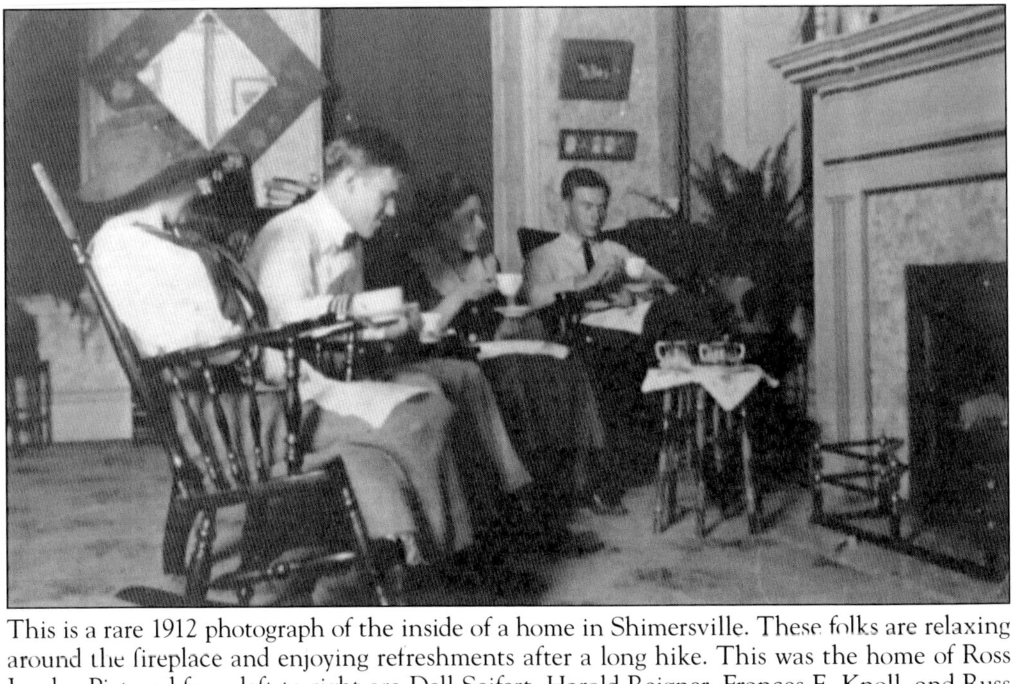

This is a rare 1912 photograph of the inside of a home in Shimersville. These folks are relaxing around the fireplace and enjoying refreshments after a long hike. This was the home of Ross Jacoby. Pictured from left to right are Dell Seifert, Harold Reigner, Frances E. Knoll, and Russ Jacoby. (Courtesy of David Jacoby.)

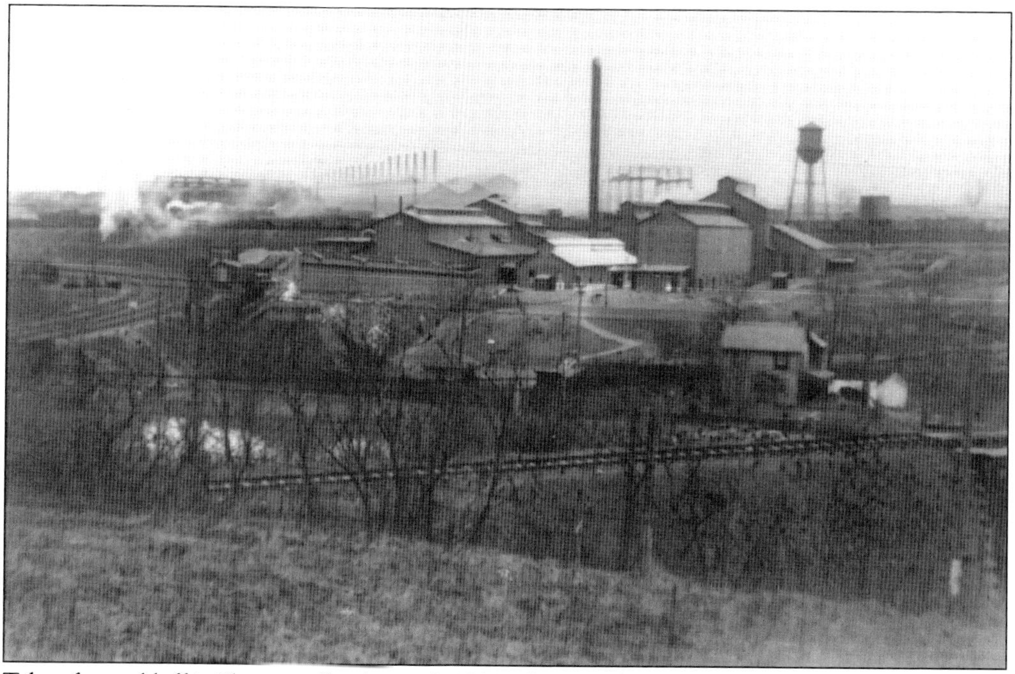

Taken from a bluff in Shimersville, this early-1900s photograph shows the New Jersey Zinc Company in South Bethlehem. The Shimersville Branch of the North Penn Railroad is in the foreground. The main North Penn Railroad tracks are seen closer to the zinc foundry. The company's furnaces were built in 1853, less than 100 yards from the South Bethlehem entrance to the Fahy Bridge. This was the first large enterprise established in South Bethlehem.

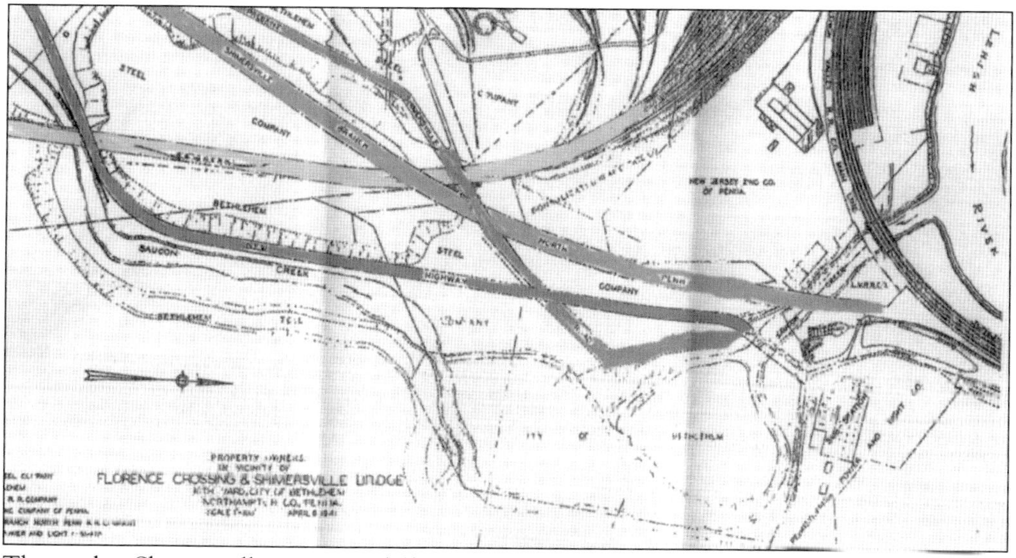

The road to Shimersville was quite different, and in a different location, than the original road. It is probably best interpreted by looking at the lower right corner and locating the "sub-station," where a bridge (or two) crossed the Saucon Creek going south toward Hellertown. From there, the current road actually runs behind the homes that lined the original thoroughfare through Shimersville. The straightest road, marked "highway," is the road as it is known today. (courtesy of Frank Fabian.)

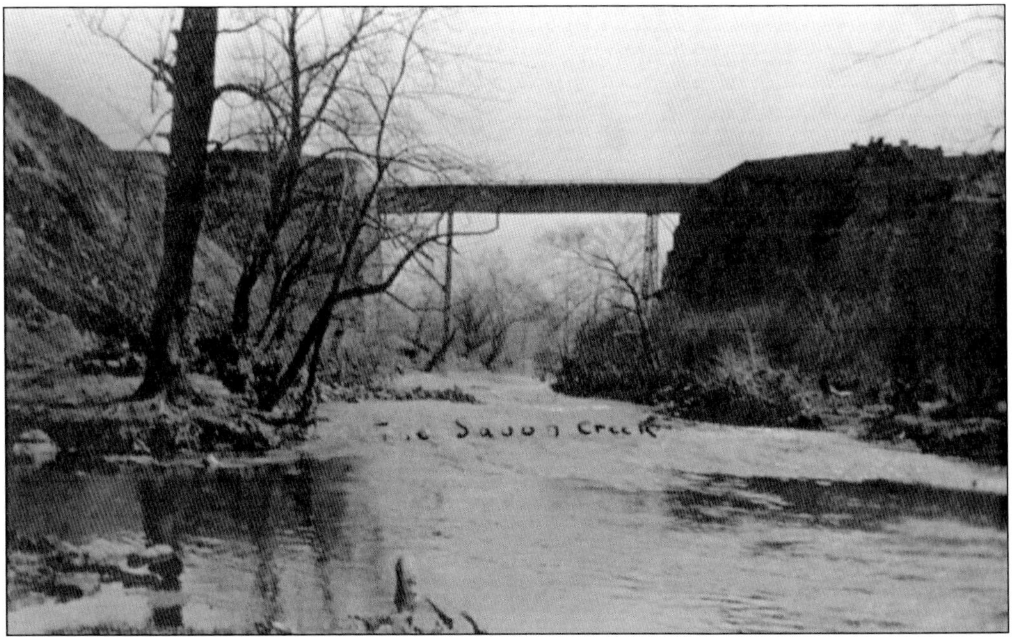

This is an early photograph of the Iron Hill Bridge spanning Saucon Creek. The bridge was located near the village of Iron Hill, one mile south of Shimersville. It once contained a marble yard and a few houses. It was a post office for a few years and had a train station. The North Penn Railroad constructed this bridge in 1856. (Courtesy of David Jacoby.)

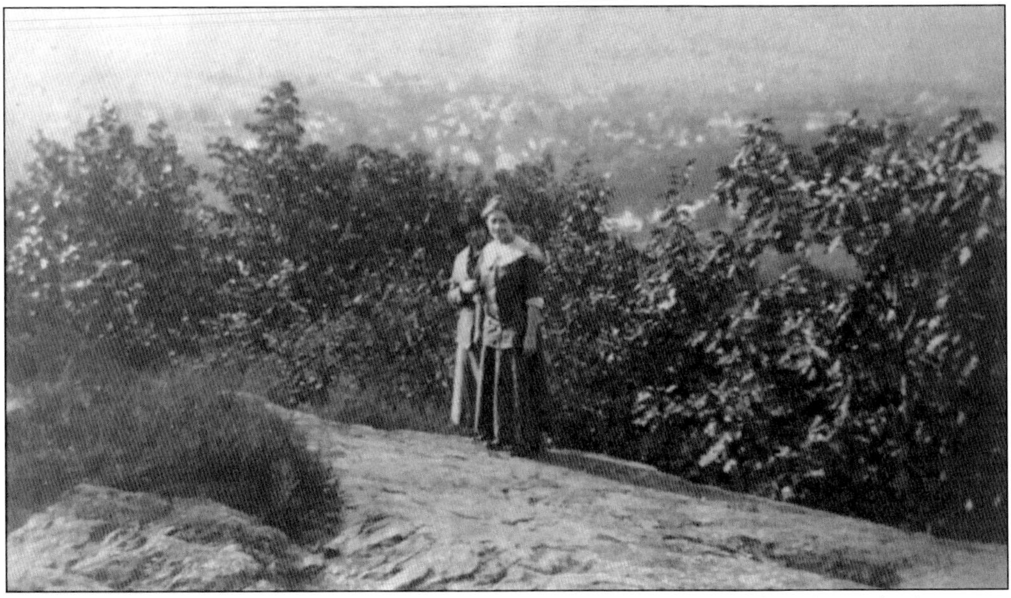

This is Flat Rock, on the summit of Green Hill in Lower Saucon Township, from which visitors had a view of Freemansburg. The legend surrounding this landmark is that it was a place where members of the Lenni Lenape tribe met Europeans to trade goods. The Indians offered animal pelts for European woven cloth, copper kettles, and sharp-edged iron tools. The woman pictured is Frances E. Knoll from Butztown. (Courtesy of David Jacoby.)

Eight

Saucon Sojourn

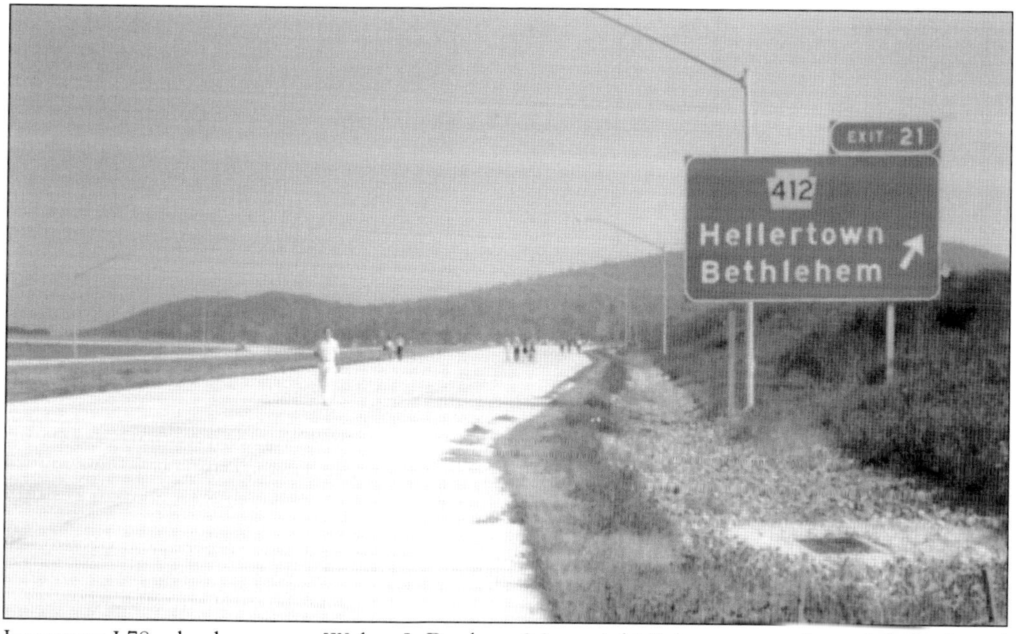

Interstate I 78, also known as Walter J. Dealtrey Memorial Highway, runs through Lehigh and Northampton Counties. It was built by the Pennsylvania Department of Transportation beginning in 1984, and it opened on November 21, 1989. Here, people walk and explore the new road just before it opened to traffic. The sign points to Exit 21, which was changed to Exit 67 in 2001. The new number for each exit matched the number of miles between that exit and the interstate's starting point in Pennsylvania. (Courtesy of Dean Shaffer.)

Historical population		
Census	Pop.	%±
1880	605	—
1890	708	17.0%
1900	745	5.2%
1910	915	22.8%
1920	3,008	228.7%
1930	3,851	28.0%
1940	4,031	4.7%
1950	5,435	34.8%
1960	6,716	23.6%
1970	6,615	−1.5%
1980	6,025	−8.9%
1990	5,662	−6.0%
2000	5,606	−1.0%
2010	5,898	5.2%

The census reports between 1880 and 2010 reveal the steady increase in population due to jobs available at local manufacturers, such as the Bethlehem Steel Corporation. The big jump in population after 1910 can be contributed to Hellertown's annex of the village of Cross Roads from Lower Saucon Township. Due to competition from foreign manufacturers and the automation of American manufacturing plants, the number of jobs began declining in the 1960s. Today, Saucon Valley residents are primarily employed in service-related jobs.

This cast-iron Keystone Marker along Route 412 (Main Street) celebrates the founding of Hellertown by Colonial settler Christopher Heller. There are two identical markers located at the north and south ends of town. Hellertown Borough restored the signs in 2012. This photograph was taken in 2009.

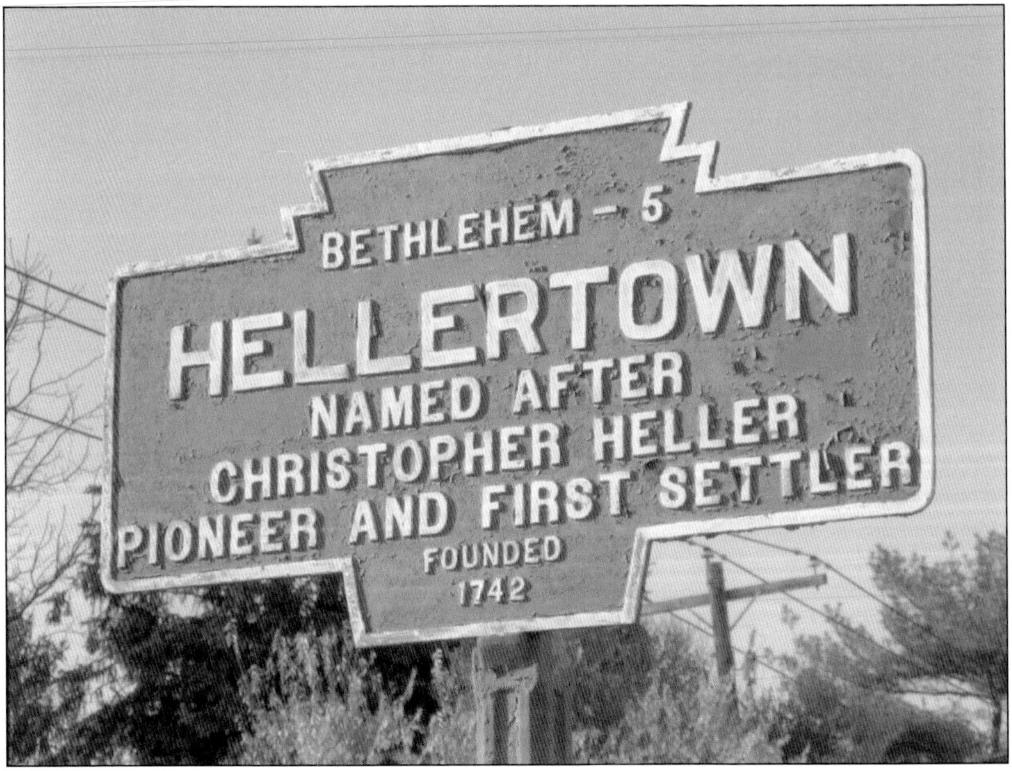

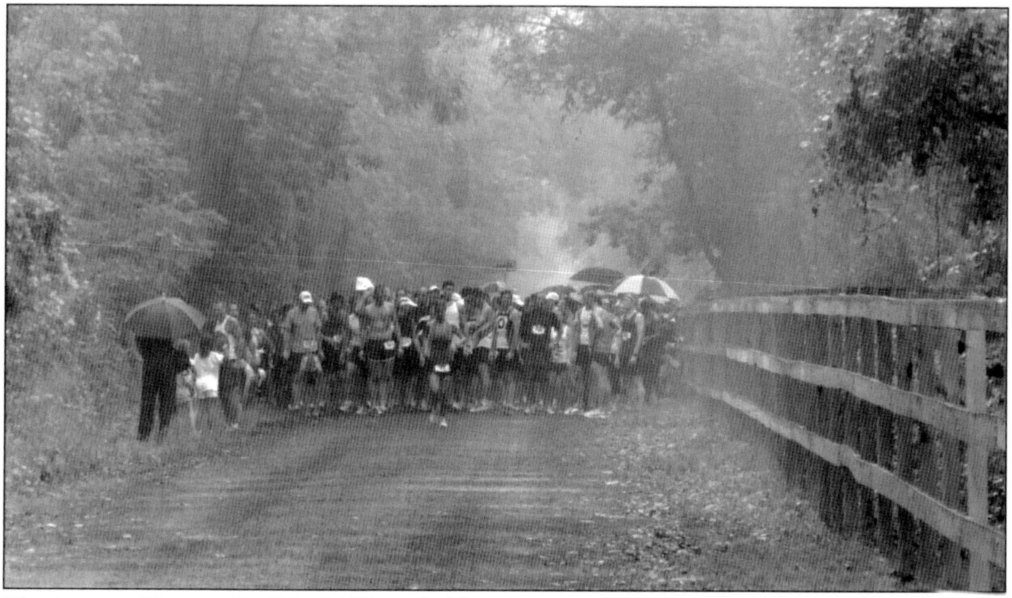

The inaugural Saucon Rail Trail 10K was held on September 3, 2012. Over 300 runners participated in the event on this rainy day. The race raised money for the Harvey C. Marsteller Foundation, which supports local families dealing with the effects of cancer. The Saucon Rail Trail, which opened in 2011, is a five-mile trail along the line of the North Penn Railroad. (Courtesy of Andrea Thrush.)

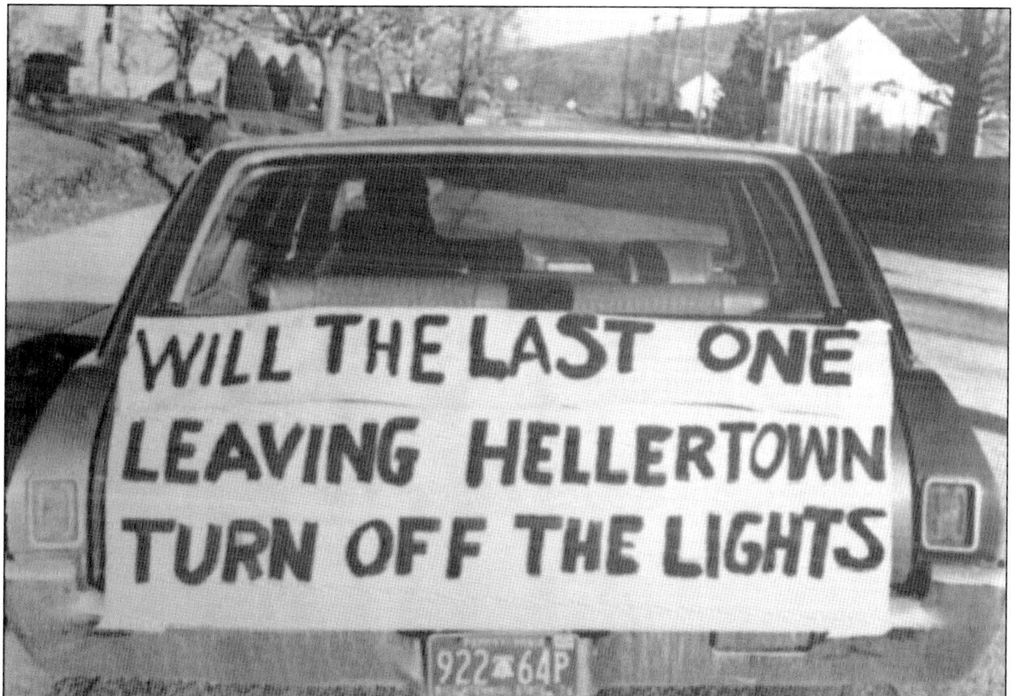

The lengthy and eventful Hellertown centennial celebration in June 1972 enlivened the community. After the event, Edward Zamiskie decorated his car to add a bit of comic relief to punctuate the festivities. (Courtesy of the Hellertown Historical Society.)

Consistent with our mission to preserve history on a local level, this book was printed in South Carolina on American-made paper and manufactured entirely in the United States. Products carrying the accredited Forest Stewardship Council (FSC) label are printed on 100 percent FSC-certified paper.

MADE IN THE USA